D1627107

Leadville's Ice Palace

A Colossus in the Colorado Rockies

by

Darlene Godat Weir

Cover Design by
Jodie Peterson

Ice Castle Editions
Lakewood, Colorado

Gilliland Printing, Inc.
Arkansas City, Kansas

Copyright 1994 by
Darlene Godat Weir

All rights reserved, including the right to reproduce this volume thereof in any form. For book review purposes, parts of the text not in excess of 350 words may be reproduced without permission in writing from the author. Photographs may not be reproduced without permission in writing from the author.

Library of Congress Catalog
Card No. 94-096368

First Printing
November 1994

Weir, Darlene Godat.
Leadville's Ice Palace: A Colossus in the Colorado Rockies/Darlene Godat Weir
   p. cm.
Includes bibliographical references and index.

ISBN 0-9637431-0-4

1. Leadville (Colo.)—History—1876-1950.   2. Ice palaces—Colorado Leadville 1. Title.
F784-L4W45 1994   978.8'46'031
                         QB194-1755

IN MEMORY

In loving memory of my dad,
Gerald (Jerry) Augustus Godat,
who started me on this journey to find
Leadville's Ice Palace,
and learn its history.

Professor Gustavas Augustus Godat

Darlene Godat Weir

ACKNOWLEDGEMENTS

To my children, Gary Longwell, Becky (Longwell) Jackson, Richard Longwell and Marcia (Longwell) Mabey, for all of your encouragement, prodding, faith and love, I leave this legacy.

To Leadville historians and authors, Don and Jean Griswold, for sharing information and their historical expertise with me, for the many hours spent reading my manuscript and making corrections to help make this book as accurate as possible, I'm eternally grateful.

To my editor, Ben McDonald, for his patience, countless hours of reading and rereading my drafts and manuscript, and for his help and suggestions in making the book readable and interesting. Thank you! Thank you!

To my husband, Wilbur, for his help, support, encouragement, and patience while I was traveling to research for the book, and hours spent in writing it, thank you!

To my brother, Larry Godat, for my painting of the ice palace, which is used as my book cover. Thank you, it's beautiful!

To my niece, Jodie Peterson, for accepting the challenge to design my book cover, and putting up with the many changes made to it. Thanks, I knew you could do it!

To Gina Brown, Terry and the late Florence Fitzsimmons, Doug Brown, Eve Cass, Francys Stalcar, Evelyn Furman, Rod Gifford and Harry Beck, Berta and "J. J." Coble, Mike Donovan, the late Olivia Reichle, Elvira N. Brown and Arthur McNair, Fred Smith, Patsy Hodgell, Velma Churchill, Francis and Freda Rizzari, Robert L. Brown, Jim Tilden, Michael Pizzuto, Earl Maddox, David Russell, Margie and Bob Gunter at American Heritage Photographs, and the many others who unselfishly shared their photographs, memorabilia, expertise and stories with me for use in my book, and to the many Leadville natives who allowed me interviews; my thanks, gratitude and appreciation to all of you.

To Nancy Manly, and the staffs of the Lake County Library, Leadville; Colorado Historical Society, Stephen Hart Library; Mesa County Library; Denver Public Library, Western Collection; Aspen Library; Colorado Springs Pioneer History Museum; Salida Public Library and Pueblo Public Library for your help and assistance in gathering information for this historical narrative. My deepest thanks and appreciation.

To Nolan J. Doesken and his staff at the Colorado Climate Center at Colorado State University for their invaluable assistance in providing needed weather information from 1895-96. Thank you so much for your time and help.

To the many members of clubs and organizations that I have presented my Leadville Ice Palace slide lectures to; for your encouragement, I thank you.

PREFACE

I came to Leadville for the first time as a child in 1937. An apartment across the street from the Tabor Opera House was home, and I attended both Central and 9th Street grade schools. Summers were spent playing around the many old mine dumps on the lower east side of town and in the old abandoned stagecoaches and buckboard wagons behind the Opera House. I remember playing hide and seek in the "cribs" along the alley down on "2" street. The Miners Club and the Bank Club, the prostitutes and gamblers are long faded memories. Sneaking into the old abandoned bank on West Fourth Street near Harrison Avenue was done on a dare. (My brother, our playmates and I thought there were ghosts in there and when we found there weren't we delighted in jumping into the piles of papers, canceled checks and other such documents that had been left many years before.)

Harrison Avenue was quite different then. Long gone are Swanson's Poolhall in the Tabor Opera House, Charlie Koch's grocery store on Second and Harrison, Robert's Variety Store, Elmer's Grocery, Cummings Grocery, the Liberty Bell theater and The Pharmacy (I. A. Taylor's drugstore). One of my fondest memories is of the beautiful lobby in the Vendome Hotel. Shops faced the Avenue and when you walked into the lobby past them, to the left of the front desk was the fountain and pond with huge Rocky Mountain trout swimming lazily. The lobby floor was marble, inlaid with silver dollars from Tabor's days when he ruled as the Silver King. Long hikes to the Arkansas Valley Smelter and picnics near the little red schoolhouse at Malta bring back happy childhood memories.

Following an eight-year education in metro-Denver schools I returned to "God's Country," Leadville, in 1949. In 1967, my Dad told me about our family's connection

vii

with Leadville's Ice Palace. As a member of Beta Sigma Phi sorority I chose the Ice Palace as the topic for my required program that year.

My curiosity of the ice palace and my family's ties to it never diminished; and in 1981, after my children were grown and on their own I started intensively researching its history and began collecting photographs of it.

I became a public speaker for Public Service Company of Colorado's PSCommunicator group and implemented a slide lecture. During my 11-year tenure as a speaker I had the opportunity to give hundreds of presentations, speaking to thousands of people about Leadville's ice colossus, throughout Colorado. I was surprised to learn of the many people who had never heard of Leadville's Ice Palace, a number of them native Coloradans. I knew I wanted to write a never before told history about it. This book is the culmination of those years of digging up the ghosts.

Very little has been written about the ice palace, most of which was general information. I wanted to learn more about this magnificent castle and the overwhelming odds the people of Leadville surmounted to make it possible. Being a novice at both research and writing, my task was long and painstaking. However, the more information I found, the more I wanted to find about Leadville's Ice Palace. (I felt my great grandad was urging me to take on this project.) Every new bit of information I found was like striking gold.

This undertaking must have been a nightmare for the newspaper reporters. There were so many activities going on with the ice palace and winter carnival during those hectic weeks it must have been impossible for them to cover every detail at length in order to meet their deadlines and get the news to the readers on time. My biggest obstacle was in tracking down the correct names of some of those involved—incorrect spellings, in some instances no first names, and if initials were used, sometimes those were transposed or wrong. Whether these were reporting or typesetting errors is impossible to determine. I can only say that I could not have made these corrections without the help and knowledge of Don Griswold, to whom I am eternally grateful. (Thank God for his razor-sharp memory.)

I felt the complete story needed to be told. Since so little had been written of its history, I wanted to be able to tell about people from all walks of life who not only built the ice palace, but of those who had other connections with it as well. The ice palace was, in itself, a colossus, but other amusements that were built and the many events held in conjunction with the winter carnival piqued my curiosity. I wanted to learn everything possible about, what I consider to be, the greatest architectural undertaking ever attempted in Colorado at that time. Considering the time in which it was built following the Silver Panic, the sagging economy in Leadville and the drastic decline in the population of that city; this was an unbelievable project. It tells of the people who made it possible, and the many trials and tribulations they faced in getting the ice palace built. It tells of the carpenters, the stonemasons, the laborers and the teamsters, and the businessmen who made it happen. These men, unskilled in ice construction, and without earth movers, cranes and other labor and timesaving tools and machinery, in **Forty-Five** days, built and finished construction of this unique, only fully utilized ice palace ever built, a colossus in the Colorado Rockies. The businessmen, led by Tingley S. Wood, in less than two months, coordinated and brought about a program of ceremonies, parades, activities and events that took place during the three-month winter carnival. The tasks they accomplished under the circumstances, and the limited communications and transportation facilities, to me, are mind-boggling.

I chose to use some articles from the newspapers for two reasons: (1) to show the type of vocabulary used during that time and (2) I felt they illustrated the incidents far better than I could rewrite them. As for the list of names; I included them with the hope that perhaps some of my readers might find an ancestor or family friend who had the opportunity to see Leadville's Ice Palace. Perhaps even send that reader to a picture album or old trunk to dig for possible souvenirs of that wonderful time.

There are no visible landmarks on the site where the ice palace stood to pay tribute to this miraculous structure. Its memory has been kept alive by the many stories handed down through the years and the limited history written about it.

It is my hope and intention, through this book, a culmination of years of digging up the ghosts, to bring the ice palace back once more.

Darlene Godat Weir

— Darlene Godat Weir
Lakewood, Colorado

TABLE OF CONTENTS

Harrison Avenue, Winter in Leadville
Colorado Historical Society

PROLOGUE

1893-1896

Worldwide—*Alfred Nobel established the peace prize in Sweden; Marchese Guglielmo Marconi received the patent for the first wireless telegraph in Britain; the first modern Olympic Games were held in Athens, Greece; Grover Cleveland was the 24th president of the United States; James J. Corbett was the World's Heavyweight Boxing Champion, and for a nickel (a lot of money in those days), deposited in Thomas Edison's 1896 jukebox one could hear a creaky "Avalon." In Leadville, Colorado, the largest ice palace ever built on the North American continent opened in 1896.*

The mining world was reeling after the Sherman Silver Purchase Act was repealed in July of 1893. The price of silver plunged from $1.60 an ounce to less than sixty cents an ounce.

The Silver Panic devastated the city of Leadville, Colorado, and brought the roaring mining camp to its knees. Mines closed, men were thrown out of work, and the city's economy plummeted. People left in droves, many with only the clothes on their backs, to seek fortunes elsewhere. Millionaires were suddenly sent into poverty. Many committed suicide; some men abandoned their families or turned to drink. In 1893, Leadville boasted a population of more than forty thousand; in 1895, the census takers reported 14,477 residents.

The years of 1893-94 were tough for the city, but by 1895 Leadville was starting to get back on its feet, and becoming a mining leader once again. Mines were being reopened, gold was the leading ore, and other metals were being taken from the hills. But the Leadville community was far from being the strong, stable mining camp it had been before the Silver Panic.

Even with this resurgence, Leadville's businessmen were concerned about the weak economy, the number of still-unemployed men, and the probable exodus of many of its citizens during the coming winter holiday season. These factors prompted the construction of the biggest ice palace ever built on the North American continent, possibly in the world!

ICE PALACES !! . . . They have been built since the 1700's. The first one in Russia, then the idea caught on and they were built in Canada and the United States in St. Paul, Minnesota and Leadville, Colorado. The Montreal palace, built in 1883, was the first to use electric lighting. St. Paul, Minnesota followed later with its first ice palace in 1886. To this day, St. Paul, Minnesota periodically builds ice palaces. The winter carnival and ice palace idea was spreading. In 1894 the people of Quebec, Canada had joined in, building an ice palace in conjunction with a winter carnival. The carnival, however, was short-lived and only lasted a short eight days. Ottawa, Canada, in 1895, built a small ice palace.

LET'S BUILD AN ICE PALACE
The Idea Takes Hold

A suggestion to build an ice palace in Leadville was first made as early as 1888. Mining magnate Roswell Eaton Goodell proposed building an ice palace near Evergreen Lakes, southwest of the city, but his idea never materialized.

Edwin W. Senior came to Leadville in February 1895, from Salt Lake City. He entered a real estate business in partnership with John C. Smith with offices at 107 East Sixth Street in Leadville. In addition to being an enterprising realtor, he was an even better promoter. Whether he came to Leadville to make money in the real estate business, or through promotional endeavors is not clear.

During a meeting of a group of thirty-nine businessmen, in the reception room of the Vendome Hotel one late summer day in 1895, discussion of Leadville's economy surfaced. The holidays were not far away and people would be taking excursions elsewhere, seeking entertainment, spending their money. This seemed to be the pattern for those who could afford it. During the discussion, it was mentioned that something needed to be done to keep the people, and their money, at home in Leadville. How could that be accomplished?

To whom is due the honor of having first proposed an ice palace for Leadville, or where the inception originated, is not clear. Senior can be given credit for creating the impetus for a winter carnival and an ice palace. The two-mile-high city was a natural for an ice palace. Leadville was blessed (or cursed) with long, cold winters, a dry climate, and an abundance of one of her natural resources—ice. (Regarding the weather, on August 20th the *Leadville Herald Democrat* reported, "Leadville, the past week has been good growing

1

weather; heavy rain on the 14th, crops growing rapidly, haying begun, slight frost during the week.") The city also had excellent railroad position.

What better way to boost the economy? There were still men unemployed as a result of the Silver Panic. Senior's plan would put them back to work, spur the economy, and promote tourism. Leadville was trying to shed its reputation as a rough, tough mining town. The idea of building an ice palace would give the city an opportunity to show the outside world its cultural side. Surely it would bring some money into the city coffers. Leadville had always been known to support other cities throughout Colorado, financially and otherwise. It was payback time. The ice palace might even cause a few excursion trains to be sidetracked. Many of them carried passengers from the east through Colorado on their way to the warmer climates of California and other points west and south during the winter months. Perhaps the passengers wouldn't mind spending some of their money in Leadville.

Senior's enthusiasm was contagious. The men liked the idea! So much so that Senior was assured by some of the gentlemen in the group that his expenses would be paid if he would promote the ice palace.

Senior told the businessmen that if Leadville were to build an ice palace it should be one that could be used and enjoyed by the community, not just a ice facade. It would, indeed, have to be unique and useable.

W. L. Temple, Senior's associate, had lived in Montreal, Canada during some of the winter carnival seasons. Temple provided Senior with invaluable service and input for Leadville's venture. It should be noted here that W. L. Temple also came from Salt Lake City in 1895. He was

2

engaged in the insurance business and resided at 128 East 8th Street.

Mr. Temple had received some figures from Montreal regarding the last ice palace they had built. The Montreal ice palace had cost approximately $5,000 to build. It was 150 feet square with a tower 75 feet high, and this was in a city of 200,000 people! Leadville had never been known to do anything halfway, nor would they now. They could, and would, outdo Montreal!

Before departing the city on business, Senior stated that the location, size of the palace, management, and the many details for the enterprise would be voted upon by the subscribers. He also proposed getting architectural designs for the palace by offering top money for the accepted plans. His intent was to advertise for qualified competitors throughout the country.

Following a ten-day business trip to Salt Lake City, Senior began promoting the ice palace to Leadville's citizens. He lost no time in talking to the working people; the merchants, the miners. However, he did not approach the bankers or the saloon keepers at that time (much to his regret, later). His intent was to contact the common people, for if they would back him, he felt that there would be no trouble getting the big money later. Those he spoke to were in favor of the project and were enthusiastically willing to subscribe. It was possible they might even get a return on their investment.

After canvassing the railroads, Senior was assured they were behind the project one hundred percent, offering to advertise the ice palace extensively along their routes, countrywide.

3

According to Mr. W. F. Bailey, General Passenger Agent for the Colorado Midland Railroad, approximately fifteen percent of the westbound transcontinental winter travel passed through Leadville. He was of the opinion that with enough advertising in the east, travel through Leadville could be increased by fifty percent.

Frank Wadleigh, General Passenger Agent of the Rio Grande Western Railroad, reassured the people through a letter to Mr. Senior, that the railroad companies who had lines into Leadville would be greatly interested in the success of this venture. They would advertise throughout the Pacific coast and the northwest territory as well as in the east, and assist with distribution of any special advertising.

The Denver papers were quick to report Leadville's plan to build an ice palace. Leadville was given a lot of free publicity when word got out that the Cloud City was going to build an ice palace and have a winter carnival. Even the outlying tabloids had their say. One Cripple Creek tabloid reported that Leadville was planning an attraction in the shape of an ice palace, "but it would be a cold day before she gets it." To which Leadville replied they were hoping for thirty to ninety cold days; they weren't advertising a summer enterprise. The *New York World* newspaper gave the ice palace a full page write-up under the flattering(?) caption "The Wickedest City in America."

On Friday, September 13th (an ominous date), Senior was in Denver to meet with the Chamber of Commerce for the purpose of securing not their money, but their support and cooperation in the ice palace venture. Senior touted this as an enterprise which would bring statewide benefits. His presentation of the project gained wholehearted support, and the Chamber's endorsement.

A mass meeting had been set up for the following Monday evening, September 16th, at the Weston Opera House in Leadville. Judge A. S. Weston had kindly consented use of the opera house (formerly the Tabor Opera House) for this meeting. The Denver Chamber of Commerce agreed to send a committee of at least a dozen members to represent Denver and back the ice palace enterprise. To show their strong support of the ice palace, the Colorado Midland Railroad provided transportation to bring the committee to Leadville, and held their night train going back to Denver until the meeting was over. Denver's daily newspapers sent representatives to give full coverage to this exciting undertaking.

Senior explained the purpose of the meeting would be to select an executive organization, and Leadville's citizens should have a voice in making those selections. Second, detailed plans for the ice palace would be presented. Broad outlines of the palace endeavor had been discussed and agreed upon by interested business men. Now it was time to bring those plans to the people.

The Weston Opera House was packed that September evening. Senior presented the plan to his audience, leading off by telling them the high altitude and extremely dry air could well support an ice palace for a two or three-month long festival. Senior asked the audience to picture a structure of pure ice, lit by various colored electric lights flashing their rainbow colors through the walls and tower. At night a bombardment and attack on the palace would be fended off by thousands of rockets. A fireworks display would shower the palace in beautiful colors, reflecting their light off the snow-capped Rockies which stood sentinel over the city. Surely an enterprise such as this would bring visitors to the city from all parts of the country.

Mr. Senior told the audience he found the Denver people ready and willing to support Leadville in their undertaking and make the ice palace a credit to the entire state of Colorado.

He had the assurance of the local ice company that they could provide all the ice needed by December first. With that in mind, it was decided to open the ice palace to the public on New Year's Day. With foresight, he told the citizens that if any of the sides of the ice palace should be affected by the sun, they could be protected by canvas. It was proposed that the main building would not be less than 200 feet square and twenty feet high.

Montreal's palace was only 150 feet square, and the same height. A prize was offered to architects throughout the country for the best ice palace design.

Senior presented preliminary plans depicting a large building with a skating rink and dance pavilion. Smaller rooms, booths and stalls for special displays might be needed. The main attraction was to be a display of the state's many industries. These, however, were going to be displayed in a most unusual and unique fashion. As the walls were built, the displays would be frozen in the ice blocks. This would allow them to be seen by natural light during the daytime and by electric lights at night. Exhibits would consist of everything from the most delicate flowers to the largest game animals. Fruits, vegetables, ore, fish, wild game, wheat and other items would be encased in ice blocks. Senior envisioned thousands of electric lights illuminating the palace. The roof would be of wood construction, but painted and decorated to blend with the rest of the structure. An enormous toboggan slide, grander than any other built, was sure to draw crowds of people. At that time the palace site had not yet been selected, but people familiar with the city knew many sites would work well for this gigantic slide. It was planned to extend a mile, with a turn or two, and end within a block of the starting point. In front of the main entrance would be a tower one to two hundred feet high. From the top, the slide was to extend to the streets. It was said Leadville's streets never lacked enough snow in winter to ride for at least a mile, and with the speed built up from the top of the tower they might go even further. Senior had no doubt the toboggan slide would be the most popular attraction of the winter carnival.

The railroads took a great interest in the festival and would exhibit, along with advertising it wholeheartedly. In 1894 more than 50,000 people traveled from the east to California, but only fifteen percent of them passed through Colorado, with only three percent stopping. It would be in the railroads' best interest to divert as much of that traffic as possible over their lines from the railroads that didn't travel through the state. The railroad representatives felt that an ice palace and toboggan slide could surely help attract more visitors to Colorado.

It was estimated at that time that the ice palace would cost less than $15,000 . . . probably not more than $12,000. Subscribers would be the stockholders and receive their investment returns from the net proceeds. Senior was so sure of their support he felt they would subscribe even if they didn't receive reimbursement.

It should be noted here, that although Senior mentioned stockholders and investment returns, it was not his intent to form a corporation. The interested parties would be an association, headed by a board of directors. It was not until Tingley S. Wood became the Director General that a corporation was established and shares of stock were sold.

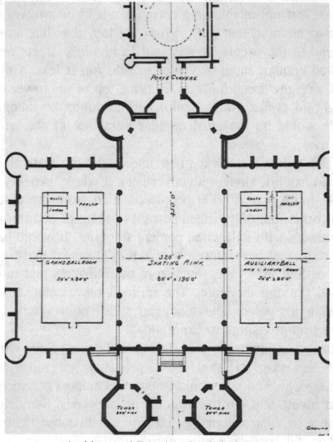

Architectural Drawing, Ice Palace Interior.
Denver Public Library, Western History Department

FUNDRAISING
Thousands of Dollars Needed

A rousing reception was held at the Weston Opera House on September 16, 1895. Senior, along with W. L. Temple, had already been seeking contributions and they were overwhelmed by the public response. Prior to the meeting they had already collected over $300, quite a tidy sum in those days. "The ice palace is the war cry. Everybody wants it. The young lady sighs for it and the baby cries for it," reported the *Leadville Herald Democrat*. The ice palace received a hearty endorsement. It was noted, however, there was very little representation from the businessmen of the community. This only supported the argument that this kind of a public enterprise was needed to unite the Leadville citizens in one common goal.

The Weston was crowded that evening, the gallery packed. Eloquent speeches, rousing music and the hearty enthusiasm of the crowd left no doubt that the ice palace would be a success. It was announced later that evening that Messrs. Senior and Temple had secured close to $2,000 in subscriptions, with additional promises that would raise the total to $4,500. The Leadville community was in agreement that they would no longer lose their people to other cities, but would make their own entertainment for them.

Although the scarcity of businessmen did not go unnoticed, women made up nearly half the audience and they were the most enthusiastic. The railroads came forward announcing their support of the ice palace on banners of gold which were displayed on the stage and arches.

Mayor Samuel D. Nicholson, L. Frank Brown, Judge Thomas A. Dickson, Reverend T. W. Jeffery of the Methodist Episcopal church and Reverend A. G. Evans of the First Presbyterian Church were seated on the stage. The proscenium boxes (box seats) were filled with lovely Leadville women, eager to applaud the speakers. The best of the local vocalists, a theatrical whistler, an impersonator and a poet, headed the entertainment bill for the evening. This mass meeting was said to be a fitting opening for the winter carnival.

Mayor Nicholson, who was said to usually be stern and severe, was beaming on this occasion. "There is no place, by nature, better intended for an ice palace than here in Leadville. If there is any doubt as to its success, that doubt has been dispelled by the presence of this enthusiastic audience I see before me."[1] The mayor then called upon the players from the Musicians Union of Leadville, who had volunteered their services, for an overture. They were followed by a quartet made up of Professor Leonard Worchester and Messrs. John Lea, H. N. Temple and Mr. Beasley.

This was then followed by the introduction of promoter, Mr. E. W. Senior. Senior gave credit to the *Leadville Herald Democrat* for suggesting the ice palace, (why the *Herald* was given credit has not been determined), then presented the layout for the ice palace venture. He compared the significance of Leadville's ice palace to what Peach Day, Melon Day, Apple Day and the Festival of Mountain and Plain meant to their respective towns. The only and biggest difference would be Leadville would have sixty to ninety days to bring tourists and their money to town, not just one day. He saw every hotel, boarding and

---

[1]*Leadville Herald Democrat*, September 17, 1895.

10

rooming house, and furnished room being occupied; every restaurant and business being well patronized.

B. L. Winchell, General Passenger and Ticket Agent of the Denver, South Park & Gunnison Railway, gave the ice palace his hearty support along with that of the Union Pacific. Agent W. F. Bailey of the Colorado Midland stood ready to assist the project in every way possible. He suggested that railroads selling tickets to Leadville should incorporate one or more admission tickets to the ice palace in their price. The Midland was prepared to offer low excursion rates to Leadville making it possible for people to visit the ice palace often. He favored a rate less than one fare for the round trip with a limited stay of not more than three days. He was proposing a round trip rate for points east as far as Chicago. These would be in line with year-round rates already agreed upon by Helena, Butte, Spokane and other points in the northwest. S. K. Hooper of the Denver & Rio Grande sent assurances that his company would cooperate to the fullest in this endeavor.

Senior went on to announce that every business in Leadville had given support to the ice palace with the exception of the bankers and saloon keepers. He said that he was not a drinking man and that the saloon keepers would not listen to him. It was later said that someone made the comment they would not support Senior. How could they trust a man who wouldn't have a drink with them? Regarding the bankers, he admitted that he had not set up a bank account in Leadville. (He had been in the city since early February and here it was mid-September!)

In 1895 there were three banks in Leadville; the American National Bank, the Carbonate National Bank and the

11

Leadville Savings & Deposit Bank, headed up by Peter W. Breene.

Senior's comment was that when he approached some of the bankers he felt as if he were already in the ice palace (about twenty degrees below zero!).

One doubting Thomas he had approached was apprehensive about the enterprise. His concern was that at Leadville's altitude (10,152 feet), the ice palace would attract lightning. Senior suggested lightning rods as protection. With that the man replied that there wasn't a man in town who knew how to put up a lightning rod. This drew hearty laughter from the audience. In closing, Senior read a poem which he wrote. (See Poetry.)

Judge Thomas A. Dickson was introduced as a man who could tell the audience all about the legal aspects of the ice palace venture. He was of little concern regarding the legalities and didn't think the lawyers would make too much of it either. He then went on to "beat the drum" for the ice palace, urging everyone's support of the enterprise that would reap a harvest of benefits for the city of Leadville and its citizens. He commented that the song presented earlier, "Home Sweet Home," had touched the hearts of the audience:

> As many of us as came here ten or fifteen years ago, came here with the idea of striking it rich and spending it some other place. We want to say we live in Leadville and take pride in calling it the greatest mining camp on earth. We ought not to stop and ask whether we can make something out of the carnival. We should stand shoulder to shoulder and say to the last that although our chief industry was struck down, yet Leadville has risen, Phoenixlike, out

12

of its ashes. Leadville is the only city in the United States that can have a successful ice palace. There is a large travel to the west that can be attracted here. Would not a beautiful ice palace cause them to stop here? This Leadville enterprise must have the support of every man and woman. We must talk about it . . . We will attract the attention of all the world to Leadville. We will hold here the first successful carnival held in this country.

His rousing speech was followed by thunderous applause. L. Frank Brown, touted as Leadville's most eloquent young lawyer, gave an excellent speech on the subject. G. A. Eldredge's recitation, entitled "The Debating School," met with resounding laughter.

W. L. Temple, Mr. Senior's associate in the enterprise, gave an eloquent speech outlining details for the venture:

The *Cripple Creek Mail* has very kindly assured us that "it'll be a cold day when Leadville builds an ice palace." This prediction has been a great relief to us. There has been, in the minds of some, a fear that nature would enter a protest against this cold proposition, and would clothe herself in Indian summer garb. (Little did he know that statement would come to pass.) But now the prophet in our sister city has stated, after careful investigation, "It will be a cold day." I trust we will be able to obtain ninety of the same kind from the same source. Never in the United States, outside of St. Paul, has there been attempted this matchless attraction. Leadville is permanently fitted for such an enterprise. She has the railroad position, she has the climate, and above all, her enterprising and pushing citizens. I see upon the canvas two names, Montreal and Leadville. Montreal, the metropolis of Canada; Leadville

13

the Cloud City, with its massive snow-covered, rock-ribbed walls, the admiration of the world. In waiting upon the businessmen of Leadville, Mr. Senior has met with hearty response in the interest of the grand carnival. The enthusiasm of this occasion cannot be doubted. Cold facts have been stated here tonight. Everybody is saying "Ice Palace." "Ice Palace," is everywhere. And so we desire everyone to talk "Ice Palace," and to be written everywhere. I received, from Montreal a few days ago, a few figures relative to their last ice palace. It cost $5,000, was 150 feet square and the tower is 75 feet high, and this is a city of 200,000. From present indications, Leadville will do even better than this. Picture to yourself, if you please, a structure of this size built of pure ice, illuminated within by different colored electric lights, flashing their rainbow colors through walls and towers. At night, a bombardment and attack on the ice palace, repulsed by a thousand rockets, a pyrotechnics display bathing in beautiful colors, the white robed sentinels all around the matchless, snow-covered Rockies, and then ask, will not the carnival be a good thing for our city. Leadville is on the transcontinental line from the east to the Pacific coast. With proper advertising thousands of visitors will be attracted to the unique road and matchless attractions, and we will see this Cloud City, around whose neck there will be a chain of travelers from east and west and north and south, and from whose breast will glitter the Kohenoor diamond of the world, the ice palace, flashing its rainbow beauty over this Eldorado of America and the entire Union.

Multi-talented Leadville lady, Ruth Ward Kahn, had written a musical composition which was sung by Mrs. Singletary.

14

A petition was voiced to elect a board to head up the ice palace project. Senior was unanimously voted Director General (since he had presented the suggestion to build the palace, and had already done some promotional work around the city). Other members elected were: S. D. Nicholson, Mayor of Leadville, who later became a United States Senator; Joseph H. Weddle, manager of the Arkansas Valley Smelter; C. N. Priddy, Superintendent of the Leadville Water Company; J. W. Smith, who was a partner with Daniels & Fisher; John F. Campion, mine owner and general manager of the Ibex Mining Company; George L'Abbe, French gambler and manager of the Board of Trade Saloon; James J. Brown, general manager of the Rex Mining Company; D. H. Dougan, President of the Carbonate National Bank, and Charles T. Limberg, President of the American National Bank.

The *Leadville Herald Democrat* on August 18, 1895 headlined:

> Novel Arctic Attraction has unique plans to make Leadville a winter resort of national reputation. Mr. E. W. Senior proposes to carry the scheme to a successful ending by getting the businessmen and others interested in the prosperity of Leadville to unite in making the carnival a success.

Senior had done a good amount of preliminary groundwork, but there was still much to do. Raising the money was first and foremost in the minds of the directors. It would be the responsibility of the ice palace board to secure funds to build the ice palace, and the duty of

15

Leadville's citizens to donate and support them. The Leadville citizens were behind the ice palace and winter carnival idea all the way.

September's weather was very rainy; not severe, but the continual drizzling rain, when combined with the low temperatures, was very unpleasant. But it didn't dampen the spirits of the hardy Leadville citizens. Their enthusiastic support of the ice palace dispelled any dreariness caused by the rainy weather.

However, toward the end of the month, the donations began to slow down and by September's end, stopped altogether. Despite Senior's efforts, the Leadville people put a hold on the money that had been collected so far, $4,000.

Winter was coming to the high country. On October 2, 1895, two inches of snow covered the ground. Two days later, October 4th, Senior petitioned the county commissioners to lease five acres of land to the Winter Carnival and Ice Palace Association. The site, then known as Capitol Hill, was part of the Stevens & Leiter subdivision, located between West Seventh and West Eighth Streets, in the four and five hundred blocks. This included lots 9 through 22 in Block 53.

The commissioners had no problem with the lease. In proceedings of the Board of County Commissioners of Lake County, Colorado, dated October 7, 1895, the following was recorded:

Petition from Winter Carnival and Ice Palace Association was read, on motion received and filed, and on further motion, the following resolution was passed. Resolved, that the chairman of the board be authorized and empowered to lease all the rights the County of Lake has in and

16

to Lots 9, 10, 11, 12, 13, 14, 15, 16, 17, 18, 19, 20, 21 & 22 in Block 53, Stevens and Leiter subdivision of the City of Leadville to the Winter Carnival and Ice Palace Association for the period of three years from this date, expiring October 7, 1898. The said premise to be used entirely and exclusively for the purposes of said association and the lease not to be assigned or subleased to other parties. The consideration to be an annual rent of $1 per year.

Edwin W. Senior *Courtesy Georgina Brown*

THE ICE PALACE FALTERS
Donations Stop Cold

In 1895 there were eighty-three saloons and three banks in Leadville.

Senior urged the Association's members to talk to the saloon keepers and the bankers, encouraging them to support the ice palace by donating money for its construction. This did not seem to work, however. By the end of September the donations had stopped cold; colder than the weather had been that entire month.

Volunteer weather observer, J. C. Paddock, reported, "There has been much more rainy weather this month. Not severe rains, but continued drizzly rains with a low temperature that made it unpleasant."[2]

Senior would not be discouraged by the sudden halt of subscriptions; winter was in the air and he was determined to build the ice palace. But the citizens would not budge. There would be no more money donated toward the ice palace venture. Senior was becoming more and more aware of this with each day that passed. He sensed the distrust and animosity of dissenters. The enthusiasm that had gripped the city in the beginning was waning, and by the end of September was all but gone.

In late September a petition was being circulated designating Tingley S. Wood as Director General of the Ice

---

[2]J. C. Paddock was the Voluntary Observer in Leadville. It was from his written reports to the U.S. Department of Agriculture Weather Bureau in 1895-96 that Leadville's Ice Palace weather information was taken. Colorado Climate Center, Colorado State University, Fort Collins, Colorado.

Palace and Winter Carnival Association. The petition was signed by subscribers as well as many other people who would substantially support Leadville's winter carnival. Mr. Wood was aware of this too, and although he had not yet consented to take the position, he was doing his homework. He sent telegrams to other cities in the country where ice palaces had been built. He requested figures regarding size and cost of the ice palaces, as well as other information pertinent to Leadville's endeavor.

Support of Wood grew stronger in the next few weeks, and Senior's was nonexistent. Finally, on Thursday, October 19, 1895, Senior sent a letter of resignation to the Association Board. He knew that as long as he stayed there would be no money or support for the ice palace. The enthusiasm he had built up among the people was weak, and donations came to a standstill. At that time $5,000 had been subscribed, but was being withheld until he stepped down. Whether he was promoting himself, incurred the wrath of the bankers and saloon keepers, or if the big-money men resented an outsider coming in to take the glory for suggesting the Ice Palace enterprise; this author will leave to the reader to decide.

Following his resignation from the Board, Senior went to Salt Lake City to promote a salt palace.

CONNED BY A HUCKSTER
Newlyweds Lured to Leadville

It didn't take long for the con-artists to appear on the scene after the ice palace was announced. The *Leadville Herald Democrat* reported this story on October 25, 1895.

———

An Ice Palace Romance

———

Tribulations of a Bridal Couple
Who Came to See the Wonderful Leadville Attraction

———

Seduced by the Goddess

———

A Bunko Steerer Gets $10 of His Money

———

A Wild Goose Chase to Leadville and
a Visit to the Court House

———

There are two persons in this city who would rather be very pleased if they were somewhere else on this footstool, not quite so close to the top. Mr. and Mrs. Charles Clauser, their matrimonial existence extending over a period of two weeks. During these two weeks they have had more experience than usually falls to the lot of

21

people who have been married for two years or more. The Clausers lived in Pueblo and were not over blessed with the world's goods, for Charlie was only a typewriter and clerk in a wholesale commission house, and his salary was not very munificent but with due economy on the part of Mrs. C., who had been a saleslady in the ribbon department of a dry goods store there, they managed to make both ends meet. After the matrimonial expense had been paid, the young couple discovered that they had a few dollars left, and decided that it would be "awful nice" to take a trip to the Festival of Mountain and Plain. This was done on a cheap rate, a boarding house was found and a glorious time was had. When the parade was over there was a young man came along on a burro carrying a banner inscribed with the magic words "Leadville Ice Palace." They had just seen the way up Leadville float, the gorgeous horses, all gold and silver, the divinely beautiful goddess who held the cornucopia from which flowed the rivulets of precious metals. Wifey had said "oh" in several different tunes and languages, and he had remarked in choice Puebloese, "Golly, ain't it fine. Wonder where it come from," said she sweetly. "Dunno," said he. But—with an air of superior knowledge—"I can find out." He soon learned that the magnificent float was the product of the great mining camp of Leadville. "She's a beaut," said he, iaconically. "Them fixin's she had on were out of sight. Say, Liz, there's an ice palace up there. We've got enough money to take us. Let's go." She looked at him reproachfully and then a tear trickled down her cheek, making a little white furrow through the liberal sprinkling of Denver dust. "I just think you are horrid, so I do, Charles Clauser. You are only stuck on that horrid painted up thing on that wagon, and only wanted to go to Leadville to see her. I don't like you any more and I'll just go back to my mother and get a divorce, so I will. Boo Hoo" and

22

here three or four more tears started to trickle down, each making a separate furrow for themselves. Poor Charles looked unutterable things (dirty looks). The crowd had begun to notice the little performance, and so he hastily took her by the arm and led her back to the hotel where after some "goo goo" talk she was "coaxed back to smiles" again, and then Charles once more broached the ice palace. "Here, we have some money left; enough to take us there and see the palace. It's all made of ice, and the finest thing in the world. I'll go out and try to find out about it." According to Charlie's tale of woe, told a reporter yesterday, he went to the Hotel Albany, where he understood there was a man who represented the ice palace. He was referred to a sleek looking man, who told him that the ice palace was already built, and that he was an agent of a company that was just about to open up a big bazaar in the palace, where they were to sell all kinds of fancy goods, curios, etc. "Now," said the slick young man, "you appear to be a bright young fellow, and if you understand clerking I think we can get you a job. Come around tomorrow." With a radiant smile Charlie rushed to the hotel and told of his prospects. He would get a job in a real live ice palace! Next day he returned to the hotel, and was informed that as a guarantee of good faith, the company would require a deposit of $10 which would be refunded at the end of the first month. Then Charlie carefully counted his cash, discovered that he would have enough money left to get to Leadville and board him for several days. So the bargain was made, the money paid over and a receipt drawn up in legal form made out, and Charlie prepared to start for the new field of usefulness in high feather. The young man had given him the name of Clark J. Monroe, Hotel Vendome, Leadville, as the general manager of the firm for which he was to work. As the train neared the Cloud City, the young couple began to watch out of the windows to catch a glimpse

23

of the beautiful palace of ice. They espied the glimmering dome of the court house surmounted by the queenly figure of the Goddess of Justice, and Charlie murmured to himself; (I'm danged if they ain't got that girl on top of the ice palace!) "Now Charlie, there you are again talking about that horrid thing, and if that's her on top of that palace, I just hope she'll stay there and freeze." Charlie assured his bride his admiration was purely harmless, and that his little wifey, need have no jealous pangs on account of the statuesque creature who crowned the glittering dome of ice. This little quarrel was settled as are all such honeymoon quarrels, and soon the train glided into the station. They took a bus to a hotel not quite so expensive as the Vendome, and concluded to take a stroll out to the ice palace. They took their bearings from the figure of the goddess and, hastened toward the massive structure. "My," said he, "it must be a big affair to be located right in the heart of the city." However, they were soon at the court house. "Why Charlie, that ain't ice, is it?" said Lizzie, as they neared the structure. "Shh," said Charlie, "you mustn't show your ignorance to these people. The ice is fixed up to look like granite, don't you see." Lizzie, like a good little wife, subsided at the burst of superior knowledge on the part of her lord and master. But as they approached the building, Charlie began to look dubious, but not liking to display any country airs, he boldly walked up the steps and into the recorder's office. It at once flashed over him that there was something wrong, but he resolved to learn the truth. Chief Deputy H. Woodward is a reader of faces, and when he saw the couple enter quickly surmised what was wanted. He reached under the counter for the marriage license book preparatory to jerking it out when the bashful swain would make his business known. "Excuse me, sir, but can you tell me how to reach the ice palace?" The clerk looked. It flashed through his mind that they might be seeking

24

the chilly chambers of the divorce court. How? "Why you see we are strangers in the city, and I want to take a walk out to the palace which I've heard so much about." "Yes," chirped the bride, "and Charley thought that this was it, but I told him I didn't think it looked a bit like an ice palace. Didn't I, Charley," and she looked unutterable things (dirty looks.) The official had recovered his equanimity by this time, and very gravely informed them that Leadville had an ice palace, but up to date it was only on paper; that-er-in fact, he didn't think the ice palace was frozen hard enough. This was sufficient and the couple promptly took their departure. "Lizzie," "Oh, Charley." This was said after they returned to the hotel. "What shall we do?" "Dunno," said the young man. "I guess I'm what they call bunkoed."

Yesterday, Clauser was out on the streets hunting up a friend whom he had met in Pueblo to borrow, if possible, the necessary funds to get back to Pueblo. The friend was found, and after some skirmishing, sufficient funds were secured to purchase tickets for the two to their home by the raging Arkansas. It is morally certain that when the ice palace finally does materialize that it will not number at least two people of the state among the visitors. "Well, I don't care," were the last words of the sweet young wife as she stood on the depot platform. "I just knew that horrid thing in that painted chariot would get you in trouble."

SENIOR RESIGNS
WHY??

At the end of September 1895, subscriptions for the ice palace came to a halt.

On October 26th, the *Leadville Herald Democrat* printed the following letter to the editor, relative to Mr. Senior's resignation:

It is unfortunate to Mr. Senior that certain parties have found it necessary in coming to his defense to have endeavored to make him out an angel and the men who differed with him a "gang of Mephistos." Judging from the tone of the defense, all that is necessary to entail the enmity of a certain people is for a man to be prosperous in his business. It is hard to believe that Mr. Senior inspired the defense, for he could have retired from the management of the Ice Palace Association without losing his self respect and have retained the gratitude of the citizens of this city for the good work he had accomplished. Mr. Senior carried on the ice palace enterprise as far as it lay in his power. He could go no further. When he got to the $5,000 limit he stuck fast. The people would not budge further. Whipping and slashing and scolding did no good. A new driver was demanded. It was well enough to look this matter squarely in the face for this was a good deal of sneaking about the bush. Mr. Senior reiterated that he had no selfish purpose in starting the ice palace, further than to boom Leadville and, incidentally, advertise Senior. He repeatedly assured the subscribers that they could choose whom they liked for their manager. The stockholders selected a board of directors that commanded the confidence of the public. Instead of permitting the board members to choose their own manager, Mr. Senior trumped up a telegram liberally signed by Salt Lake bankers and businessmen vouching for his honesty and ability. While the stockholders were dazed at the purport of the telegram, Mr. Senior swung himself into the managerial chair, clean over the heads of the directory. This was against all precedent for it is everywhere the business custom of corporations to name a manager of their own selection, who shall be responsible to them for his acts. The directors must have felt this indignation keenly, yet they were determined to go ahead and make a success of the enterprise. But they found that the enthusiasm had died out and subscriptions had come to a standstill. Many of the bankers and businessmen refused to subscribe as long as Mr. Senior was at the head of the procession. The directors, seeing that more money could be raised without Mr. Senior than with him, intimated that his resignation would be acceptable. Mr. Senior, rather than stand in the way, discreetly placed his resignation in the hands of the directors. When Mr. Senior saw that he could do more for the ice palace by getting off rather than staying on, he got off. By this act he raised $5,000 it is said. His action met with the approval of the stockholders who made their subscriptions for the sole purpose of securing an ice palace regardless of who should be the Director General. The man who can inspire confidence and raise an additional $5,000 is the man the people want. The businessmen of Leadville are committed to the enterprise. It must go through. No man nor set of men must stand in its way. It belongs to the people, and when any man is in the way he must step aside. Neither newspapers nor croakers can prevent its success. It is no one-man enterprise, but belongs to the people. Let the right man take hold and the people will follow. Hotheaded, malignant and malevolent malediction will accomplish nothing. Let the right man take hold and the people will follow. Smile and join the procession. ss: Ice Palace Subscriber.

On October 27th, E. W. Senior replied to the accusations in a letter to the editor of the *Herald Democrat*.

I am sorry to notice in the columns of your valuable paper of this morning, that some individual signing himself "Ice Palace Subscriber," has seen fit to open an attack upon me, which I consider entirely uncalled for and a very ungrateful return for what he, whoever he may be, admits in the article I have done in the interests of the enterprise. He says, "Mr. Senior rather than stand in the way of the enterprise discreetly placed his resignation in the hands of the directors." What more does this person hiding behind the nom de plume want? This assertion that I carried the enterprise as far as lay in my power is untrue as is the statement that I reached the $4,000 limit and stuck fast. "Subscriber" further says, "Mr. Senior repeatedly gave assurance that he had no selfish purpose in getting up the ice palace." Do not my actions, from the very commencement to the time of my resignation, prove I have conclusively, to any fair-minded person, acted unselfishly? I am perfectly and fully satisfied with the credit given me in the above paragraph of "getting up the ice palace." Further on subscriber says, "He (Senior) repeatedly assured subscribers that they could choose whom they liked for manager." This they did and by a standing vote elected me to that position without a dissenting vote. Rather inconsistently subscriber added, "The stockholders selected a director that commanded the confidence of the public. Instead of permitting directory to choose its manager, Mr. Senior trumped up a telegram. While the stockholders were dazed at the purport of the telegram, Mr. Senior swung himself into the managerial chair clear over the heads of the directory." Here "subscriber" not only insults Salt Lake City, who voluntarily sent out the telegram to show their goodwill towards

Leadville and its enterprise, and only incidently mentioned me in the same, but insults every subscriber who attended that meeting. Every one of them present knew that their subscription was made with the express condition, in writing, that such a meeting should be held for the purpose of electing a General Manager. They know also that the vice president of the Board of Directors, unsolicited, read the telegram referred to, to the subscribers after I had been placed in nomination by one of the identical board of directors, with the president and vice president of that board at the meeting, all three casting their standing vote with every subscriber present. "Subscriber" further says, "The director, seeing that more money could be raised without him, intimated that his resignation would be accepted." The above statement is the keynote to the whole situation. I stood in the way of certain moneyed men subscribing and when I found they had expressed a willingness to put up if I retired, I did so. The directors, so far as I know, have no doubt as to my ability or honesty, or any ill will toward me, and I certainly have none towards them or any living soul in the Cloud City. I am not built that way. I say that the enterprise is a good one, and will be of great benefit to what, in my mind, is the greatest mining camp on earth. And I am perfectly willing to "smile and join in the procession," without any sneaking around the bush, I am one who is not ashamed to sign his real name. ss: Edwin W. Senior.

The following article was contributed to and printed in *The Free Lance*[3] on October 28, 1895 following Senior's resignation.

Editor, *Free Lance*: If you will permit me to infringe upon sufficient space in the columns of your enterprising paper in order to place myself correctly before the Leadville public, I assure you it will be appreciated. In the *Herald Democrat* of Saturday morning there appeared what I consider an uncalled for article, headed, "What The People Say," and signed, "Ice Palace Subscriber." As your paper, through the columns, has seen proper to make some comments upon the change in management, and in the face of the article referred to, I consider it a matter of justice and right that *The Lance*, as well as the *Herald Democrat*, who kindly agreed to publish my answer to "Ice Palace Subscriber," should do the same if it thinks proper. I know not who this individual hiding behind the nom de plume of "Ice Palace Subscriber," is, nor do I care, and if it were not for the insinuations thrown at my friend by implication and innuendo, I would let the article go unnoticed. . . . In answer to this, let me say that at a meeting of the Board of Directors, held on October 8, 1895, I presented those gentlemen plans for the pavilion, bids from the contractors for erecting same, bids from the ice men, and then and there informed those gentlemen the amount of cash subscribed and prospects for further subscriptions. I read to the Board a joint letter from the three railroads, as to the position they took in the matter. Also informed the gentlemen that I had secured a three-year lease from the

---

[3]The Free Lance at that time was said to be the same caliber tabloid as the *Atlantic Monthly*.

county, upon a site for the building. Then stated in substance as follows: "Gentlemen, it is necessary that I leave for Salt Lake this evening and from the progress I have made, and which is presented here before you, if you think the enterprise is not in a proper shape to proceed with, there will be no necessity of my returning. Should you believe as I do, that everything is in good and proper shape to go ahead, I will return within a few days and use my best efforts to push the same to a successful issue." It was decided by every director, seven in number, that we should go right ahead. That the secretary should proceed to collect fifty percent of the subscriptions, and when that was done, the contract let for the building according to the plans then before the directors. Accordingly, I returned from Salt Lake. Found the secretary had collected within a few hundred of the fifty percent, and started right (away) to walk in good earnest, when one day I was informed by Mr. Temple that someone had intimated that if I would resign, certain men had said they would pay handsomely. I answered very readily if the directors think this is the proper thing, you can tell them I will cause no trouble on that score and handed the secretary, a few hours later, the following letter which explains itself.

Leadville, Colo., Oct. 19, '95—Board of Directors Ice Palace and Winter Carnival Association, Leadville, Colorado—Gentlemen—My attention having been drawn to the fact that you gentlemen believe there exists in Leadville today feeling against myself acting in the position of General Manager, by many who would contribute toward carrying the enterprise to a successful conclusion, and while I may differ with you gentlemen regarding the advisability or necessity of securing the support of those referred to, still I realize that it is very essential your general manager, whoever he may be, in order to carry an enterprise of this kind to a successful issue, should and in fact: must have the confidence, and assistance and hearty cooperation of the Board of Directors. And while I fully appreciate the fact that personally you gentlemen have no objections to me, yet in an official capacity I am informed that you're present subscribers, and the enterprise would be subserved were I to resign. As you are well aware, I have faithfully devoted two months time in the interest of the plan to the exclusion of other business. On October 1, I neglected accompanying my excursion to Salt Lake, in order to go to Denver in the interest of the Ice Palace. You are aware I have neither directly or indirectly received no enumeration for my services, and while I have repeatedly assured you that I did not wish any salary or pay for past work, still I had in mind, and so stated to you, that I should be paid for my services from the time building operations were actually started. Again, I had in mind that to carry such an enterprise financially and otherwise to a successful termination, would place me not only in a creditable light before the people of your city, but the whole state. This to a young man, ambitious and trying to forge his way in the world, is the greatest consideration. My resigning would deprive me of both of the above.

I would therefore respectfully submit for your consideration, should you decide it advisable that I withdraw my subscription of $100, and further pay me the sum of $200 in lieu of money I have personally expended, and services up to date. Respectfully, E. W. Senior.

Reader, in view of the above facts, do you believe, "Further I could not go" or that, "I stuck fast," or, "that the people would not budge further?" Do not my actions from the very commencement to the time of my resignation prove conclusively to any fair minded person I have acted unselfishly. I am perfectly and fully satisfied with the credit given me in the above paragraph of, "getting up the Ice Palace." Further on, "Subscriber" says, "He, Senior, repeatedly assured the subscribers that they could choose whom they liked for manager." This they did, and by a standing vote elected me to that position without a dissenting voice. Rather inconsistently subscriber adds, "The stockholders selected a directory that commanded the confidence of the public. Instead of permitting the directory to choose its manager, Mr. Senior swung himself into the managerial chair clear over the head of the directory." Here "Subscriber" not only insults Salt Lake City, but insults every subscriber who voluntarily sent out the telegram to show their goodwill toward Leadville and its enterprise and only, incidentally, mentioned me in same, but insults every subscriber who attended that meeting. Everyone of them present knew that their subscription was made with the express condition in writing that such a meeting should be held for the purpose of electing a general manager. They knew also that the vice-president of the Board of Directors, unsolicited, read the telegram referred to the subscribers, after they had decided to elect their general manager, and after I had been placed in nomination by one of this identical Board of Directors, with the president and vice-president at the meeting. All three cast their standing votes with every subscriber present. This is the telegram that so dazed the stockholders and directors present at the meeting (where) I was elected, "Ice Palace Subscriber" does not attack their common sense and intelligence by such an assertion? . . . — E. W. Senior

The *Salt Lake Tribune*, the following day published the telegram.

This paper is known all over the West and is published by one of the signers of the dispatch:

Leadville's Ice Palace—Salt Lake sends greeting and received a fitting response (*Salt Lake Tribune*, September 24, 1895). Salt Lake City has during the past three years secured a great number of Leadville's moderately wealthy citizens as permanent residents. This has mainly been brought about by judicious advertising done by Edwin W. Senior throughout Colorado, and the excursions he has promoted from there to this city. On account of this a brotherly interest is now manifested between the two burgs, and a constant intercourse by rail, mail and wire is kept up. So when in the Cloud City they proposed to build an ice palace for their winter museum, Salt Lake City yesterday wired their congratulations as follows, "To the citizens of Leadville: The citizens of Salt Lake City send you greetings in your ice palace enterprise. May your public spirit meet the appreciation it deserves. You have in E. W. Senior all the abilities required to make it the success you desire. Salt Lake is always glad to welcome as its

35

inhabitants the Colorado people, and such cour-
tesies are therefore opportune and becoming.
This greeting was signed for the Chamber of
Commerce by James Bacon, president, and
Edward F. Colborn, secretary; the Real Estate
Exchange by Charles E. Monro, secretary,
Frank Harris, Receiver United States Land
Office; Byron Groo, Registrar United States
Land Office; W. S. McCormick, Governor West
G. F. Culmer and Bros.; H. L. A. Culmer,
Samuel F. Walker; J. C. McNally, Probate
Judge; W. E. Hubbard, Immigration Agent
Union Pacific system; C. C. Goodwin, Editor
Tribune; Harvey Hardy, Sheriff Salt Lake Coun-
ty and F. A. Wadleigh, General Passenger
Agent Rio Grande Western Railway.

The following was late in the day received by wire
from Mr. Senior, who is now in Leadville: "Charles E.
Monro, Salt Lake City: I heartily thank you and every gentlemen on the telegram. (ss) E. W. Senior."

Shortly after Senior resigned from the Board, he left
Leadville and went to Salt Lake City to promote a salt
palace.

THE ICE PALACE IS A GO!
Tingley S. Wood Takes Charge

On October 29th, the following notice appeared in the *Herald Democrat*.

Ice Palace Notice. An important meeting is called for tonight at the Vendome. The following Directors of the Ice Palace and Carnival Association will please take notice of a meeting of the board will be held this evening at 7:30 in the parlors of the Vendome Hotel: Tingley S. Wood, S. D. Nicholson, C. E. Dickinson, J. M. Maxwell, J. E. Miller, H. M. Blakely, Harvey T. Brown, C. H. S. Whipple, D. D. Sullivan, C. N. Priddy, A. V. Bohn, D. H. Dougan, J. W. Smith, C. T. Limberg, John F. Campion, Peter W. Breene, H. I. Higgins, W. R. Harp, J. H. Weddle, Hugh Kelly, Albert Sherman, Frank O. Stead, S. F. Parrish, George E. Taylor, Franklin Ballou, Charles Hayden, George Campion, James W. Newell, Norman Estey, S. W. Mudd, J. A. Ewing, Dr. S. A. Bosanko, A. S. Weston, George P. Brown, Francis X. Hogan. As very important business will be transacted at this meeting it is desirous that every member of the board should be present. ss: W. L. Temple, Secty.

Tingley S. Wood was highly respected in the community, as a businessman and a supportive citizen. There was no such word as failure in his vocabulary. He did request some time to study and inquire into the feasibility of the venture. He was not about to lead a project that would not be successful. With the information he was able to gather in the short time given, and the resounding favorable response he received, Wood agreed to accept the position of Director General. He did, however, stipulate that he be guaranteed plenty of money to complete the project. It must

37

reflect the willingness and enthusiasm of the Leadville citizens, nothing less would do. The Tuesday evening meeting was called to order by selected chairman, A. V. Bohn, with W. L. Temple acting as secretary. Temple read the following communication:

Leadville, Colo, Oct 24, 1895. Tingley S. Wood, esq: Sir, a general feeling pervades the community that we should make the projected ice palace a success only second to that of the recent carnival at Denver. To do so it is necessary that someone be selected as Director General of the enterprise whom the people will at once recognize as the man for the occasion, and with one accord we name you as the man and beg that you accept the duty. It is not our wish to impose on you the burden of the routine work that will be necessary, for this the Board of Directors will provide under your direction. If you will consent to our desire and give us the benefit of your name, your ability and your energy, we pledge to you our best efforts to make the enterprise one that will benefit our city and reflect credit on all connected with it. ss: (One hundred fifteen signatures were on this document.)

To this letter Mr. Wood replied as follows:

Mr. J. H. Weddle and Others — Leadville, Colo..Sirs — Reply to your communication of the 24th, instant has been delayed in order to communicate with gentlemen who have conducted, in other cities, enterprises similar to your proposed "Crystal Carnival and Ice Palace." Consequent upon information received from these sources, I am of the opinion that the conditions here are favorable to such an undertaking; but it is also evident that the cost will largely exceed estimates heretofore made, if, as I suppose, you desire to attract more than local attention. I think that the creditable construction of the principal building or "palace" together with the more permanent inside buildings, will entail an expenditure of not less than $20,000. With this sum you can make a showing which will bear comparison with any previous structure of the kind, and will again demonstrate that "Leadville does not do things by halves." If you find it practical to raise the amount named, I shall be glad to render such assistance toward success as may be in my power, and to serve you in any capacity you may indicate, but with a decided personal preference for a minor position. Yours very respectfully, ss: Tingley S. Wood.

Mr. Wood stated that letters and telegrams had been sent to Montreal and St. Paul with reference to securing a man from one of the two cities mentioned. A letter was received from Mr. Charles E. Joy, an architect from St. Paul, who was highly recommended and had designed, and been in charge of construction of ice palaces in that city. Mr. Wood felt it was necessary to enlist a man who had experience with this type of construction.

Dr. Dougan asked for an opinion from those present on forming an association to be known as the "Leadville Crystal Carnival Association." Response was overwhelmingly in favor of it.

Many questions were raised that evening regarding obtaining subscriptions, labor, materials, and clarity of the ice. It was pointed out that unless the ice palace was built on a scale that would attract significant attention it should be dropped. They did not want to advertise their palace unless they had the backing to make it a success.

There was some talk of approaching Denver for contributions, but the majority was strongly against it. This was going to be Leadville's Ice Palace and they should do this on their own; Leadville's palace, Leadville's money. It should be noted here, although, early on, it was determined that solicitations from other than Leadville's own, would be downplayed; the Adolph Coors Brewing Company of Golden, however, donated $300.

Tingley S. Wood was emphatic that the money raised would be used to hire local labor and buy supplies locally. The only outside expense would be to hire a man to superintend the construction, and that man's experience and expertise would be worth the money.

He also told the members that the ice palace was to be built for all the people and no person, group or organization would be given privileges of the palace that others could not enjoy. There would be no private entertainment of any kind within the palace. All applications for its rental for such purposes (there had been several from societies and lodges) would be promptly refused by the management.

After much bantering and concern about the fundraising, it was proposed that a minstrel show be held using the very best local talent. This would bring in at least $500.

The consensus was that everyone was in favor of the ice palace venture if the money could be raised. Finally, a voice from the crowd . . . "Gentlemen," said James J. Brown, "it is useless to talk longer until we see some money in sight. I subscribe $500." "Put me down for $500 also," said Tingley S. Wood. "I subscribe the same," said John Campion. The announcement of the three subscriptions brought a rousing burst of applause.

A motion was made to appoint a finance committee to begin operations immediately. The committee was composed of C. N. Priddy, John Harvey, Emanuel Katz, Adolph Baer, C. T. Limberg, George P. Brown, J. W. Smith, J. H. Weddle, John F. Campion, R. B. Estey, F. O. Stead, C. H. Bennett and George A. L'Abbe. Within minutes, nearly $4,000 was raised. Added to the $4,000 already collected, a total of $8,000 was available.

Tingley S. Wood was quick to point out that this fell far short of the needed funds and it would behoove the committee to get busy at once. He also stated that acceptance of his position of Director General was purely tentative and if necessary he would be glad to be relieved of the responsibility of directing the enterprise. Mr. Campion pointed out that Mr. Wood was the only man for the position. His well known ability, his public spirit, his matchless executive abilities made it imperative that he should be Director General. A. A. Blow stated, "that the success was not dependent upon the enthusiasm, but on the man, and the only man for the job was Tingley S. Wood." (This was followed by resounding applause.)

John Harvey, Williams Lumber Company, John E. Miller, C. T. Limberg, Agassiz Mining Company, Adolph Schayer, H. M. Blakely, D. H. Dougan, C. N. Priddy, S. W. Mudd, Tomkins-LaSalle Hardware Company, Citizens Electric Light Company, Patrick Crowe, A. V. Bohn and E. J. Gaw each subscribed $100; the Crystal Carnival Minstrel Aggregation gave $400; H. I. Higgins and George A. L'Abbe each promised $250; Leadville Improvement Company, Dr. S. A. Bosanko, Harvey T. Brown, Theo Nollenberger, C. H. S. Whipple and Thomas Robson each subscribed $50, and H. C. Dimick donated $25.

41

Director General Wood had no firm plan in place, but proposed to the audience that the palace would contain an ice skating rink 150 x 200 feet covered by a wooden trussed roof. The roof would be supported by a row of posts set in the center of the rink and on the sides. He contemplated starting construction immediately. The outside walls would be ice blocks, frozen together using water instead of mortar. By making the roof self-supporting it would add to the safety of the palace. When the ice began to thaw, the roof would not be impaired and the building would be intact. This way it could be preserved and used from year to year. When the ice started freezing again they would be able to wall the building up with ice blocks and have an ice palace and winter carnival for many winters to come.

It was estimated that by charging twenty-five cents admission, the skating rink alone would raise $5,000. The rink could probably be built for $5,000. Some revenue would also be realized from the many concessionaires. The toboggan runs were estimated to cost no more than $1,500. The site selected for the toboggan runs was on West Seventh Street near the intersection of Leiter Avenue. The route was originally selected for the toboggans to run a downhill course to the crossing at the (Colorado) Midland bridge, and with good sleighing, it would be possible to run to the Arkansas Smelter. Those who did not want to participate in such a long run could cut across to Sixth Street on a downhill run, back on Sixth Street to Leiter Avenue. This would require the tobogganers to walk the short distance of a block back to the palace.

The skating rink and the toboggan runs could be built at once and put into use at the earliest snowfall, thereby generating revenue for construction of the ice palace proper. That way, along with the skating rink, the stockholders would earn money for two or three years. The walls of the ice palace could be erected within two weeks by rushing construction. The target date for opening the palace was Christmas Day. By doing this, excursions could be routed to Leadville during the holiday season. The businessmen of the city were behind this all the way for they, too, would benefit from all the visitors to Leadville. It was anticipated that hotels, rooming houses and restaurants would do a landslide business. The merchants operating ladies' and men's "clothing houses" would profit the most. The ice palace would initiate the wearing of heavier wraps, and seal coats and caps would certainly be in vogue.

The gloom of winter would be replaced by the winter carnival, Leadville would make its own fun and invite the world to join in. An ice palace 10,000 feet above sea level would be an unheard of and unique attraction that would attract a multitude of sightseers to the two-mile-high city.

Having Mr. Wood's name associated with the ice palace lent credibility to the project. Much more enthusiasm and support was evidenced after Director General's acceptance of the job. By early November Director General Wood had turned his responsibilities as manager of the Lillian, Antioch & Benton mines over to others. This allowed him to devote full time to getting the ice palace built. This project would prove to be no small task. (He received no pay or compensation of any kind as Director General.)

Director General Wood had the land which had been leased surveyed for exact location of the ice palace. He rented the George S. Phelps house at 400 West Eighth

Street to be used for construction offices while the palace was being built, and he temporarily relocated from the Delaware Block on Harrison Avenue.

LEADVILLE SOCIETY
A Whirlwind Social Season Planned

The social impact brought on by the ice palace was beginning to gear up as early as late October. Leadville society, which normally was at its peak during the holiday season, slowed down considerably, awaiting the winter carnival. There was some entertaining; card parties and dinner parties were on the social calendar but for the most part Leadville's citizens held off until the ice palace opened and many of their friends were visiting the Cloud City. When the winter carnival began, whirlwind entertaining was taking place. A number of socials, card parties and elaborate dinners were given for out-of-town guests. Local events were crowded with spectators as guests began pouring into the city.

If the carnival atmosphere became a bit wearisome, entertainment could be found at the local theaters. On January 2nd, the Lyceum Theater offered "The Private Secretary," a three-act comedy, which played for a week. Those looking for a good laugh were encouraged to visit the theater. Later that month, "Passion Slave" was featured. Matinee tickets sold for ten cents, evening performances, twenty-five cents.

The Weston Opera House featured Burt Hodgkins as "Uncle Josh Spruceby." John E. Kelly starred as the villainous Luke Fay; Will W. Johnson as Major Wellington; W. K. Jones as Hank Mont, Fay's accomplice; songstress and dancer Pearl Hight was played by Sally Spruceby. Lillian Berkley was featured as the wronged daughter of the old farmer. The sawmill scene was described as realistically horrifying. Nancy was rescued by her father just as she was being carried to the teeth of the menacing saw.

Oscar Ellason made his first appearance in Leadville at the Weston Opera House. Ellason, from Salt Lake City, was hailed as the new wizard of the West. He was advertised as skillful in palm reading, mind reading, and magic. Seats in the gallery sold for one dollar, others were fifty cents.

THE LAND IS CLEARED
Construction Begins

Architect C. E. Joy arrived in Leadville on Thursday, November 6th, to assist in designing and overseeing construction of the ice palace.

After Joy's arrival in Leadville, building plans for the ice palace were changed. The size of the palace was increased from 150 x 200 feet (originally announced by Director General Wood) to 320 x 450 feet. The ice skating rink design was enhanced, and the support pillars were redesigned.

Director General Wood worked very closely with Architect Joy on the ice palace building plans. Norman-style architecture was chosen for the ice palace's design because it was easily adaptable to the creation of spectacular effects with the ice blocks. This type of architecture was used in building most of the ice palaces during that time.

The site selected for the ice palace was located between West 7th and 8th Streets from Spruce to Leiter. At that time it was barren land covered with sagebrush and rocks. Today, it's covered with beautiful old Victorian homes.

The ice palace was designed to sit diagonally on the property. The reason for this being that passengers on the trains coming into Leadville would be able to see all sides of the ice palace setting on Capitol Hill. Perhaps the curious travelers would be encouraged to lay over in Leadville to visit the site.

It was determined by the way the ice palace was designed, and the enlarged size, additional land was going to be needed.

In proceedings of the Board of County Commissioners of Lake County, Colorado, November 25, 1895, the following was recorded:

47

On motion it was ordered that lots 20, 21, 22 & 23 of Block 46, Stevens & Leiter subdivision be leased to the Leadville Crystal Carnival Association upon the same terms as the lots already leased to said association.

Explosions rocked the two-mile-high city when clearing of the land on Capitol Hill began in early November. Sagebrush, rocks and tree stumps shot into the air. Windows shook, and crockery rattled in the pantries of homes in the area around the ice palace site. (More crockery was broken in one day by the dynamite, than it would take a pantry maid a week to shatter.)

By November 13th all of the tree stumps had been removed and the land was clear of debris. Surveyors were staking the site and marking the levels for the ice skating rink. That same day lumber began arriving at the ice palace site.

The ice palace was finally getting underway!

On November 16th the local railroad agents were invited to visit the ice palace site. Agent B. L. Winchell of the South Park Railroad, Mr. S. K. Hooper of the Denver & Rio Grande, and Mr. W. F. Bailey of the Colorado Midland, stood on the proposed site of the palace. It was the consensus of the men that Mother Nature had made Capitol Hill just for the purpose of erecting an ice palace. A more breathtaking, picturesque site could not have been chosen. The agents viewed the city lying at the proposed castle's feet, winding its way up the gulches east of town. The hillsides beyond were dotted with mine shafts, smoke streams rising from the engine houses and smelter stacks. To the south below other smelters, lay the beautiful valley. The slow-drifting Arkansas River threaded its way through the snowy blanket that covered the valley floor. Frosted tree-covered mountains surrounded the valley and climbed to timberline where the trees gave way to the lofty white-capped peaks of Mt. Massive and Mt. Elbert. Nowhere else in Leadville could a more beautiful scenic panorama be found, and nowhere else was more fitting for the ice palace.

The agents came away filled with enthusiasm and excitement at the prospects of revenue to be reaped from the ice palace, and the multitude of visitors that would come to see Leadville's diamond in the sky.

A reporter on the site asked Mr. Winchell if the carnival would attract many people to Leadville from faraway. His reply was, "Only two cities have attempted to give winter carnivals on this continent, and they were too far north to attract the patronage of the Western states. We shall try to get the (rail) roads to cooperate with us to get excursion parties from the Missouri River points. One excursion, at least, I believe can be worked up from Missouri River points, and it may be possible to get excursion parties from Chicago." The reporter asked Agent Winchell if it was difficult to get people to travel in the winter. He answered, "It was very surprising, but the railroads carried a large number of passengers during the winter season."

W. W. Coble and W. J. Kerr, contractors and builders at 131 West 5th Street, were hired to erect the inner building which would consist of 307,000 board feet of lumber. The men were diligent in their efforts to get the building started. The first man to be hired by Coble and Kerr was Fred R. Arnold. It was said he was a careful and accurate timekeeper. Mr. Arnold resigned on January 1,

49

1896, before the ice palace was finished, to become a deputy in the County Treasurer's office.

The seventy-five laborers and craftsmen hired were anxious to get to work. Construction of the wood building began and Capitol Hill became a frenzy of activity. Lumber wagons were being unloaded as fast as they arrived on the hill. Echoes of teamsters yells and hustle of the workers resounded down the valley. The sounds of sawing and hammering soon filled the crisp winter air.

It was almost as if Christmas had arrived in Leadville a month early; men were back to work, earning wages again, receiving weekly pay of $20 to $30. An honest day's labor for an honest day's wage was the hue and cry of the workmen. When construction on the ice palace began, eighteen carpenters and fifty-seven others were hired. They were laborers and bricklayers, and stonemasons were hired to cut the ice into blocks, but lacked the experience to get the work done quickly.

One of the greatest benefits realized from building the ice palace, was the number of men that were put to work. Because of the demands for materials purchased from Leadville merchants, it created a demand for laborers as well as craftsmen.

Many of the workers walked to and from their jobs, others came in wagons or sleighs. Some of the Finlanders, who lived east of the city, used their "old country" skis as transportation back and forth to work at the ice palace.

From the beginning, problems began arising. Construction was slowed down by the inability of the local lumbermen to furnish the proper type of wood from their own lumber yards, or keep up with the demand. Because of these delays much of the lumber was brought from the sawmills, and some was shipped by rail from other nearby lumber camps. Despite this fact, the workers managed to make good progress. Due to time constraints, some of the lumber was still green. Although the lumber did not have time to cure, the workmen used it; however, construction on the wooden buildings did not begin in full force until December first because of this problem.

Slow though it was, the Director General was extremely pleased with the contractors and the progress made on the building, now that it was underway. This was no small undertaking. Plans called for 182,000 feet of lumber. There was no lumber used for flooring in the skating rink. Only three sides of the ballroom and dining room had boarded walls. Glass partitions were used in the rink sides of the walls.

Director General Wood was unable to find a contractor who would lay the ice blocks at a reasonable price, so he elected to have the job done by day laborers. Coble, in addition to his interior wooden building contract, was given the job of superintending the laying of the ice blocks. Even with the added responsibility, Coble insisted on being on the job site to oversee the ice work. Most of the time he and his partner, Kerr, spent more time at the ice palace than they did at home.

The weather was cooperating, much to the relief of the Director General, Architect Joy, the Association, and the workers. The temperatures were below normal, and during the last week of November they were unusually low. The cold weather added to the enthusiasm of the community. Colder weather is just what the city needed to erect the ice palace, and cold it would get!

"TEAMS WANTED — TO HAUL ICE.
LIBERAL WAGES OR CONTRACT.
ENQUIRE JAMES MCCORDIE,
POND NEAR ELLSMERE."

So read the ad in the *Herald Democrat* on December 3, 1895.

Cole & McCordie, of the Leadville Ice Company[4] (not to be confused with the Leadville Ice & Coal Company which came later), were awarded the contract to provide ice for the palace. By terms of their agreement they were required to provide 200 tons a day, but if good sledding weather set in they expected to be able to deliver from 300 to 350 tons daily. Twenty-four drivers with four-horse teams were hired. The ice was harvested then transported from the ponds near Ellsmere, approximately two miles northwest of Leadville. The reservoir at the mouth of Big Evans Gulch provided beautiful transparent ice. Ice was also hauled from Evergreen Lakes, Twin Lakes and the Arkansas River. The ice from these sources was also clear and transparent that winter; perhaps a gift from Mother Nature to the Leadville people.

The inexperienced stonemasons hired to cut the ice into blocks, used axes and saws. The blocks ranged in sizes from 20 inches by 30 inches to blocks 5 feet x 2 feet x 2 feet. After being cut, the blocks were moved by the derricks or slid along the pond's surface to the shoreline.

---

[4]The Peoples Ice Company, 213 E. 4th St., was the only other ice company in Leadville at that time.

The ice blocks were then loaded on sleighs or wagons drawn by the four-horse teams, and hauled into town.

The ice was weighed at the Frank E. Brown grocery store, located at 10th and Poplar Streets. Mr. Brown had a drive-on platform scale, the only one in town strong enough to handle the many tons of ice. The wagons or sleighs (having been weighed prior to being loaded) were then driven onto the platform. The ice was weighed and recorded, then hauled to the construction site on Capitol Hill.

The drivers earned $6-12 per day. They were paid fifty to seventy-five cents per ton and averaged three tons per load, four loads per day. It was estimated it would take 27 days to deliver the 5,000 tons of ice required to build the ice palace.

Work on the ice palace was delayed because of the shortage of teams to haul the ice. Mine owners lodged the same complaint. They, too, were unable to get enough teams to haul their ore.

One teamster turned greedy. He was going to make money while the ice was freezing. He worked his mules all day hauling ore from the mines and then hauled ice at night. One mule fell in its tracks. It was so exhausted, it died. The mule skinner was fired on the spot and told not to set foot on the property again.

No fanfare heralded the laying of the cornerstone for Leadville's Ice Palace during the afternoon of November 25, 1895, and no formal ceremony was conducted. Architect Joy set the ice block while Director General Wood watched with intense interest. Superstitious thoughts crossed the Director's mind as the first block was put in place. The ice

53

cut on that day was thirteen inches thick. Was this the second foreboding omen[5]?

There were no trenches dug, nor foundations laid for the ice palace. The ice walls were started by freezing the ice blocks to the ground. The unevenness of the ground was overcome by carrying the layers of blocks in benches from the lowest to the highest point reached, then laid in regular rows.

The thickness of the blocks depended upon the ice depth at the time it was harvested and the blocks were not always uniform in size. When the ice was unloaded at the ice palace, the blocks were then put in wooden forms and covered with boiling water. The blocks froze to a uniform size and were set in place.

Instead of mortar, boiling water was used to cement the ice blocks because it froze faster than cold water, thus speeding up the construction. As the water was poured over the blocks the excess ran down the walls to the ground. It froze, adding thickness to the bottoms of the walls, giving them additional strength and support. The walls were as strong as if they were made of stone.

During the nights and early morning hours after the ice palace's cornerstone had been laid, the temperatures dropped below zero. This was miserable for the icemasons. Some wore double layers of clothing to keep warm. On many nights, teamster James Murray wore two overcoats to protect himself from the biting frost. The workmen told of the thermometer standing at thirty-five degrees below

---

[5]The first omen being E. W. Senior's Friday the 13th meeting with the Denver Chamber of Commerce.

zero. That was greatly exaggerated, however, although it may have felt that cold working on the ice walls in below freezing weather.

The coldest temperature recorded during the month was November 28th, when the temperature dropped to seven degrees below zero. During most of November the temperature fell below freezing and on a few nights even below zero. Snowfall during the month totaled twenty-one and one-fourth inches, but by month's end weather observer J. C. Paddock reported zero snow depth and an average temperature of 22°.

It had been suggested that instead of sentencing city prisoners to work the streets on the chain gang, why not give them a night shift on the ice palace? (Whether this transpired or not is known.)

The townspeople were less reluctant to grumble about the cold weather since they knew it was necessary for the erection of the ice palace. Another benefit derived from building the ice palace, there were fewer complaints about the freezing temperatures.

The *Cripple Creek Times* reported "This is excellent weather for the Leadville Ice Palace and the structure is growing under the influence of the blasts from Old Boreas."

On November 30th the work force of carpenters and ice masons was doubled to 150.

Construction progressed, but not quite as fast as Director General Wood had hoped. He determined that if the palace were going to open by Christmas Day, night crews would have to be added. To speed up construction of the palace, the Director General had seventeen street lights placed around the construction site. By doing this the men could work night and day; and they did, in two 12-hour shifts, seven days a week.

By December first the ice walls were being extended along the west side of the property. Ten of the poles had been set and arc lights were strung along the west and north sides of the construction site. The first night crew went to work. That same day the carpenters hoisted sections of the cantilever trusses over the 250-foot span of the interior building. Ten men were required to keep the snow shoveled off the ice palace's roof.

In addition to working full shifts during the day, many nights Coble and Kerr were on the job making sure things were going smoothly. When Coble was stricken with pneumonia in early December, Kerr took over and was instrumental in keeping the project on schedule. At times he worked 16 to 24 hours or more. Coble was ill for almost three weeks and returned to work during the third week of December, much to Kerr's relief. Once Coble was back, work progressed at a rapid pace.

Messrs. Wood and Joy were relieved when the cold weather set in. The ice walls were beginning to climb. To lift the ice to the higher walls, the men used horsepowered quarry ginpoles, and block and tackle. Leather horsewhips were wrapped around the ice blocks; the blocks were then lifted up the walls and swung into place. The blocks weighed from 300 to 600 pounds apiece. The men setting the ice blocks worked from tall ladders. The snowfall of four inches recorded on December 2nd made good sledding for the ice haulers. There were three sleds to one wagon in the parade from Big Evans Gulch to Frank Brown's grocery store.

CHINOOK!!!

HOT WINDS ATTACK THE ICE PALACE!

Tingley Wood was probably cursing the wind, shaking his tightly clenched fist at the unrelenting sun beating down on his beautiful ice castle.

The elation felt by Director General Wood and Architect Joy, relative to the cold weather in November, was short-lived. The first two weeks of December were pure hell for Director General Wood, Architect Joy, the workers, and the Association.

Following the snowstorm of the previous night, by midday of December 2nd a Chinook wind blew into the Cloud City, elevating the temperature to 35°. The next day it rose to 46°, jumped to 60° by the 10th, and by the 12th of December the temperature was 65° above zero!

When the Chinook winds struck, Director General Wood immediately ordered muslin to protect the ice walls. In order to save the ice palace, he used $5,000 of his own money to purchase 10,000 yards of muslin to cover to protect the walls from the sun and the wind during the day. After the sun went down, the muslin was removed and the ice palace walls were sprayed with a fire hose. The freezing night temperatures did their job solidifying the walls, allowing the men to get on with the construction. However, the warm daytime temperatures slowed the workers down and set the construction schedule back more than a week.

By December fourth the ice walls were reaching outward and upward. The great octagonal towers at the main entrance were beginning to take shape and the buttresses were going up.

It had been suggested that an elevator company would get plenty of free advertising by installing an elevator in one of the palace's towers. The elevator could take visitors to the roof of the ice palace from which they could view the city, the mines, famous gulches, and smelters. They would be able to enjoy the beauty of the mountains in the surrounding area from atop the ice palace roof. However, the elevator was never installed.

The walls of the palace grew massive, and Leadville's citizens were ecstatic, excitement was on the increase. By December 5th the ice walls were 12 feet high and climbing. Two days later, the first tier of ice blocks was laid on the south side of the palace. By the following day, the ice walls were looming 20 feet high in places.

"Ice Palace" was heard everywhere. The palace walls could now be seen from the Vendome Hotel on Harrison Avenue. The ice on the ponds had increased from 13 inches to 18 inches in thickness, and was as much weight as the workmen wanted to handle.

On December 7th, fifteen carpenters were brought in from Denver. This caused some unrest due to the imported carpenters trying to take charge. After some discussion, the locals set the newcomers straight and it was business as usual.

On December 10th there was another delay, caused by a shortage of ice haulers. At that time the mines were experiencing an enormous output of ore. The suggestion was made that either the mines or the ice palace would have to be shut down.

The following day, Mr. Kerr took charge of getting the ginpoles and tackle in the towers as the walls began to climb skyward. A major problem cropped up as a result of this. For two days there was extensive settling of the ice walls, causing more concern for everyone. But with each night that passed the temperature dipped below freezing and dropped to 5° below zero on the 18th.

Prior to December 13th the south end of the east walls were being honeycombed because there was not enough canvas to cover them. The ice walls were being dried up and shrunken by the Chinook winds. The air was so dry it sucked the moisture out of the blocks like a sponge. There was no visible thawing. One could lay hands on the ice blocks without feeling any moisture. In places the ice disappeared as if big bites had been taken out of the blocks.

The cost of additional canvas set the Director General back $200. The west walls suffered the most damage having been exposed to the daylong sunshine. The northwest walls withstood the onslaught. By the time the sun moved around to that side of the palace, the heat of the day was starting to subside and the sun was beginning to set.

A reporter from the *Herald Democrat* visited the ice palace site to examine the damage. He interviewed Director General Wood about the fate of the ice palace. The reporter, doubtful of the palace's completion, asked Mr. Wood, "Suppose the thing melts down?" to which the Director General replied, "We'll build it up again!" The tone of the Director's voice left no doubt in the reporter's mind that it would be done. The reporter left the site convinced that Wood did not intend to fail or give up.

Following four days of colder weather, when the daytime temperature was close to, or below freezing, the ice palace was hit again. In the next forty-eight hours the temperature rose to 46°, then climbed to 58° during the day. During the 13th and 14th there was serious settling of the walls. Thankfully, the night temperatures were well below freezing and sometimes dropped below zero. After sundown, when the walls had been sprayed with a fire hose, and the water froze, the ice palace resembled a fairy tale castle. The ice blocks turned into beautiful mother-of-pearl walls with myriads of colored light reflecting through them.

Despite the setback caused by the Chinook, Architect Joy was very much on top of the project ensuring the work was being done quickly and efficiently. More men were hired as the need for ice increased and the ice palace grew. Between 250 and 350 men were working on the palace when the project was in full swing (approximately the number of men working in the Little Jonny Mine). The men were paid wages ranging from $2.50 to $3.50 per day depending on their skills. Carpenters were paid $3.00 to $3.50, laborers were paid $2.50 - $3.25. Three dollars per day was union scale at that time.

Passengers on the trains coming into Leadville while the ice palace was being built were able to see the immense frozen structure, and were awestruck by its beauty. If anyone had their doubts about the immensity of the ice palace they had only to visit Eighth Street and their doubts were tossed to the four winds.

On December 14th, a strike was brewing at the ice palace and was another threat to its construction. The trouble began when night foreman Floyd W. Bartlett was fired. Charged with unsatisfactory work, he and a dozen icemasons were laid off for incompetency. Some of the ice had to be removed because of defective construction. The irate men moved among the workers trying to breed discontent. Their efforts were futile and they finally left the construction site, probably cursing under their breaths. Three days later Bartlett, still angry, said he was not discharged for incompetency. He claimed the firing came as a result of a dispute between Bartlett's father, who was working for contractors Coble & Kerr, and Kerr. Young Bartlett took offense at being referred to as an incompetent.

By December 17th, the cold weather returned to the high country. The cold spell came much to the relief of the Director General, who was ecstatic, and to Architect Joy, who grinned ear to ear. It was said the weather was cold enough "to freeze the hair off a hairless monkey."

This change in the weather also changed the minds of the naysayers who were predicting there would never be an ice palace in Leadville, "Until hell freezes over." The pessimists pulled their hats down over their eyes, and slunk away.

More setbacks for the ice palace . . . On December 19th Leadville's Ice Palace was blasted again. Another Chinook wind blew in, elevating the temperature to 46°, then climbing to 58° the next day. The east and north walls were not affected but the west and south walls were damaged. The sun and blowing wind took an inch thickness from the walls in some places. A troubled Director General Wood and the management team, concerned about the damage, were assured by Architect Joy that the walls would stand, even if shrunk to 10 inches thickness.

61

On December 20th, the main towers of the ice palace reached a height of 37 feet. Work had progressed so far that visitors could no longer be admitted to the palace without seriously interfering with the workmen or endangering themselves to the falling ice blocks. Director Wood had been very lenient in allowing the visitors to inspect every part of the ice palace, but it became necessary to restrict them from the work areas. The visitors were asked to stay away and not make it necessary for the watchmen to perform the unpleasant duty of ordering them out. Everyone was pushing to get the project finished in time for the grand opening. Mr. Wood had targeted a completion date of December 25th. He wanted to open the ice palace to Leadville's citizens on Christmas Day so they could enjoy their palace before it was open to the outside world.

The Christmas of 1895 was unlike any other in Leadville. Although there were poor people, there was less need and want than the previous two years in the Carbonate Camp. Idle men were a rarity now, and although work on the ice palace was no picnic, it brought in a paycheck. At that time many felt that beggars couldn't be choosers.

On Christmas Eve, $5,000 in wages were paid to the ice palace workers. On Christmas day, the men working on the ice walls were given four hours off for reporting to work on the holiday. Had the work not been so urgent, Director Wood would have given them the entire day. By that time it was reported that more than $40,000 had been collected by the Association but costs had risen to well over $60,000, and the ice palace was still not finished!

Christmas day dawned with a chilling zero degree temperature. By 2:00 p.m. the temperature reached the high for the day of 18°. The work was delayed again, and a full day was lost when Cole and McCordie moved the derricks from the one of the reservoirs at Ellsmere to another. The icemasons were laid off for the night and told to come back at 6:30 the next morning. Another two days were lost when the ice contractors failed to furnish their quota of ice. They had erected their derricks directly on the ice to hoist the ice blocks, but the weight drove the ice under water. This made it necessary for the contractors to move their derricks back to the shoreline. The derricks were back in place the next morning and more ice was ready to be hauled. The ice that was harvested at that time was eighteen inches thick.

The first reported outside visitors to see the ice palace were Santa Fe Railroad engineers. On December 18th a wire was sent by George B. Dougan of the Santa Fe railroad in Newton, Kansas, directed to C. N. Priddy. Dougan requested special permission for a group of Santa Fe engineers to visit the ice palace. These men, representing every major city between Denver and Kansas City would only be in town overnight, arriving on December 24th and departing Christmas Day. Their visit to the ice palace would be great way to get free publicity throughout the country. Permission was granted.

Problems of one kind or another beset the Director General, and the palace was not finished as planned. Another week of warm weather had delayed the construction again. Finally, it was announced that the formal opening would be held on New Year's Day, 1896.

Director General Wood and his board members were attending to the many final details necessary to bring the ice palace to a successful opening.

Excitement in the town rose to a fevered pitch during the closing days of December. People flocked to Capitol Hill in droves to watch the finishing touches being added to the beautiful crystal castle. They were not deterred by the freezing weather that hovered over the city.

Construction was proceeding at breakneck speed as New Year's Day drew near. The Capitol Hill grounds were a beehive of activity, and the push was on to complete the palace in time for the January 1st formal opening. Local merchants brought their displays to be set up and deliveries of all kinds were being made to the palace in preparation for the forthcoming gala affair.

On December 27th the east bay of the castle walls was topped out and the flagstaff set in position. Old Glory, with 44 stars[6], or Colorado state flags flew from each of the towers that embellished the Norman-style medieval ice castle. The flagpoles were 120 feet high and painted the official carnival colors; gold at the top with a silver base, tapered with burnished copper and lead blue.

Three turnstiles[7] were placed at the main entrance on December 28th. Director General Wood had purchased turnstiles that would admit one person at a time and count the

---

[6]Utah, the 45th state was admitted to the Union on January 4, 1896.

[7]The turnstiles were manufactured by the H. V. Bright, M.A.K.E.R. Company of Cleveland, Ohio. One of the turnstiles, #639, is still in Leadville. It stands in the courtyard at the Healy House Museum, between the Dexter Cabin and the main house.

daily attendance. In this way it enabled the gatekeepers to keep a more accurate account of visitors. Tickets were dropped in glass boxes attached to the turnstiles. This provided an accurate check on the ticket sellers. Three ticket takers were on duty for opening day. On special events days another three ticket sellers would be on duty. Two of those hired were John Ten Eyck and Tom Van Valzah. Director General Wood's, son, Tingley C., was also a gatekeeper and a short time later was put in charge of the gates. Some of the gatekeepers were letting their friends in without paying.

Architect Joy had calculated the exterior walls to be completed by December 29th and moved the icemasons inside to work on the arches that spanned the spaces between the ice pillars around the ice skating rink.

December 30th was reportedly a record breaker. The icemasons laid 254 tons of the translucent. Never had there been such furious activity since the first ice block was laid. The arches between the ice rink pillars were completed on two sides and the third side was finished before noon.

On December 31st, the last load of ice was hauled to the ice palace. In forty-eight hours, twenty-four drivers with their horse-drawn sleighs had hauled 304 tons of ice to the construction site.

During the last days of December the weather was miserable for the laborers. The highest daytime temperature was 26° on the 27th, and dropped to an early morning low of 19° below zero on the 29th. Three inches of snow fell on the 30th, bringing the total snowfall for the month to fourteen inches. Although it was not easy for the workers, they joined the carnival mood of the Leadville community. Winter had set in again; perfect ice palace weather.

The ticket office was a small wooden building that sat away from the palace. When the ice palace opened on January 1, 1896, the ticket office was placed near the Seventh Street entrance. After the main entrance was completed the ticket office was relocated to the front of the ice palace. (The ticket booth now graces the backyard of the Terry Fitzsimmons home on West Seventh Street.)

The Cloud City, that for forty years had been buried in winter snows and enveloped in dark depression, was getting ready to shed that cloak of gloom and put on the dazzling colors of Leadville's winter carnival. The people were ready to cast their cares and troubles aside, to enjoy the wonderful winter festivities.

The *Victor Record* gave glowing coverage — "The Leadville Ice Carnival, which opens on January 1, promises to be a grand success and will attract a big crowd of visitors from all parts of the state. Victor and the rest of the great Cripple Creek district will doubtless be well represented during the festivities. The *Record* wishes its Leadville neighbors all success for their enterprise."

The Pueblo Chieftain stated that "If the Leadville Ice Palace is half as dazzling as newspapers describe, it will be worth the trip across the country. If the railroad men have their way, half the country will be in Leadville."

In talking about the method of setting the ice blocks *The Chieftain* reported, "There must be a good deal of mica in that Leadville water."

The *Littleton Independent* — "The Ice Palace being built in Leadville will be opened January 4, at which time the enterprising citizens of that place will entertain their numerous guests in a most lavish manner. The palace, it is said, will by far eclipse anything of the kind ever built in the United States."

The *Colorado Mining Era* reported, "It will not do to tell any man from Leadville that they 'could cut no ice,' in the camp. Their ice palace is growing rapidly and nearing completion."

But more problems and delays continued to plague the Director General and his work force. The ice palace was not finished by New Year's Day. The main towers were still being worked on, some of the displays were yet to be set, and other construction details had to be completed. On January 4th, work on the interior buildings continued, and as beautiful as the ice palace was, it was not completed.

By the end of the first week in January, the Association had paid out $6,500 in wages to the workers; yet there were people in Leadville who still failed to appreciate the benefits being derived from the ice palace such as some of the businessmen who were not profiting directly from the ice palace.

The last nail was driven into the building's woodwork on January 11th. By the following night the remainder of the ice work was completed and the grounds were put in tip-top shape. The workers were paid off, and the last week's construction payroll amounted to $960.

Director General Wood and the Association members were ecstatic, and relieved that the ice palace was finally completed and open to the world. They paid high compliments to architect Charles E. Joy and contractors William W. Coble and William J. Kerr for the miraculous accomplishment. The Director General could not say enough good things about the little people—the carpenters, laborers, icemasons, and ice haulers. For without them this magnificent structure would never have gotten off the ground. Special recognition went to some of the icemasons, though untrained at the beginning, became award winners by the time the ice work was finished. John Saum was outstanding and deserving of a gold medal, but none was given. Wiley Murray and Jim Murray could "trim more cubic feet of ice than any three or four common hackers." Oscar Shellman was another first class icemason deserving of special recognition. William Kerr, in charge of erecting the ginpoles and tackle, "had no superior in Colorado."

INCORPORATION PAPERS ARE FILED
Board of Directors Restructured

A corporation was formed by Charles T. Limberg, Tingley S. Wood and Charles N. Priddy on November 7, 1895, for the purpose of "Erecting and maintaining a place of amusement, and conducting sports and amusements therein." Twenty thousand shares of stock were to be sold at a dollar par value. The Association was to exist for a period of five years. Incorporation papers for the Leadville Crystal Carnival Association were filed at the Lake County Courthouse two days later, at 10:30 a.m., November 9th (only days after they had begun clearing the land for the ice palace).

The Board of Directors had been restructured. Nine trustees and the Director, whose names appeared on the incorporation papers were: John F. Campion, J. H. Weddle, C. N. Priddy, J. W. Smith, D. H. Dougan, C. T. Limberg, S. D. Nicholson, George L'Abbe, James J. Brown, and Tingley S. Wood.

At that time, Colorado certificates of incorporation were filed in the county in which they were formed, not at the State Capitol in Denver.

Know all Men by these Presents, That we

Charles J. Limburg,
Tingley S. Wood, and
Charles K. Priddy,

residents of the State of Colorado, have associated ourselves together as an Association under the name and style of The Leadville Crystal Carnival Association for the purpose of becoming a body corporate and politic under and by virtue of the laws of the State of Colorado, and in accordance with the provisions of the laws of said State, we do hereby make, execute and acknowledge in this certificate in writing of our intention so to become a body corporate, under and by virtue of said laws.

FIRST. The corporate name and style of our said Association shall be The Leadville Crystal Carnival Association.

SECOND. The object for which our said Association is formed and incorporated is for the purpose of Erecting and maintaining a place of Amusement, and conducting Sports and Amusements therein.

THIRD. The capital stock of our said Association is Twenty thousand dollars to be divided into Twenty thousand shares of One dollars for each share, and said stock shall be Non assessable.

FOURTH. Our said Association is to exist for the term of Five years.

FIFTH. The affairs and management of our said Association is to be under the control of Nine Directors or Trustees, as follows: to wit; and Geo. F. Campion, J. H. Weddle, C. K. Priddy, J. F. Smith, D. H. Dougan, C. J. Limburg, S. D. Nicholson, Jas. L. Abby and J. F. Brown, are hereby selected to act as said Directors and to manage the affairs and concerns of said Association for and during the first year, and until their successors are elected and qualified.

SIXTH. The operations of our said Association will be carried on in the County of Lake State of Colorado, and the principal place and business office of said Association shall be located in the City of Leadville, County of Lake and State of Colorado aforesaid.

SEVENTH. The Directors shall have power to make such prudential by-laws as they may deem proper for the management of the affairs of this Association according to the statute in such case made and provided.

IN TESTIMONY WHEREOF, We have hereunto set our hands and seals, on this Seventh day of November A. D. 1895

Charles Limburg [SEAL]
Tingley S. Wood [SEAL]
Charles K. Priddy [SEAL]
[SEAL]
[SEAL]
[SEAL]
[SEAL]

Leadville Crystal Carnival Association Incorporation Papers.
Lake County Courthouse

INVEST IN THE ICE PALACE
Become A Stockholder

As early as November 6, 1895, Leadville was confident that in the hands of Tingley S. Wood, who always made a success of whatever he undertook, the ice palace would be one of Leadville's biggest money makers.

By the 7th of November $15,000 had been collected. The Leadville people had donated more than was ever raised for a similar purpose by the people of Montreal or St. Paul, but Director General Wood was still insistent that more money was needed.

On November 23rd the office of the Leadville Crystal Carnival Association released the following announcement:

> To Whom It May Concern: The *Leadville Herald Democrat* is authorized to open a special subscription for shares of its capital stock, and the certificate issued by said paper, bearing the official seal of the association are hereby declared valid. ss: Tingley S. Wood President, Board of Trustees.

Each stock certificate was numbered and beautifully engraved with a half-tone photogravure of the ice palace. The golden corporate seal was embossed in the lower left hand corner and signed by W. L. Temple, Secretary, and Charles Limberg, President of the Leadville Crystal Carnival Association. The certificates were framed in an elaborate printed blue edging.[8]

---

[8]Description courtesy of Evelyn Furman, Tabor Opera House, Leadville, Colorado - 1993.

71

The *Herald Democrat* was selling stock in the ice palace venture for one dollar per share. They advertised heavily, urging everyone to buy at least one share of stock. Readers were encouraged to buy shares as gifts to send to their friends and relatives within or out of the state. Every Leadville citizen would own a part of the palace; it would not belong to any one individual or group, but to the entire city.

The subscription list was growing day by day. On December 5th the *Herald Democrat* printed a list of more than sixty subscribers. Names of all subscribers were printed as they invested their dollars.

The ice palace coffers continued to grow and the Association was close to collecting the designated amount to build the palace. Director General Wood indicated much more was needed to complete the interior decorations, and the many other items needed to make it the most beautiful ice palace the visitors would ever see.

The *Herald Democrat* continued to advertise daily, that every man, woman and child should become the owner of at least one share of stock. This ice palace was going to be their playground and each of them should be willing to become an owner of this majestic crystal castle.

One merchant on Harrison Avenue was publicly reprimanded for refusing to subscribe even one dollar to the ice palace. To add insult to injury, the man was advertising carnival merchandise. It was suggested that he and others like him should be frozen in ice blocks and placed on exhibition as bad examples!

The *Herald Democrat* also sold lithographs of the ice palace, suitable for framing, for ten cents each. These were the same as the one shown on the front page of the "Crystal Carnival Edition" of the *Herald Democrat*.

George Wallace Williams, publicity chairman for the Association, made arrangements with W. J. Morgan & Company of Cleveland, Ohio, to reproduce lithographs of a special day scene of the ice palace by W. H. Jackson. The lithograph was the best and largest picture of the palace. It was done in seventeen colors, was 28"x42" in size and sold for $15. Limited supplies were available at the *Herald Democrat*, and Nowland's or Whipple's stores. Revenues collected from the lithograph sales added more money to the ice palace coffers.

Leadville Crystal Carnival Association Stock Certificate
Courtesy Evelyn Furman

MAKE ROOM FOR THE TOURISTS
Accommodations Scarce

Leadville was incorporated in 1878, and the winter carnival was the first public celebration of its kind or magnitude ever held within the city's boundaries.

On November 11, 1895 the *Leadville Herald Democrat* reported:

> The present hotel lodging of Leadville is ample under normal conditions, but will be severely strained once the carnival season is inaugurated. The management of the great enterprise will doubtless early recognize the necessity of so distributing the leading events over the lifetime of the celebration as not to attract too large a crowd at any one time. It will be better for all concerned to have an even influx of visitors from the opening to the closing of the function.

Director General Wood was aware that lodging for the visitors was going to be a problem. Fifteen hundred people from the Leadville Club of Denver alone were expected on opening day. The city could not begin to accommodate the crowds that were anticipated.

It was suggested that good money could be made by someone who was interested in building a lodging house near the ice palace. Director General Wood owned some property near the ice palace site and was willing to assign it to anyone who would put up a building to accommodate the visitors. It is not clear whether Director General Wood intended to give, lease, rent or sell the property or whether the lodge was even built.

Early in November, Horace A. Bixler, Lake County deputy clerk and recorder, resigned to go into business for

75

himself. He opened a "rooming bureau," on the Avenue, north of Seventh Street, to make lodging reservations for visitors coming to see the ice palace. This "rooming bureau" was perhaps the forerunner of modern travel agencies.

On November 14th, the following notice was published in the *Leadville Herald Democrat*:

> To Whom It May Concern . . . Mr. Horace A. Bixler has been officially recognized as quartermaster by the Leadville Crystal Carnival Association for the charting of such apartments and rooms as may be available for the use of persons visiting Leadville during the Carnival of 1895-96, and arranging with such of the owners of rentable rooms as may desire to avail themselves of his services in the renting of rooms and apartments. The said Association assumes no responsibility in the connection, but has required of Mr. Bixler a bond in the sum of $1,000 for the faithful and satisfactory performance of his undertaking, and for the accounting to the proper parties for all monies that may come into his hands in this connection. ss: T. S. Wood, Mgr.

In early December Bixler requested permission from the city council to post flyers on the telephone poles between the Denver & Rio Grande and Colorado Midland depots, directing the visitors to the "only authorized rooming agency, officially certified by the Crystal Palace management." Permission was granted.

There were seven hotels, twenty-nine boarding houses, and sixteen restaurants in Leadville in 1895. In addition, there were four lodging houses: The American House operated by Mrs. Kate Groy at 110 West 2nd Street; the

White Front Lodging House, 127 West 2nd Street; Leadville House, 222 East 3rd Street, and the Leadville Lodging House at 1407 Poplar Street. Private homeowners with extra rooms provided board and lodging for some of the working people employed in the city.

One homeowner in Leadville had a room in her house rented to a local miner, who had been a long time boarder. When news of the possible lodging shortage came out, she evicted him. She planned to become rich by renting his room to ice palace visitors. (What happened to the ejected miner is not known.)

It was estimated they could rent a room out from $2 per day to $60 a month.

In mid-December only 80 rooms on Harrison Avenue were available for visitors. By that time, Leadville's citizens were being urged to make ready any spare rooms in their homes to prepare for the onslaught of visitors expected when the ice palace opened. It was a matter of utmost importance that every homeowner in Leadville should prepare every bed, cot, and bunk in rooms that could be used to house the visitors when they arrived. It was suggested that rooms be shared, if possible. Local citizens were urged to write to their out-of-town friends, offering whatever accommodations they could, inviting them to their homes to alleviate crowding the hotels and rooming houses. By doing so this would make facilities available to others who were dependent upon the hotels, boarding and lodging houses.

The ice palace opening was drawing closer and the sleeping accommodations for visitors were still short in supply. The Denver & Rio Grande offered accommodations to Leadville visitors by sidetracking several first class sleepers near the depot.

A telegram sent to Director General Wood on December 18th, from C. H. Morse of Denver, urged the Director to contact Howard Chapin in Denver regarding arrangements for rooms and accommodations for the ice palace opening. Chapin, who was in charge of the Leadville Club of Denver, expected 800 members to attend the grand opening and were requesting rooms for that night. He needed to be able to report the information to the Leadville Club the following day. The city was able to provide accommodations for the club members.

(There seems to be conflicting figures as to how many club members would be attending. Denver was reporting one total, while Leadville reported another.)

THE CARNIVAL TAKES SHAPE
Winter Sports Clubs Are Organized

Little had been reported or discussed about the social side of the carnival activities. In mid-November an interview was conducted with Architect C. E. Joy for the purpose of obtaining information about entertainment and events held during St. Paul's winter carnival. Leadville's Ice Palace management felt the information would be helpful in arranging events for their Crystal Carnival.

The most important thing done, socially, was the organization of winter sporting clubs. Club members were identified by special carnival uniforms they wore. Contests were arranged among the many carnival clubs; hockey, skating, snowshoeing, curling, and other winter sports. Prizes were awarded to the winning clubs. The clubs were limited to men 18 or older; women were honorary members. The goal of the Association was to enlist 1,000 members; St. Paul had signed 10,000.

Other prizes were offered for the best float in a given parade and best representation at an event. Mr. Joy expounded on the attraction and interest the ice palace would create. He remarked that when the first ice palace was built in St. Paul, the population was 45,000. Three years later the city had become home to 110,000 inhabitants. The ice palace would be a financial boost to Leadville by organizing events which would attract people to the city's winter carnival. Perhaps, in visiting the city and meeting Leadville's citizens, some might want to relocate to the area.

Leadville's enthusiastic citizens organized clubs of every winter sport imaginable, at a furious rate. Snowshoeing, tobogganing and skating costumes were the order of the day. It was ruled that clubs of twenty or more members

79

were to wear brightly colored uniforms, but not necessarily identical in style, provided a distinctive club badge was worn. Snowshoe clubs were limited to a membership of one hundred. Each club was held responsible for the character and conduct of its members.

Club uniforms were made of white blanket cloth coats and pants, piped with red, red stockings, white buckskin moccasins, toques[9] of Yale blue, with Harvard red tassels and red fingered mittens. Red blanket cloth coats, piped with black piping and buttons, black hose, buckskin moccasins, and red toques with black tassels were worn by some. Gray blanket cloth coats with blue piping, suede moccasins, blue stockings and blue toques were also uniforms of the day.

David LaSalle, captain of the Leadville Carnival Snowshoe Club, received a complete set of rules from the Montreal Amateur Athletic Association. Those rules governed the sporting events held during Leadville's Winter Carnival.

On November 24, 1895, the Leadville Carnival Snowshoe Club was organized, modeled after those of Montreal, Canada.

Members of the Snowshoe Club dressed in colorful costumes including a blue toque with a red tassel, a coat made of white blanket with a red stripe, and a hood. The knickers were also white blanket and worn with red-striped stockings and buckskin moccasins. Their snowshoes were Canadian-webbed.

---

[9]A small, round, close-fitting hat, usually brimless hat, sometimes plumed.

The snowshoe clubs made treks to Twin Lakes, Evergreen Lakes, Evansville, Oro City, Ibex City, Iowa Gulch, Soda Springs, McMahon's, Sugar Loaf and Lake Park,[10] and other points of interest near Leadville during the carnival season. Moonlight cross-country trips were favored by many of the club members. Even though the evenings were cold and clear, a number of participants made the long journeys.

The Juvenile Ice Palace Club was organized. Members included: Edna Howell, Theo Austin, Bertha Williams, Buena Alverson, Eva Hale, Lyda Little, Becky Cohn, John Ellsworth, Hume White, John Pritchard, Robert Little and Sam Cohn.

The Ladies Carnival Club consisted of 70 members.

Near the end of December the Leadville Toboggan Club received a sample uniform from St. Paul. The suit was black and red. The Toboggan Clubs adopted this sample as their official uniform which was red and black toboggan suits, with brilliant red stockings; official carnival colors decorated the shoulder epaulets. Five hundred club medals were ordered. The badge consisted of three parts: the first or top bar was gold, with the name of the club engraved on it, the second bar was silver, with engraved lettering, "Ice Palace," and the third bar was lead with "Leadville, 1896" engraved across it.

---

[10]From "Memories of the Leadville Ice Palace 1895-1896," an unpublished paper by Ezra Dickerman. Stephen Hart Library, Colorado History Museum.

Members of the Scottish Caledonian Society organized Curling teams. The teams held practices at Ellsmere Pond. The Curling Club provided exciting entertainment for the ice palace visitors during the carnival season. A number of Curling competitions were held on the palace's ice rink.

The Military Athletic Association Hockey Club members, under Captain C. H. MacNutt, wore maroon sweaters in place of blanket coats. The team colors were maroon and white. Members of this club were some of the best skaters. The club contacted teams from Denver, Aspen, Colorado Springs, Pueblo and Cripple Creek to compete with. Leadville's home teams were not left out of the contests. Hockey tournaments were one of the main attractions of the winter carnival. Officers were: President C. H. MacNutt, Warren V. Jones, Secretary/Treasurer. D. G. Houghton, Willard G. Riggs and George P. Brown served as the committee.

The Gee-Whiz Ski Club used Norwegian skis instead of webbed snowshoes. The webbed snowshoes other clubs used varied in shape.

By December first, H. M. Blakely had received the regulation toques, sashes and stockings for the Snowshoe Club's 60 members. He also had blankets for pea jackets and knickerbockers that could be made to order at any of the Leadville tailor shops. The regulation uniforms gave considerable employment to the 18 local tailors and numerous dressmakers.

Skating clubs were organized, the craze set in, and merchants couldn't keep up with the demand. More skates were sold during the end of November and the first of December than all of the previous winter. One merchant ordered 150 pairs, and had to wire for more. C. H. Musser, at 108 East 5th Street, offered Barny & Berry ice skates — ladies' ice skates for $1.25 to $5; men's $.75 to $5, and children's at all prices.

Members of the Carnival Snowshoe Club included:

Andrews, H.
Blakeley, C. H.
Bloss, A. F
Boehmer, Mrs. Max
Bohn, Charlie
Brockway, Helen
Brown, George P.
Brown, Harvey T.
Church, H. P.
Davis, Mrs. C. C.
Davis, Ed
Davis, Madeleine N.
Dickinson, Ethel P.
Dye, C. T.
Edwards, Miss
Edwards, Mrs. T. W.
Felker, W. B.
H. D. Follett, Frank
Follett, Fred
Frantz, Miss J. J.
Frisbie, George F.
Gilbault, Miss
Gould, Mrs. F. J.

Gould, Fred
Hanley, Mrs. Maud
Harp, W. R.
Harvey, Alex
Harvey, John Jr.
Havens, Mrs. H. W.
Healey, Mrs.
Heath, Mrs. Agnes
Heath, J. H.
Horner, Mrs. Edward
Horner, J. F.
Horner, Mrs. Joseph
Houghton, D. S.
Hurd, W. F.
Jones, W. V.
Kahn, Dr. Lee
Kahn, Tillie
Kringen, Lena
LaSalle, David
LaSalle, Mrs. David
Leppel, Amelea
MacNutt, C. H.
Mahana, Miss

83

Maxwell, Emma L.
Maxwell, J. M.
Maxwell, Mary W.
Mayer, Mrs. Carrie
McDonald, Mrs.
McKeon, J. W.
Miller, Mrs. J. S.
Milner, John A.
Moore, W. A.
Norton, Mrs. Mary
Nowland, John
Parks, Miss
Peyer, Mrs. P. P.
Pitney, Miss
Porter, F. K.
Reef, Mrs. Joseph
Riggs, Willard

Robinson, A.
Rose, Mrs. C.
Rose, Lena
Ruggles, H. D.
Sands, Mrs. Charles
Smith, F. T.
Smith, Mrs. Mark
Stotesbury, Mrs. J. H.
Weeks, Mrs. W. C.
Whipple, Mrs. C. H. S.
White, Della
Wilkins, Estelle
Williams, T. J.
Wood, T. C.
Woodley, S. V.
Yothers, Mrs. M. C.

PARADING FOR THE CARNIVAL
Marchers Flood The Streets

The Grand Minstrel Parade
November 16, 1895

The first of many parades held during Leadville's Winter Carnival brought crowds of spectators to Harrison Avenue. On November 16th, a Grand Minstrel Parade was held in support of the ice palace. The citizens turned out in force to show their enthusiasm and support of the Crystal Carnival.

The parade was not very colorful, but the lack of variety was broken by some of the marchers dressed in linen dusters, or wearing a mum in their lapel. Whatever they lacked in color was made up in enthusiasm and noise; as much as a band, a drum corps and a steam calliope could make. The Crystal Carnival Minstrel Aggregation was topping off its advertising campaign with a showy demonstration for their ice palace fundraiser. Although the show was sold out, they wanted to draw public sentiment and support for the ice palace, and incite the carnival spirit.

The parade was led by Brigadier General Nat Daniels, "the prophet of Scott's Bar," mounted on a magnificent, snow white horse whose only failing was going around corners backwards. General Daniels was dressed in regulation uniform, and their noble appearance drew applause all along the parade route.

Only one float was entered. Melodious selections drifted into the afternoon air from this "musical" float, a half dozen steam whistles, which had been placed on the water company's thawing machine. The entertainer, disguised in blackface, played Beethoven's sonatas, Strauss waltzes, and several unpublished selections. The float, designated as a calliope, was the sensation of the parade and created excitement all along the way.

The parade, after traveling the Avenue, marched out West Seventh Street to the site of the ice palace, returning by way of West Eighth Street.

The New Year's Day parade was the first of the carnival's official parades that occurred every day throughout Leadville's winter carnival.

The revelers would march up and/or down Harrison Avenue. Every train that came into Leadville was greeted by a band that accompanied the visitors to the ice palace.

The Carnival Snowshoe Club took part in all the carnival parades and acted as a Committee of Entertainment for the Crystal Carnival Association. The members of the club were at the depot on the arrival of trains to meet visitors, and put forth their best efforts to provide entertainment for all who attended the Carnival.[11]

---

[11]*Olden Times in Colorado* by Carlyle Channing Davis, copyright 1916.

THE CONCESSION AND EXHIBITS
Display Your Wares At The Ice Palace

Concessionaires would contribute to support of the ice palace expenditures. As early as late November, exhibition space at the ice palace was already in great demand. The Colorado Midland Railroad was the first company to sign a contract for exhibition space.

H. B. Hardt was recommended by Director General Robert W. Speer[12] of the Festival of Mountain and Plain, to manage the exhibits for the ice palace. Hardt was no stranger to these kinds of fetes, having been associated with Chicago's World Fair, the Midwinter Fair in California, the Atlanta Exposition, the Crystal Palace in London, the Colonial Fair in India, and others in cities of Europe and Australia. Mr. Hardt had been in charge of the exhibits for Denver's Mountain and Plain Festival and was reported to have done an outstanding job.

In late November, Mr. Wood met with Hardt, and heeding Mr. Speer's recommendation, hired him at once. Hardt lost no time in presenting plans for exhibits to be sent to Leadville. He guaranteed that the displays in the ice palace would be more novel and spectacular than those seen at the World's Fair in Chicago.

His first plan of action was to personally visit cities and towns throughout Colorado and contact businesses around the country that he felt would be willing to send exhibits to the ice palace. He found tremendous response to his requests.

-----

[12]It was erroneously reported that Speer was mayor of Denver in 1896. Speer served as Denver's mayor from 1904-1912 and again from 1916-1918.

On December 5th, Superintendent Hardt opened an office in the Albany Hotel in Denver, and for the next three weeks he contacted 40 wholesalers and manufacturers for the purpose of enticing them to display their merchandise in the Leadville Ice Palace, pointing out the benefits of the publicity. He stayed in Denver until shortly before Christmas.

Concession space bids were let by the Association Secretary, W. L. Temple, for the restaurant, cigar stand, confectionery, and hot popcorn and peanut stands. Others who wanted to sell their merchandise, curios, knickknacks, or had amusements were also invited. The bidders were required to pay a fee to the Association, plus a percentage of gross receipts. Bids had to be submitted to Mr. Temple no later than December 8th.

The concessions went faster than hotcakes. John A. Milner, F. T. Smith and Frank Hurd were awarded the cloakroom concession. They were required to put up their own storage lockers, hire help at their own expense, and be responsible for lost articles. Fifty percent of the gross receipts were to be paid to the Association.

Harvey Brown, submitted a cash bid, and was awarded concessions for soft drinks, candy, popcorn, hot peanuts and offered a specialty drink of hot soda. He was also awarded the cigar concession.

John E. Miller, popular Leadville confectioner, baker and restauranteur, was awarded the restaurant concessions.

Charles Salter was allowed to sell peanuts on the street, without a license for a week, "so he could get a little ahead."

H. M. Blakely won the skating concession which required him to have lock boxes for those who wanted to leave their skates. He also had skates to rent.

F. W. Bartlett & Company had exclusive rights to sell mineral specimens and gems, and another concession to sell furs and taxidermy goods. A large shield, covered with various kinds of furs, hung on the wall in back of the company's display case.

A studio concession was granted to C. F. O'Keefe and Frederick Stockdorf (O'Keefe & Stockdorf), 501-503 Harrison Avenue. The latest equipment for taking photographs, said to have been the finest in the West, was installed. Top of the line lighting equipment was ordered from Chicago and a variety of background props were available.

The railroads came through with their support. Any business that would send frozen exhibits to Leadville would be given a special freight rate, one-half the regular rate. Freight business into Leadville had increased to the point that the Colorado Midland added more switch crews.

The exhibits were arranged in a manner that gave the appearance of a vast art gallery. Exhibits frozen in ice blocks were placed within the palace's walls and interior walls of the towers as the walls were being erected. Exhibits, not frozen in ice, were placed in the dining room, part of which became an exhibition hall. Although space was limited, Hardt was complimented for being able to arrange the exhibits without overcrowding the dining room.

The first block of ice placed on exhibit contained a photograph of Tingley S. Wood. It was Mr. Hardt's intent to show early visitors to the ice palace what the frozen displays would look like.

Displays began arriving in Leadville the last week in December and on Christmas Eve, Hardt began the layout for the exhibits. Time was of the essence and the men worked like beavers.

The firm of Craffey & Crowell had a pyramid of their company's brooms placed in the West Annex.

Harry Kahn & Company had a large showcase of souvenir ice castle spoons made of gold and silver for sale. The bowl of the spoon had an engraving of the ice palace with the lettering "Leadville Crystal Castle, 1896." There were also spoons engraved with the Colorado coat of arms, the state flower (the Columbine), a silver dish with, "The Ice Palace," engraved in the bowl. A number of other items were also sold.

Newspapers were among the numerous businesses that had displays in the ice palace halls. The *Leadville Herald Democrat* displayed their December 22, 1895 special edition. It was arranged so that the cover page and two others were shown. The *Denver Republican,* the *Denver Times*, and *Rocky Mountain News* also sent editions to be displayed.

W. H. Jackson displayed twenty views of Colorado scenery.

On December 17th, Stephen N. Thayer asked the city council for and was granted permission to erect a portable phonograph gallery on a lot at the corner of West 7th and Spruce Streets and was awarded a concession to sell phonographs and records. Thayer also exhibited a phonograph collection.

The Carbonate National Bank exhibit displayed $150,000 in bars of pure gold from the Little Jonny Mine in the bank's lobby. Each bar weighed fifty to sixty pounds, valued at six to eight thousand dollars each. Although not displayed at the ice palace, the exhibit was considered to be part of the palace's exhibits.

A $1,500 working model engine of the Denver & Rio Grande Railroad, trimmed in gold, was displayed along with photographic views of their scenic line. This working miniature locomotive, that had attracted so much attention at the World's Fair in Chicago, arrived in Leadville on December 30th and was placed in the northeast corner of the exhibition hall.

Hungarian Flour Mills heralded the merits of its flour with a huge pyramid of sacks. It contained enough sacks of flour to feed an army. This display was located in the southwest corner of the exhibition hall.

Hardt made arrangements with a Denver ice company to freeze the exhibits into the ice. F. A. Callenburg, of the Denver Ice & Refrigeration Company at 1722 Blake Street, was manager in charge of decorating Denver's frozen exhibits for the ice palace. The exhibits were frozen in ice blocks weighing 400 pounds. Pictures, samples of merchandise, and other displays were suspended in the water by a thin white thread. The water froze from the outside toward the center, holding the exhibit in place during the freezing process, which took anywhere from 54 to 62 hours. The frozen exhibits were then shipped to Leadville and set in place at the ice palace.

On January 8th, Mr. Callenburg traveled to Leadville to inspect the frozen ice palace exhibits that he had designed and produced in Denver. He remarked, "that the Castle was beyond all imagination." This was his first visit to the Cloud City and he complimented the Association officials for their congeniality and found the city to be, "a hummer."

The Vendome Hotel of Leadville and the Windsor, Albany and New St. James hotels of Denver took spaces and displayed table delicacies of all descriptions, all frozen in ice, topped off with bottles of champagne. The Albany also had its name carved in ice.

The Conforth Fish & Oyster Company of Denver displayed fish and deep sea delicacies in two ice blocks.

A collection of Rocky Mountain trout taken from a Colorado stream created local interest. One oversized ice block contained two Rocky Mountain trout that almost filled it. These were brought in from the Leadville Fish Hatchery.

The Denver Fish Company exhibited eight blocks of ice containing fish and vegetables. Their name spelled out in vegetables made this display stand out.

The Booth Packing Company displayed fish, oysters and canned goods in eight ice blocks. They proposed to outshine all competitors with every kind of fish that the connoisseur was fond of, all frozen in ice.

C. Rathe displayed a tenderloin and other meat cuts in "cold storage."

The Colorado Packing & Provision Company displayed hams, meat and other products.

The Colorado Orchard Company displayed red apples.

Bowman & Burleson Candy Co. displayed delicious sweetmeats, "frozen so securely they couldn't be eaten."

The Longmont Creamery sent rolls, fancy imprinted pats of butter, and cheese. They were all frozen in ice blocks, and "guaranteed to make your mouth water."

Fleischmann & Company displayed their yeast products.

The Alamosa Milling Company displayed wheat flour in ice blocks.

The Kuner Pickle Company displayed four ice blocks full of their appetizing wares.

Wineries, breweries and distilleries sent their wares to be displayed in the ice palace. Beer seemed to be the most prominent.

Coors beer was frozen into a pyramid. This display, rated one of the finest, occupied the entire space of the northwest tower of the ice palace. The Coors banner, an inch thick, was made of silk, and was considered the best one in the crystal castle. Contractor Kerr began setting up the ice for this display on December 30th, and Hardt began working on the display the following day.

An amusing story spread about Mr. Adolph Coors, of Golden, who sent six kegs of bottled beer to Leadville; he also sent along twenty-four extra bottles. In case some of the bottles in the barrels were broken, he could replace them with the extras and proceed with the display. However, a couple of days before the ice palace opened the twenty-four bottles had disappeared. Mr. Hardt, in charge of the exhibits and Mr. Murray, one of the foremen, went looking for the missing bottles. A short time later they were found but only six of the bottles were lying on the ground. They were puzzled that all of them had not been emptied. They removed the top from one of the remaining bottles and tasted it. Mr. Coors, being a smart business-man, knew that when the bottles froze they would break, and that would ruin his display; so, in some of the bottles he put colored salt water, and that's what the culprits had confiscated. Served 'em right, "Thou Shalt Not Steal!"

Neef Brothers Denver Brewery's Wiener/Maerzen display was an eye catcher. Their sign encouraged their customers to,

"Help Home Industry, Drink Wierner/Maerzen." The display was contained in eight blocks of ice.

Pabst Brewing Company had one of their signs on display.

Zang's Brewery sent one of the most elaborate collections, having ordered twenty ice blocks. Their display was built into a pyramid with a row of bottles in the center and every other block contained specimens of the signs it gave to its customers. Their sign, 15" x 20", was placed above the display.

Railroad Agent Anthony Sneve, of the Colorado Midland Railroad, hired one of the foremost artists from the Chicago Art Institute to paint the Colorado Midland's logo. The artist was brought to Leadville to work on the display. Mr. Sneve was fearful that shipping the glass plates from Chicago would be risky. The logo, a life-size American Indian, was painted on plates of glass, 2 feet x 5 feet. Scenic photographs of their route were frozen in twelve colored ice blocks, along with the logo. The display was placed inside the Seventh Street entrance.

South Park Railroad's artwork, showing photographic scenes along their route, were displayed in the west annex. These photos were reportedly, "some of the grandest scenery of the Rocky Mountains."

The May Clothing Company of Denver reserved eight blocks of ice containing clothing displays.

The T. J. Underhill Company displayed overalls, shirts and pants from their Denver factory.

George Kendall displayed a comic advertisement of his mattresses in an ice block.

Harrison Avenue druggist, George Taylor, displayed different kinds of medicines in twenty ice blocks.

Dunwoody Soap Company displayed their fine goods, carved faces and figures of beautiful women in soap, frozen in ice.

F. D. Cameron, local manager for the Singer Manufacturing Company, displayed sewing machines. The latest sewing machine model "that would embroider snowflakes without a flaw," along with samples of needlework were included.

Capitol Hill Greenhouse, and florist R. C. Gallup, both of Denver, displayed flowers in two ice blocks each.

General Electric displayed many of Thomas A. Edison's inventions including electrical appliances "of almost every imaginable kind," and a 15-inch high induction motor model which generated 15 horsepower, had no commutator or moving contacts. There was also displayed a large frame containing an illuminated monogram, "G.E.C.," made of miniature, multi-colored incandescent bulbs. A bronze bust of Edison and two ornamental arc lights completed the display.

The Mountain Electric Supply Company of Denver had requested space from Mr. Hardt for an exhibit of dynamos, motors and other electrical equipment.

The Solis Cigar Company put several boxes of their dry climate cigars in ice. M. Grossman & Company displayed boxes of Perfecto cigars. Silver State Cigar Company had two blocks of ice filled with their finest brands.

A. E. Meek & Company of Denver froze one of their trunks in ice blocks.

Dunn & Blass displayed leather goods in three ice blocks.

Grove & O'Keefe exhibited H. L. James, and M & M Companies' paints and colors in blocks of ice.

Celebrated badgeman, John E. Miller of Denver (not to be confused with John E. Miller of Leadville), had his extensive collection of fraternal organization badges, pins, society and secret order emblems frozen in ice blocks. This was said to have been one of the most unique and eye-catching displays.

C. R. Galleys displayed an exhibit of Masonic emblems.

The Denver Tent & Awning Company display was located in the west annex and had an entire camping outfit on exhibition. A small tent was filled with ore sacks.

The Denver Fire Clay Company gave their local agent, George E. Taylor, carte blanche for a display of their products. This was the most extensive display of assayers' supplies exhibited; some of which could only be identified by "a graduate of the (Colorado) School of Mines."

A. M. Donaldson & Company filled one ice block with assay supplies.

George W. Lancaster, local agent for Studebaker Brothers wagon manufacturers of South Bend, Indiana, displayed a newly patented ore dump wagon that would "leave other models lost in the dust." In addition, three kinds of snowshoe bicycles on slats were exhibited.

Mr. Hardt was protective of the largest exhibit, one of the best kept secret displays, the Midway Pleasance[13]. This was an immense, 29,000-square-foot painted canvas representing Cairo, Egypt. This panoramic view of the Cairo streets was placed on a wall near the entrance. "The streets of Cairo were presided over by Turkish maidens with lustrous dark eyes and delicious wicked winks."

---

[13]A pleasure ground, that which pleases.

It was reported that Hardt had a herd of camels on the desert somewhere in New Mexico which he proposed to bring to the carnival. The camels were to be available for visitors to ride. They would have been quite an attraction, but they never arrived.

Director General Wood, who was a personal acquaintance of Senators Teller and Wolcott, planned to secure a government exhibit for the crystal palace, including the famous Rescue of Greely[14] collection. He would request the Senators to ask Congress to make a small appropriation of $5,000-$10,000 to defray the expense of sending a small government exhibit.

Leadville created the greatest exhibition of winter life and sports that was ever undertaken in this country at that time, and since it was the purpose of the government museum to preserve valuable historic relics for the education of the people, it was argued there wasn't any reason why the people of Colorado and the west should not be able to see a small part of the government's collection. Even if Congress would not pay the freight there was little doubt that they would send an exhibit and there were enough enterprising people in Leadville who would raise the necessary money to ship it. Leadville had contributed more of the precious metals to enrich the nation than any

---

[14]In 1881, Adolphus Washington Greely, arctic explorer, was in charge of a U.S. Government expedition to establish a meteorological station in the Far North. All but Greely and six of the expeditioners starved or froze to death when relief expeditions were unable to find them. The survivors were rescued from Cape Sabine in 1884.

97

other city during the fifteen years previous to the raising of the ice palace. Now Leadville's citizens felt they should be honored with an exhibit from the nation's capital.

Other exhibits included local and imported beers, pickles, biscuits, saddles, candles, mining machinery, brooms, musical instruments, marble, jewelry, drills and more.

In mid-January H. B. Hardt traveled to Denver to oversee the shipment of frozen merchandise to Leadville. On January 21st, the third carload of exhibits was sent from Denver. Among them were displays from the Colorado Orchard Company, Skinner Bros. & Wright, Knight & Atmore, Kuner's Pickles, and an ice block display of peanuts grown in the Arkansas Valley.

THE TOBOGGAN SLIDES
A Spine-Tingling Thriller

A petition was read at the city council meeting on November 26, 1895 that requested the area on West Seventh Street from Harrison Avenue to the ice palace site be closed to traffic. The street was to be used as toboggan runs during the carnival season. The petition also empowered the Association to install additional arc lights. Charles T. Carnahan and a number of residents undersigned the petition, which passed by unanimous vote.

There was a lot of haggling among the city council members during that meeting. Some councilmen strongly urged that the Association should be made to put up a $5,000 surety bond and be responsible for any accidents that might happen on the toboggan slides. One councilman was of the opinion that if the Association didn't want to indemnify the city, then they should run the toboggans the other way on Seventh Street, away from town. Other aldermen opposed the idea of the bond, arguing that it was unfair to make the Association responsible when the carnival was being run for the benefit of the entire city. Following a motion by Alderman C. C. Joy, (not to be confused with C. E. Joy, architect for the ice palace), a five to one vote was passed, granting the Leadville Crystal Carnival Association use of West 7th Street for the toboggan slide, as long as it didn't interfere with the public's safety; and the Association would be responsible for all damages that might be caused by their use of the street during the carnival season.

With permission granted to use West Seventh Street, Director General Wood now set to work estimating costs for the toboggan runs. His biggest concerns were the possibility of accidents and purchasing toboggans. He figured the cost of the toboggan runs would be $1,500.

On December first, the Director General let bids for two toboggan runs to be built to his specifications, erected at the successful bidder's expense, and operated by the bidder as well. A number of bids were submitted, including one by Wallace T. Perkins of the American National Bank. But he and some of the others were unwilling to comply with some of the conditions imposed by Director General Wood regarding the construction and maintenance of the electric lights.

The winning bid of $2,000 was submitted by H. C. Dimick, a Leadville building contractor. Director General Wood was pleased with the success of the toboggan contract, and the fact that he would be relieved of that responsibility.

Dimick had his work cut out for him. He was not only responsible for building the runs, but also seeing that they were kept free of snow, and sprinkled every day to maintain the proper surface. There were ticket sellers to be hired, and guards along the streets. He had to have his concession built and operating before he would be able to pay a percentage to the Association and realize any return on his investment. When Dimick was awarded the contract to build the toboggan slides, it was agreed that twenty-five percent of the gross receipts would be paid to the Association. He was anxious to have the toboggan runs completed and operating as quickly as possible.

When the toboggan runs were designed, Architect Joy directed that eight feet distance would be needed on either side of the toboggan runs, with 20 feet in the center left free for vehicles. (It was later decided to close West Seventh Street off to all but foot traffic.)

Dimick immediately began construction as he planned for the runs to be in operation by December 15th. By December 6th the air was filled with pounding and sawing as the framework for the platforms began taking shape. Holes were being dug for the light poles along West 7th Street. Construction of the toboggan runs drew the attention of many sidewalk superintendents and gawkers. The *Herald Democrat* reported on December 6, 1895, "The curious may transfer their attention from the Ice Palace proper now, and for a while, watch the toboggan slide grow under the hands of the carpenters."

The toboggan runs were made of wooden planks eighteen inches wide, about the same width as the toboggans, with eight-inch grooves. These guides were tapered out on the top so the toboggan had about the same amount of play as the flange on a railroad car. They would also keep the toboggan on track and prevent it from jarring from one side to the other.

Dimick elected to build the toboggans in Leadville. He was instructed not to use the old model, which was made of a single board with one end turned up like a sled runner. This old style toboggan could prove hazardous in that it could split and cause the sled to crash. The progressive Director Wood ordered the toboggans to be fashioned after a newer model. This entailed using rounded wooden strips that were steamed, then turned up in sleigh runner fashion on the front end. The strips were held together by cross strips, and a cushion placed on the toboggan for the rider's comfort. Along each side of the toboggan, guide ropes were attached to metal rings for the riders to hold onto. In

101

this way they were guaranteed a fast, but safe ride unless the toboggan overturned.

Contractor Dimick hired three men to work on the toboggans and had ordered enough yellow pine from Denver to construct seventy-five toboggans. He planned to build fifty of them as soon as the timber arrived and the runs were completed. The toboggans were from 5 to 19 feet long and 2 feet wide. The longer ones could accommodate up to twelve persons.

By December 22nd Dimick had put the finishing touches on the toboggan runs and was anxiously awaiting a snowfall to "Let 'er rip." The snow was needed to cover the wooden planks, fill out the edges and shape the runs. Dimick has special scrapers made which would fit the grooves and mold the track, leaving the needed amount of snow for a base. After the scrapers had been run over the slides, the snow was frozen by sprinkling it with water. This was accomplished by using lengths of rubber hose. Mr. Dimick had secured permission from the homeowners along the toboggan runs to attach his hoses to their water hydrants.

Shortly after Christmas the toboggan runs were in a state of disuse. Mr. Dimick had a team of workers scouring for snowdrifts and moving them to Harrison Avenue near the toboggan runs. Two inches of snow was needed for a base on the wooden planks. After the runs were packed they were sprinkled with water. Thankfully, on December 28th, Leadville received two inches of snow, followed by three inches more on the 30th. The toboggans were back in business and being readied for the ice palace's grand opening.

The palace run was 900 feet long, with a pitch of 48 feet. It began on a platform 20 feet above the ground at Spruce Street on the south side of West Seventh Street, in line with the first house east of the ice palace. The toboggans slowed to a stop at a small rise on Pine Street. The riders would then disembark and walk to Harrison Avenue for the return trip to the palace.

The Avenue slide was 1200 feet long and had a pitch of 64 feet. The slide, 26 feet above the street, started at the Vendome Hotel on the north side of West Seventh. For one block, between Spruce and Pine Streets, the toboggans ran side by side.

The tobogganers mounted wooden stairways to a platform edged by a wood railing. After all the riders were seated, a toboggan assistant would give it a shove, and the riders were off! The ladies riding the toboggans were assisted. Screams of fright and delight resounded through the crisp mountain air and the looks of sheer terror on some of the passengers faces may have changed the minds of some of the waiting riders.

The runs were so fast four to eight people could be sent down every thirty seconds! The toboggans were pulled back to the starting points by young boys who were paid a small wage.

Two station houses, twenty by twenty-four feet, were built at each end of the toboggan runs for the comfort of the visitors who awaited their turns down the slides. The stations were furnished with benches, and heated by coal stoves. The station house on Harrison Avenue, called the Toboggan Lunchroom, contained a small kitchen and lunch counter.

The cross street (Pine) was closed off, and a rope strung across 7th Street at the Avenue. The purpose of this was to control the crowds and the rope could be removed quickly in case of fire. Traffic was limited to pedestrians on West Seventh Street during the carnival.

The late Arthur McNair passed this story along about one "Jim Dandy" who was going to pull a fast one on a toboggan full of young ladies. He had agreed to accompany them down the slide from the palace. His devilish scheme was to get the toboggan started down the slide and then jump off, but his plan backfired. As the dastardly coward was preparing to jump from the toboggan back onto the platform, his britches caught on a nail protruding from the handrail. It ripped them quite badly and he had no choice but to ride the toboggan down the hill, pants flapping in the breeze. The women's screams caught the attention of the viewers who then focused on the embarrassed man. When the toboggan got close to the bottom of the hill, but was still moving, the gent jumped off and hightailed it to Snell's Saloon[15] for refuge, and a change of trousers. Ladies did not patronize saloons in those days, so the rounder knew he was temporarily safe from further embarrassment.

Director General Wood specified that 2,000 candle-power arc lights be placed every one hundred feet along the toboggan runs. The globes covering the lights were colored glass in shades of red, green, orange, white and yellow, which at night radiated dazzling colors. On the nights of

---

[15]Although the establishment changed names many times, the saloon, now called the Manhattan Bar, is still doing business in the same location today.

104

special events, more colored lights were strung between the arc lights. The lights reflected off of the snow, tinted the houses, and sprayed the tobogganers, in their picturesque costumes, with a myriad of beautiful rainbow hues.

To add to the splendor of this gala Crystal Carnival, West 7th Street was arched with countless varicolored globes of light, suspended over the toboggan runs. As the tobogganers streaked down the icy chutes they were covered with an array of kaleidoscopic colors.

Twenty arc lights, ten on each side of the street, were placed every hundred feet between Harrison Avenue and the palace. The lights burned continually during the carnival season. The cost to install the poles, lights and wiring was $250.[16] This figure was exclusive of the lights that would be used at the ice palace proper. The installation of the lights along the toboggan runs was equal to one-fourth of all the lights that were used to illuminate all the streets of Leadville at that time.

For the sake of the children's safety, the City Council members granted the school board's request that an elevated platform be built over the top of the toboggan runs at the corner of 7th and Spruce Streets. This would enable the school children to cross the street without danger on their way to and from school.

Street signs were installed at the intersections and a special crossing was put in on the north side of West 7th Street at Leiter to accommodate travel to the palace.

---

[16]Those same lights, installed today, would cost an estimated $12,753.

The official opening day for the toboggan slides was January 1, 1896, having been delayed by the Chinook wind that hit the high country in December. Unofficially, however, the Avenue run was opened on the evening of December 11th when a few small boys christened it.

Construction of the toboggan runs was finished. The workmen had picked up their tools and left the site. A group of boys were standing out of sight in a doorway at the rear of the Vendome Hotel, watching as the workmen departed. As little imps plotting some devilish prank, they decided to christen the toboggan run. They made a toboggan from two barrel staves with two slats nailed across the bottom. Being a little faint-hearted to start from the top, they climbed about a third of the way and began the initiation from there. When they found that to be safe, some of the more daring ones climbed to the top. They determined that was a little too tame, so one of the boys suggested they freeze the slide. They rounded up two buckets and filled them with water. The older boys carried the buckets to the top. They continued sprinkling water on the boards which soon froze to an icy surface. They then cautiously ventured onto the slide again, starting part way up until they bravely reached the top. At the bottom, they began extending the end of the slide by adding more boards. When they overshot those boards they laid more planks to make it even longer. One of the daredevils said that if only they had more planks they could have gone all the way past Pine Street.

The ten little pranksters, the first to fly down this daredevil ride, were: Frank Quigley, Leo Ragen, Frank and Joe Jennings, Will Cully, Frank Putkamer, Frank Hale, Jimmy Hays, and Bob and Harry LaSalle.

106

Fares for the toboggan slide were announced. A single ride was a nickel, round trip cost a dime. Toboggans could be rented for a single ride at $.25; a five-foot, two-man toboggan was $.75 per hour; a seven-foot, four-man toboggan rented for a dollar an hour; a twelve-foot toboggan rented for $2.50 per hour; fourteen-foot toboggans were $3.00 per hour; the nineteen-foot toboggans, carrying six persons, rented for $4.50 per hour. Those who furnished their own toboggan or belonged to one of the toboggan clubs, rode for .50 cents, $1.50 or $1.75 an hour, depending upon the number of passengers.

The toboggans operated all day and well into the night. The first day Dimick was in business, he collected over $850. The toboggan slides proved to be a roaring success.

Railroad agent, B. L. Winchell, made a contract with the toboggan managers to have an ad painted on the side of the Avenue station, facing the hotel. The sign depicted the Denver, Leadville & Gunnison, the Union Pacific and Denver & Gulf Railroads.

On February 3rd, Anthony Sneve, Colorado Midland agent, was involved in a accident while taking a ride on the toboggan. His leg was broken below the knee. His unnamed companion was also badly injured. The toboggan jumped the track, causing the unfortunate mishap. This was the only other[17] news-reported accident that happened during the winter carnival.

The toboggan concession came under new management on February 13th. The new owners spared no expense in

---

[17]Sam Olds' accident on December 15, 1895 was the other.

getting the runs in shape. To celebrate the new grand opening, the east end of the toboggan run was decorated with carnival colors, and Shriners and Elks Club flags. In a news release from the *Colorado Springs Telegraph* in late November, it was reported:

> Those of us who have been envious of the fun which the eastern people have had on their toboggans need not be worried any longer for the Leadville Ice Palace there is to be a genuine toboggan slide constructed in a really humane principle, that is one may coast both ways, down hill, up an elevator (an erroneous report, there was no elevator), down the hill again. It will be all fun and no hard work.

ELECTRIC LIGHTING INSTALLED
The City Lights Up

In early December, the Citizens' Light Company, located at Fifth and Leiter Streets, and the Leadville Electric Light Company, owned by Charles Boettcher, with offices at 305 Harrison Avenue and plant at 12th Street and Harrison Avenue, were merged. Talks had been going on between the two companies for some time, and finally an agreement was reached between them. The new utility, the Citizens Electric Light Company, was valued at $150,000, with each company investing $75,000. Leadville once again had but one electric light producer.

The consolidation meant better service to their customers with no increase in cost. At that time, electric service rates to Leadville's citizens was 20% lower than Denver, Colorado Springs, Pueblo and Canon City. Both plants, operating as independent companies, were running on overload. By merging, the same distribution system could be used, eliminating the overload. The Citizens Light Company had been started in 1894 because of the exorbitant rates charged by the Leadville Electric Light Company. Following the merger, the company immediately installed a substation near California Gulch, to provide lighting for the ice palace. The plant was equipped with an alternator and a generator, having a capacity for "one thousand incandescent lights."

On November 26th, Councilman Royal J. Donnen suggested additional electric lighting be installed around the city during the winter carnival. A special committee of councilmen Donnen, Warren F. Page and Charles C. Joy were appointed to meet with George P. Brown, manager of the Citizens Electric Light Company, to determine the number of lights, locations, and price.

After canvassing the city, it was agreed that lights would be installed on Harrison Avenue at the crossings of 4th, 5th, 6th and 8th Streets; at the corner of Hemlock and East 6th; 8th and Hemlock, 7th and Poplar; 8th and Hazel, and 7th and Hazel. The lights were to burn all night and the price per light was estimated to be $5 per month. This was the rate the Association was being given for the lights at the ice palace.

On December 10th, George P. Brown attended the City Council meeting and he reported the light company and the City Council committee had reached an agreement on the location of the additional electric lights for the carnival. The committee had asked for a rate of $12 per light per month but Mr. Brown's company (The Citizens Electric Light Company) could not afford to concede this amount because all but four of the lights would require new installation. His company gave the city two lights and the city would be charged $15 per month for sixteen lights. A total of twenty new street lights were installed for the winter carnival.

The light company would be responsible for installing the necessary wiring and poles at its own expense. The cost of construction would be equivalent to a month's electric usage, about $300 (estimated on the low side).

Two street lights were requested to be installed near the South Park depot, and were paid for by the railroad. The Denver & Rio Grande also wanted extra lights placed around their platform.

A special report issued on February 9th by the city council finance committee stated that $1,920 had been expended, to date, for extra police officers and electric lighting during the carnival season. The council was

110

operating in the red, and expenses needed to be cut as soon as possible.

On March 10th, a motion was passed by the city council to disconnect all of the extra street lights that had been installed for the carnival. The motion was voted down. A committee was appointed to meet with representatives of the light company to get a cost estimate to light some of the streets with arc lights, and others with incandescent lights.

On April 9th the city clerk was instructed to notify the light company to discontinue all of the carnival street lights. Exceptions were the fire station on East Second Street, the light at the intersection of Fifth and Orange, and the intersection of Ninth and Pine.

THE CARNIVAL MOVES FORWARD
More Work To Be Done

Director General Wood was relieved that he was able to turn responsibility for construction of the toboggan runs over to Mr. H. C. Dimick. This allowed Wood time to tend to the many other tasks required to keep the ice palace project moving.

Wood knew it would not be a financial success unless the word was spread. The citizens of Leadville, themselves, were not going to be able to financially support this massive project. Leadville had to toot her horn to let the world know the city was going to accomplish the biggest ice palace ever attempted. The masses had to be told about the ice palace and winter carnival in every way possible. Promotion and publicity had to start immediately and getting the word out was one of the first and foremost assignments. Those is charge of this task were: George Wallace Williams, W. H. James, Charles Smith, W. K. Burchinell, W. S. Ward, Howard Chapin, E. H. Bush, C. Pearson, Robert Schrader, J. C. Mitchell, W. M. Clark and George W. Cook. Not only was it important to promote the ice palace statewide, but national publicity was needed to draw the people and their money to the Cloud City. The committee's efforts were a tremendous success.

In addition to getting the palace built, it would be necessary to delegate the other directors to oversee many of the winter carnival activities. There were the responsibilities of letting bids for the concession stands; ordering the souvenir medals; arranging various contests and prizes as well as other entertainment. Obtaining musicians and bands for the many functions that would be held during the winter carnival was important to Director Wood. People to work as ticket takers, maintenance staff, and ice skating and

113

dancing instructors also had to be hired. The city council, through the Carnival Association, was requested to hire extra policemen to keep the order and protect the citizens during the carnival season. The policemen were paid by the city council.

There was even an "official handshake." One of the most important things was the style of handshake that would be adopted as the proper greeting for visitors to the Crystal Carnival. It was important that the greeter look the visitor directly in the eyes and "no grip would be too high for Leadville."

A thousand and one details were continually arising that demanded Wood's attention, and although he delegated many of the responsibilities, he made it a point to be aware of what was taking place in every aspect of the palace's construction and the winter carnival activities.

Director General Wood's operating plan determined that the money earned from the toboggan slides and the ice skating rink would be needed to pay the bills. The cost of the electric lighting was estimated to be $1,000 per month and the music would be twice as much; the fireworks displays would cost $5,000. Construction workers and ice haulers wages were paid from the revenue earned from sales of the stock.

TREASURED KEEPSAKES
Get Your Souvenirs Here!

Director General Wood announced the official colors of the carnival were to be burnished copper, burnished silver, old gold and French gray (lead).

Leadville would not be outdone by the Chicago World's Fair. The event had offered metallic souvenirs, and so would the Crystal Carnival. By the first week in December Wood had ordered 10,000 beautifully designed souvenir badges, at a cost of $30,000. By December 21st a number of Leadville's citizens were sporting the keepsakes.

Most of the medals depicted the mining industry, and were designed to recognize and honor the miners who, through their hard labors, had brought so much wealth and prosperity into the city of Leadville.

Director General Wood learned the Association had competition for its souvenir medals. One hustler came into town intending to make a bundle selling counterfeit souvenirs.

The largest of the four counterfeits was a badge in the shape of a shield with the ice castle etched on the face and the inscription, "Crystal Carnival, Leadville, Colorado, 1896." It was suspended from a pin bearing the word "souvenir," and was minted by W. W. Frisholm Company. Another medal, the size of a nickel, had a white background. It pictured the ice palace with colored flags waving, and was inscribed, "Leadville Ice Carnival, Leadville, Colorado—1896." The third medal was made of white celluloid and was about the size of a nickel. It was imprinted with black lettering, "Crystal Ice Carnival — 1896 — Leadville, Colo." It pictured a replica of the ice palace with colored flags flying from the towers. The fourth medal was made from silver aluminum, suspended from a gold-colored pin that was engraved, "Colorado." The medal was a little larger than a modern-day fifty-cent piece and embossed with a replica of the ice palace on one side. It read, "Leadville Ice Palace — 1896 — Leadville, Colo.," and the back of the medal was blank. These medals were not sanctioned by the Crystal Carnival association.

The *Leadville Herald Democrat* reported in its December 25, 1895 edition, "Do not buy a spurious medal, for as soon as people understand the fraud, it will not be safe to wear it under your night shirt in a dark room." They warned that buying medals from this gentleman was not supporting the ice palace project. The public was urged to buy only the genuine round gold, or gold or aluminum medals. The profits realized would help build the ice palace. After the huckster was exposed to the public he made his peace with Director General Wood and left the city.

The largest medal designed by Director General Wood was a hoisting bucket, heaped with ore, embedded with a horizontal bar imprinted with the raised figure, "$200,000,000," representing the metals of the Carbonate Camp. On the back was a picture of the Crystal Palace. The pin from which the barrel was suspended was embossed with miner's tools, a pick, shovel and doublejack. The medal was made of gold plated aluminum.

For the smelters, a round medal about the size of a gold eagle coin was designed to show miners loading bullion onto a handcar. On the reverse side was a picture of Leadville's Ice Castle.

For the ladies, Director General Wood designed an "idealized love heart," made of brass on which was engraved "1895-1896 Crystal Carnival & Ice Palace," and a picture of the ice palace. This was intended to be a romantic and affectionate love souvenir.

The medals authorized by the Leadville Crystal Carnival Association were minted by the Schwaab S&S Company of Milwaukee, Wisconsin.

BANDS AND ORCHESTRAS
And The Bands Played On

As with every other facet of the carnival, Director General Wood was emphatic that the music provided for the dancers and skaters would be the best the budget would allow. Although Director Wood favored using hometown talent, he notified the city's Musicians Union that outside musicians would be brought in if the local musicians didn't measure up. The committee did invite bands from other cities on special events days, to allow visitors the opportunity of hearing some of the top-notch bands in Colorado. Bands from Pueblo, Grand Junction, Aspen, Denver and Colorado Springs, said to be the best at that time, were among those who came.

Harry S. Phillips was appointed chairman of a twenty-three man committee in charge of the music and dances at the palace. The Music Committee corresponded with state musical organizations and secured the First Regiment Band and several other musical groups from across the state. The musical program was changed every week, and concerts were given each afternoon and evening.

When Director General Wood and his committee began soliciting music for the ice palace, Jack St. Clair was high on the list. St. Clair and his Fort Dodge Cowboy Band were very popular and much in demand throughout the country. Director General Wood was successful in bringing them to the ice palace at a cost of $2,100. They were contracted to play for twenty-one days at $100 per day (an enormous salary at that time), beginning on January 1, 1896.

After their contract expired, (Fen G.) Barker's Dance Orchestra, Cook's Drum Corps and the Leadville Drum Corps, the Finn Cornet Band, and other local bands and orchestras were hired to provide the music. At times they were entertained by musicians whose talents were questionable.

The Fort Dodge Cowboy Band stayed in Leadville for a time and participated in a number of the parades. Whether this service was included in their contract is uncertain.

Harry Phillips was assisted by the following aides:

Beman, F. W.	Keith, F. A.
Bohn, C. A.	Korn, Will
Brown, H. T.	Milner, John F.
Cummings, L. C.	Moore, W. A.
Ferguson, John	North, G. F.
Follett, Fred	Perkins, W. T.
Foster, F. K.	Raney, Thomas
Frisbie, G. E.	Thomson, A. C.
Harris, A. C.	Schlessinger, B
Harvey, John Jr.	Sherwin, F. L.
Heichemer, H. E.	Stead, F. O.
Keith, F. A.	Wood, T. C.

GETTING READY FOR THE VISITORS
Clean Up, Fix Up, Paint Up

The spirit of the townspeople was one of support and enthusiasm. It was time to make ready for the thousands of guests who would pour into their city via the three railroads. Merchants advertised that it was time to clean up, paint up, and fix up in readiness for the visitors.

Homeowners were asked to paint their houses and "spruce up" for the many visitors who would be coming to see the beautiful ice palace.

Carpenters, painters, paperhangers, decorators and upholsterers were in great demand as the realization of the impact the ice palace was going to have on Leadville set in. Harrison Avenue was bustling with excitement. In anticipation of the crowds, the many restaurants busily prepared for the masses they would feed. Many restauranteurs enlarged their dining rooms to double capacity. Mrs. K. Matheson opened a new restaurant across the street from the post office. It was a "short order" house, but a fine dinner could be had for thirty-five cents

Old buildings were repaired and renovated, new furniture replaced old, and the town was filled with energy as they made ready for the multitude of visitors.

Director General Wood invited Ben Cirkle, the Chicago World's Fair Decorating Director, to assist with Leadville's decorations. This was noted in the following letter:

Chicago, Ill, December 18, 1895 — W. L. Temple, Secretary, Leadville Crystal Carnival Ass'n. Leadville, Colorado. Dear Sir: Yours of the 12th on hand and contents noted. Our Mr. Cirkle will arrive in your city with a very large stock of bunting, flags and streamers of all sizes to help decorate your city for the opening, and the

119

prices will be within the reach of all. We will want space in the exposition. Very truly yours, Ben Cirkle.

The city's businessmen were encouraged to incorporate the ice palace carnival colors into their store decorations. Store fronts from Chestnut to Ninth Streets were colorfully decorated with buntings, streamers and flags, and pictures of the ice palace. Merchants decorated their windows with articles depicting Leadville's Ice Palace and Winter Carnival. The only building, shamefully obvious, was the courthouse. It was left undecorated, and stood out plain and unadorned amid the sea of red, white, blue, and carnival colors. Was it going to be dressed in carnival garb?

J. D. Thomas & Son, 107 East 7th Street, advertised in December 5th's *Herald Democrat*, "Fix up for the great 'carnival' opening. The Ice Palace will bring thousands of visitors—Paper & Paint now."

On December fourth, Theodore Eck asked for the city council's permission to erect a billboard, for the purpose of business advertising, on the south side of 7th Street, at the east end of the ice palace. Mr. Eck also painted artistic advertising displays for some of the merchants' wares on the fences that enclosed the side streets.

Safety of the visitors was of major concern. It was noted that exit doors in some of hotels, lodging houses and other establishments were unsafe, opening to the inside rather than out. This would be a life threatening problem if fire broke out or other danger occurred. A suggestion was made that owners consider making this inexpensive, but significant change to their buildings, and that the authorities enforce this safety issue.

Although it would be of some cost to the city, the ditches and alleys needed to be cleaned up and cleared of debris and the streets cleared of large rocks. The money invested in this cleanup would be well worth it. Leadville was going to be welcoming thousands of visitors and if they were going to make a lasting impression of their city, it had better be a good one!

First impressions are lasting impressions, and the Colorado Midland put on its best bib and tucker. A month was spent painting and decorating its big depot between 3rd and 4th on Leiter Street. The walls were wallpapered and the ceiling was re-covered with gold-figured wallpaper. The lunchroom was repainted and papered and the dining room was refitted with electric lights, and murals were hung on the walls. The waiting rooms were refurnished. The men's and women's lounges were renovated; the wainscotted walls were repainted terra cotta, with wallpaper to match; figured moldings were installed. The offices of the trainmaster, the dispatcher, the operators, the roadmaster and building departments were all redone. The exterior was painted three shades of olive, with California white-sand trim and the roof was redone in bright red. Improvements to the building cost $1,500.

ADMISSION TICKETS/SEASON PASSES
It's Worth The Price

There was some quibbling about the price of admission tickets. It was argued that people were paying fifty cents to dance in other ballrooms in the city. Why couldn't they pay that much to dance at the ice palace? Fifty cents was thought to be a fair price.

The $.50 admission fee was decided upon for adults, and $.25 for children twelve and under. The ticket included all privileges of the ballroom and the skating rink, and maid and valet services in the dressing rooms. Director General Wood was firm in his decision of the fifty-cent admission charge to outsiders, and yet was willing to lower that rate, if necessary. Even though it meant a loss of revenue, his intent was to make it possible for everyone to have a chance to attend the winter carnival and enjoy the ice palace.

Season tickets were available from Director General Wood's private secretary, located in Room 7 of the Delaware Block. The tickets sold for $15 for the month of January. Ten additional dollars, paid by February first, would extend that pass through the remainder of the carnival season. Twenty-five dollars bought 180 passes that entitled one person admission to the palace on all carnival days and granted him or her all privileges of the ballroom and skating rink. Ten-dollar season tickets for clubs were available, but limited to a total of one hundred men, or one hundred fifty women.

In addition to the season tickets, commutation tickets were sold to those who could not afford $10 or season passes. The plan called for a certain number of tickets to be sold at a reduced rate of $5 or less for fewer admissions. These tickets were available for those who could not afford the $10 or $25 passes. Wood was emphatic that everyone should be able to see the ice palace and this was an affordable method.

One young "society blood," who was using a commutation ticket, disregarded the conditions of the purchase. He let another gentleman use it to save a few pennies. The ticket takers had been alerted to possible ticket violations. Much to the owner's sorrow, the ticket was confiscated by the gatekeeper and the young borrower was left out in the cold. After the opening on January 1st, Director General Wood announced that some members of the carnival clubs were taking advantage of their tickets. The tickets were sold with the agreement that the holders would not be admitted unless in costume. It was the Director General's intent to lend color and carnival atmosphere to the ice palace through this directive. Management sold tickets for this purpose at a loss of $3,700.

One, of possibly many love stories, involved one of the ticket takers at Leadville's Ice Palace and Winter Carnival.

In an interview with Pat (Mrs. Owen) Hodgell, I was told of her family's association with the ice palace. A young girl named Daisy Drucilla Perry, Pat's grandmother, was a ticket seller at the ice palace and Otis Richmond, Pat's grandfather, was a miner and the palace's skatemaster. When Daisy began working at the ice palace, little did she know she was destined to meet her future husband. Otis and Daisy became attracted to one another while they were both working there. Otis wooed her and pursued her as they danced or skated at the palace. They would sometimes go sleighriding after work. He romanced her and won her heart during the moonlight rides they took in Otis's cutter, pulled by his horse, Billy.

Daisy's father, Walter Perry, was one of the carpenters who helped build the ice palace and kept a watchful eye on Otis and Daisy.

Richmond opened a dance school in Leadville, teaching the miners the latest ballroom techniques. Dance instruction was the career he followed after the ice palace closed.

Exhibition Skaters - Leadville's Ice Palace. (Ernestine Kuehl, fourth from the left.) *Author's Collection*

ICE PALACE FASHIONS
Brightly Colored Costumes A Must

By late December, suggestions for appropriate dress at the ice palace were being heralded. Colored costumes were the order of the day. The *Herald Democrat* reported on December 20, 1895, "It is hoped the ladies will take kindly to the idea of bright costumes. Nothing is lacking in color and design of the palace itself, yet nothing will dim its beauty more than the people in dull-hued costumes."

The Association reiterated that it was every citizen's duty to add to the beauty of the carnival by appearing in appropriately bright, attractive costumes.

It was advertised that costumes could be made at a cost of $1 to $4. "There was no excuse for a person living in carnival times to be without a costume."

Charles H. Bennett of Beggs Dry Goods appeared in the first carnival costume on December 14th and attracted considerable attention. His costume was made from a white woolen blanket, with a blue striped border and his knickers were white with a blue waistband; a blue toque with elaborate trim covered his head. Mayor S. D. Nicholson, a short time later, was the first city official to appear in carnival garb.

A $25 season pass was awarded to the lady and gentleman wearing the best costume of carnival colors. When first announced, they were to have received a $60 gold piece. Women who agreed to come in costume were awarded $10 season tickets.

Fashionable gowns of light colored velvet with muffs and hats of a darker colored velvet, trimmed in fur, were popular carnival attire. Popular winter fabrics included

Moire silk and poplin; crepon[18] with alternate dark and light stripes; dark fabrics embroidered with gold beads; dark shades of mohair and alpaca, plain and prints.

A number of costumes caught the attention and admiration of the palace visitors to the Ballroom. Mrs. A. A. (Jennie) Blow wore a blue cloth, trimmed in Angora; Marce Denman caught the attention of many admirers with her lovely green cloth gown; Mrs. C. E. Dickinson's green velvet design with mink trim was greatly admired. Mrs. Charles H. Bennett's brown cloth ensemble with fur trim was a favorite and the envy of many ladies. Miss Mahana's blue cloth costume, trimmed in fur, drew a number of compliments. Mrs. C. Street received many compliments with her snug red and white blanket costume. Miss Martin, attired in a gray cloth ensemble trimmed in marten fur caught the attention of the fashion-conscious ladies.

Most of the skaters were dressed in colorful attire which added a festive mood to the carnival. Many of the costumes were loosely fitted allowing the skaters to move more freely on the ice.

The gaily colored regalia worn by the many winter sporting clubs, fraternal and social organizations added greatly to the carnival atmosphere. The clubs were identified by the costumes worn by their members.

---

[18]A thin "stuff" resembling crape (crepe), made of either wool or silk, or both.

NEAR TRAGEDY AT THE ICE PALACE
Worker Injured

A daily parade of Leadville's citizens visited the construction site to inspect the palace's progress. It became a Sunday ritual for many Leadvillites to climb Capitol Hill to watch the workers, and "sidewalk superintend." Many of them would go home after church, pack a picnic lunch and spend the day at the ice palace.

It was on one such Sunday (the 15th) that a near tragic accident happened at the site. Onlookers were horrified as two of the workmen were thrown from one of the towers. A ginpole toppled, throwing two of the workmen to the ground.

On December 17, 1895, the *Leadville Herald Democrat* reported:

> While thousands of spectators were admiring the grandeur of the crystal walls Sunday afternoon and watching the huge cubes of ice as they were being lifted to the walls, a serious accident occurred. Two men were standing on a platform on the inside of the big octagonal tower on the east side of the main entrance, when the ginpole used to lift the ice crashed down beside the men, breaking the joist that supported the platform on which the men stood when at work. The two workmen were thrown to the ground and landed among the blocks and chips of ice. One of them escaped uninjured, but Sam Olds, who boards on Elm Street, was picked up when found to have received a bad gash in his scalp. Owing to the fact that he retained consciousness it was believed that his brain had not been affected. Dr. Samuel P. Johns was telephoned for and was soon at the scene. The patient was taken to his boarding place as he said he preferred to go there than to the hospital.

Later, on closer examination, Dr. Johns found that the man's spine had been injured, and that the cut on his scalp was only trivial. However, the injuries sustained by Sam Olds appeared to have been misdiagnosed. His doctor pronounced him well enough to go back to work, and he returned to his job on December 19th.

DEATH TOOK NO HOLIDAY
FROM THE CARNIVAL
Fatality Toll, Four

Dr. S. Arthur Bosanko, died of pneumonia on November 23, 1895. Dr. Bosanko was a staunch supporter of the ice palace. He passed away two days before the ice palace's cornerstone was laid.

Tragedy struck on New Year's Day when a Denver & Rio Grande train bringing a group of *Rocky Mountain News* reporters to Leadville derailed at Malta. Shortly after 8:00 a.m., J. G. Baker, engineer, and Harry Hartman, fireman, were killed when the lock on the switch failed to catch. The switch, about 100 feet south of the depot, was hit by the engine, causing the front wheels to go onto the siding. The rear driving wheels left the main track, but failed to take the switch and fell to the left on the ties. The tender tore loose from the engine and left the track; the baggage car and the coach car of the two-car special stayed on the main line. The engine toppled onto the platform and the tender was pushed into the depot by the momentum of the other cars. The tender broadsided the depot moving the building four feet off its foundation and demolishing the platform and depot. The two men attempted to jump from the train, but the engine turned over before they got out. Fireman Hartman was thrown approximately 25 feet across the platform and was pinned beneath the car. He was killed instantly. Engineer Baker fell from the cab. He was badly bruised and scalded, and his left leg was broken in several places. He died about noon that day. The passenger and baggage cars remained on the tracks and the passengers, although not injured, were shaken up and terrified.

The train had left Denver at 1:37 a.m. In charge were Conductor Bunbury and Brakeman A. L. Paul. On board were J. C. Heckler, General Roadmaster; A. C. Ridgeway, Assistant Division Superintendent; C. A. Parker, Superintendent of Telegraph, Guy Adams, Editor of the *Official Road Guide*; A. S. Gregg of the Passenger Department. R. W. Butler of the *Rocky Mountain News*, Frank E. Kelly and express messenger Edwards were in the baggage care at the time of the accident and escaped injury.

High winds during the morning had filled the narrow spaces between the rails with snow, preventing the switch from closing. When the accident was reported they were unable to reach the company doctors and Dr. Lee Kahn of Leadville was called to the scene. A special train from Salida brought two company surgeons, Drs. Mattoen and Cochran, later that morning.

On January 12th Peter Egger, a cook at the Toboggan Lunchroom, stepped into the restaurant, collapsed and died. He was in poor health and came to Leadville to be cured of tuberculosis, (then called consumption). His brother was working in the mines in Victor at the time. Coroner Nelson notified him immediately.

NO LIQUOR AT THE ICE PALACE
Petition Granted!

On December 10th, Messrs. Andrew N. Coyne and J. G. Stewart made application with the city council to build a saloon on vacant lots 28 & 30 of block 46, at the corner of 7th and Leiter Streets, "for the benefit of the Crystal Carnival sufferers." Alderman George N. Easum, who lived across the street from the proposed saloon was opposed to turning West 7th Street into a "saloon row." Alderman C. C. Joy remarked, "that if the ice palace people were to undertake regulation of the liquor business on the outside, then the lemonade sticks and other refreshments sold at the ice palace would come to grief." The application was referred to the License and Ordinance Committee for review.

The committee heard arguments regarding the liquor question. Bottled beer and other malt beverages were served in the cafes at Chicago's World Fair. If someone preferred beer to coffee, why not allow it and the Association profit? If there were to be saloons around the palace grounds, why not have a bar in an annex that the Association would control and conduct properly? The concession for handling bottled beer could be the most profitable money maker the Association could have. Why not profit, "instead of outsiders who might cover Seventh Street hill with all kinds of joints?"[19]

The liquor debate was finally put to rest on December 17th. A petition was presented to the city council by residents of the neighborhood where the proposed saloon

------

[19]Leadville City Council Minutes, December 12, 1895 — Leadville, Colorado City Hall.

was to be built. The citizens' petition was "unalterably opposed" to the establishment of a saloon in their community and they petitioned, "your honorable body to refuse license to all applicants for the same." Sixty-seven signatures were affixed to the document . . . Petition granted!

LAW & ORDER
Special Police Hired

On December 18th, the City Council granted Director General Wood permission to have John Greenlaw appointed Special Policeman to the ice palace. Four other officers were appointed at a later date. Two detectives from Denver came to Leadville offering their services. Some of the city council members thought it was a good idea, since the detectives could move among the crowds, undetected, and apprehend would-be thieves. The Association was satisfied that Leadville's capable police force could handle the job very well, thank you very much!

On February 18th the city council ordered the discontinuance of the extra policemen. Two of the policemen, were retained at the request of the Association.

At the city council meeting on March 17th, Charles E. Joy, representing the Leadville Crystal Carnival Association, requested that the two policemen's salaries be paid for by the city. The petition was voted down, 4-2.

SPECIAL!

BEN LOEB, the olp reliable and popular amusement caterer, has rented
The Mascot Theatre, 122 State street, Leadville, Colorado, and will
re-open his Variety Theater for the Winter Season under the name of

Ben Loeb's Novelty Theater

~~December 2, 1895.~~

Special
Announcement:

Having Redecorated. Repainted Refitted and Remodeled and thoroughly
Renovated this place of Amusement, I
shall open my regular season as stated
above, with the most complete organization of Vaudeville celebrities ever
produced before the Leadville public.

Now booking

Artists of recognized ability and versatility, secure your dates at once.

BEN LOEB THEATER ADVERTISEMENT
The Free Lance

LADIES OF THE NIGHT
Prostitutes Solicited to Leadville

The *Leadville Herald Democrat* reported this story in their December 19, 1895 edition:

GIRL INDUSTRY IS BOOMING
Denver Being Drawn on Heavily to Secure "Scenic" Attractions for the Beer Halls.
For Uncle Ben's Scheme
He Keeps an Agent in Denver to Look Out For Helpers and Blooded Stock.
"Good Lookers" and Well Dressers Are the Hot Stuff That the Old Man Must Have.

The coming carnival has caused an activity in every line of business in town, even to the dance halls. These institutions, that have been in a state of semi-coma for several years, are now scenes of activity that portends, at last, that great things are to come. The owners are busy painting, polishing, and in many other ways making ready for the harvest that will soon be ready for them. Of course, Ben Loeb is to the front in the mad rush for public favor (the public that he caters to), and it is even said that he will launch a new enterprise in the way of a variety theater, which he will run in connection with his dance hall. But it is the latter place that is now in question. Ben wants to run nothing, if not the best so he says, and to do this he must have the prettiest girls that can be had. His rules are strict on that score. To get pretty girls, he must send out of town for them. 'They are scarce here,' says Ben.

A reporter called at his house last evening and showed him a spicy bit of news from one of the morning papers. Loeb read it through, then handed it back to him, and with a shrug of his shoulders, said, 'It's the same as they all do. We need the girls to run a business of this kind and have no other way of getting them. I never employ girls that are under age. If I know it, and you can see by this (showing one of his letterheads, on which the rules of the place were printed), that they are requested to state their age before coming to work."

The item of news in question is the following, 'Mike Annacito is charged by the police with procuring young girls for immoral purposes. The detectives were first made aware of Annacito's transactions by inquiries made by 2 young girls, who called on Chief Farrington and requested his assistance in regaining their trunks that had been shipped to Leadville despite their protests. When the Italian was searched at the city hall, several telegrams were found upon him, all from Ben Loeb, relative to the shipping of girls.

The following letter was also taken from him.

Mike Annacito: Worthy Friend—received your dispatch and have answered same. You want to be very careful what girls you select, some that have some sense, that are good dancers and not bashful to sell drinks. Send them just the way you get them, one or two at a time, but look out so they have baggage, as I secure checks from the railroad company so that they can't jump my tickets. Look out for good lookers and well dressers. Telegraph at any time for tickets. As soon as the girl is ready, bring her trunk to the depot, where she gets her ticket and the agent secures the baggage checks.

Hoping that you will be successful and secure the address of a good man there which can always send me girls if I pay him a commission.

138

If you come across some good lookers that don't want to come now, secure their addresses. Don't mention anything about advancing fares, some of them have got the money. Yours Respectfully, Sam Loeb.

How many girls have been sent to Leadville is unknown to the detectives, but they say at least six have been prevented from going. Two were engaged to leave Saturday night, but after reaching the depot they awakened to a realization of their situation and returned to their homes. Their trunks had been checked through to Leadville by Annacito, and for this reason they called upon Chief Farrington. Two more were engaged to go last night.

Loeb did not deny that he had an agreement with Annacito to furnish him girls from Denver, his only comment being that they were not compelled to come against their wishes, and that "slinging" beer and dancing is no worse than the business they follow in Denver.

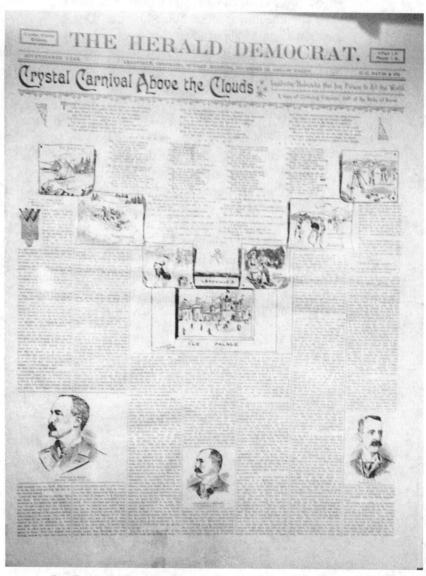

Ice Castle Edition, The Herald Democrat December 22, 1895.
Author's Collection

A SPECIAL CRYSTAL CASTLE EDITION
Souvenir Copies Distributed

On December 22, 1895, the *Leadville Herald Democrat* published a special "Crystal Carnival Edition" of their newspaper. It was announced that this souvenir edition would be delivered to the customers' doors by the carriers to ensure that everyone received their copy. The "Crystal Carnival Edition" was a twenty-eight page issue and sold for ten cents. On December 21st the *Herald* published the following notice:

> To avoid loss to subscribers by theft or otherwise of our holiday edition, Sunday morning December 22nd, our carriers will not start out as early as usual, thus necessarily making the delivery late. It is hoped subscribers will render material assistance by taking in their papers at once and waiting patiently for its arrival. The paper will be too large for letter boxes and to go under doors. It will be impossible for carriers to deliver extra copies ordered from the office, but will be prepared to serve the people by sales, and patrons ordering at the office will be expected to call for them—not before noon. Newsboys are not to appear until 7 o'clock, as they cannot be served before that time.

This special edition issue contained a detailed story of the ice palace. Pictures of Tingley S. Wood, C. E. Joy and Charles T. Limberg, a lithograph of the ice palace, and sketches of the many winter sports to be enjoyed at the carnival, graced the front page.

A poem by Frank E. Vaughn was given front-page honors.

The special edition also contained:

"An Ode to the Ice Palace," by George P. Wallihan.

"Dante's Ice Palace, or a Crystal Carnival in Sheol," a gruesome story of the nether regions by A. S. Petterson (pen name, Steve Joy).

"Reunited After Peril," a thrilling tale of the early days in Leadville by George P. Wallihan.

"In the Horseshoe, or Love in a Snowslide," a romantic tale of the wooing of a Colorado prospector.

A true story of cannibalism in California Gulch, never before published, by J. J. Guenthrodt.

An elaborate review of the mining and smelting interests of the districts, to which was appended a number of articles by prominent mining men of the Carbonate Camp.

Leadville merchants advertised their wares in big, bold ads.

A later ad in the *Herald Democrat* stated that customers who had ordered extra copies of this special edition, had not picked them up. Unless they were called for by December 30th, they would be sold.

"Colonel Davis is to be congratulated on his 'Ice Palace Edition,'" reported the *Greeley Sun* on January 8, 1896.

FINANCIAL PICTURE NOT GOOD
More Money Needed

On December 29th, George P. Brown issued a financial statement, reporting to members of the Association that the ice palace fund was in the same condition as the United States Treasury, "a little short." A little over $15,460 (in stock sales) had been collected, and with some concentrated soliciting, they hoped to raise another $540, bringing the total to $16,000. This was still $4,000 short of the $20,000 agreement made with Director General Wood.

Mr. Brown was emphatic that the additional $4,000 had to be raised, and a way had to be found to do it. The original $20,000 had already been exceeded, but Brown said that the Director General intended to handle that, "in his own way." By that time more than $30,000 had been paid out and there was still more work to be done.

Brown was apologetic in stating that he would like to help, but was unable to do so. Albert Sherman doubled his subscription on the spot. Charles Limberg and Charles Hayden had already doubled theirs. George L'Abbe donated another $250. Mayor Nicholson gave another $100 as did Charles Priddy, George E. Taylor, Herman Strauss, and John Nowland. Another $1,035 in contributions was raised at the meeting.

Will Dickinson, Mr. Sherman and George Brown were appointed to "do a little missionary work," to raise the additional $3,000.

Skating Rink, Leadville's Ice Palace.
Denver Public Library, Western History Department

THE ICE SKATING RINK
A Sparkling Jewel

Director General Wood's plan for the ice rink, located in the center of the ice palace, was set in motion.

By December 8th work on the ice rink was begun and instead of excavating the frozen ground, which would have been expensive, the low ground was flooded and a reservoir of water was dammed up with banks or walls of ice. Nothing was wasted; chippings from the ice walls were used on the rink floor. When construction began on the rink, ice chunks and chips were thrown onto the uneven surface. They were scattered over the low spots to even up the ground. Just enough water was released each night to fill in the crevices and low spots and freeze solid. The water froze to the ground giving the rink a firm base. This method of layering and allowing the layers to freeze solid was used until the rink was covered with eight inches of smooth, clear ice flooring.

Coble & Kerr's building contract called for the ice skating rink to be turned over to the Association on December 15th, and the remaining wooden buildings by the 20th. It was necessary to have the rink done earlier because it would take some days to freeze the ground to an even surface for skating. When the icemasons had completed their work, flooding of the ice rink began. By the 20th the rink was slushy, but it had several inches of solid ice foundation and the surface was almost level.

Visitors to the ice palace entered the nave of the castle by way of a crystal ice stairway to the foyer of the breathtaking, main attraction of the ice palace. Directly ahead was the ice skating rink, 80 feet wide, 190 feet long; spacious enough to accommodate a thousand skaters.

The trussed roof, with eight cantilevers, covered the 250-foot span. When the roof was designed, Architect Joy had allowed for 1/16-inch depression of the joints, but when placed on the wooden partitions there was no give at all; every section fit like a glove. The cantilevers rested on the wood framework, designed to maintain the building as a permanent structure. The ice pillars, five feet in diameter and one foot thick, were separated by ice arches, placed every fifteen feet on the long sides of the rink. On December 12th, lights were placed in the rink pillars. Down through the center of each of the pillars was suspended a different colored electric light bulb. The pillars radiated beautiful lighting, creating a rainbow-hued effect throughout the skating rink. Electric lights hung from umbrella-shaped chandeliers, fourteen feet above the ice. Electric lights had also been placed in the ice blocks and covered with an ice veneer that looked as if they were imbedded in the walls and over the archways.

Above the arches the walls were extended upward by rows of ice blocks to a height of twenty feet. The ceiling was 35 feet high. The crushing resistance (capacity) of the ice, by actual test, was 17 tons per square foot.

Multi-colored light wheels made of isinglass[20] were placed in each corner of the skating rink. These lights could be directed onto the skaters as they circled the rink in their colorful costumes, or flashed onto the frosted roof.

---

[20]Sheet mica, a monoclinic mineral that occurs in Colorado in thin translucent sheets. Used as a substitute for glass.

The roof was studded with stalactites of ice, myriads upon myriads of them hanging from the great trusses and the rafters and rods and every inch of timbering and iron was covered with an ice frosting that gave the whole roof the glistening of a large bed of diamonds.[21]

Dozens of exhibits, frozen in the ice walls, could be seen from the rink. Ice sculptures were placed in some of the archways surrounding the rink. The skating rink was said to have been the most beautiful of all the rooms in the ice palace.

To see the rink at night was breathtaking. The great ice pillars were aglow and glistened with pale yellow, orange, green and blue colored lights of every description. The colors blended and separated, faded and deepened, creating an ice cave of indescribable beauty. At certain times the arc lights were turned off, leaving the incandescents burning. This intensified the colored lights in the ice blocks and created a beautifully romantic atmosphere.

Wooden promenades encircled the ice rink to ensure the non-skaters had firm footing. Benches were placed next to the outer rink walls where the skaters could rest or spectators could watch the various contests. Many chairs were also available.

The carpenters built a wooden platform that could be moved onto the ice rink and removed very quickly. A number of events were performed on this portable stage.

---

[21]*Olden Times in Colorado* by Carlyle Channing Davis, copyright 1916.

An elevated platform, encased in glass panels, was built between the ice skating rink and the ballroom. This enabled both the dancers and the skaters to sway and skate to the music provided by the variety of orchestras and bands who played there. The enclosed band stage was accessed by a ladder stairway on one side of the platform.

The skating rink was used for a number of events as well as public skating. There were speed skating contests, tugs-of-war, figure, free style, solo, and pairs skating exhibitions, and skate dancing competitions. Championship hockey tournaments were held there.

Curling, one of the oldest outdoor ice games played, found its way into the ice palace and spectators were entertained by Scotch Canadians competing in curling contests. The "rink," as the space was called, was 110 feet long and 20 feet wide. At either end were a marked series of circles resembling a target, the outer circles being 10 feet in diameter and the others reduced in size to the bulls-eye in the center. Ten feet from the outer circle and from the parallel size lines was drawn a mark called the "hog line." The game was played alternately from one end to the other, the rink being marked the same at either end. Four men played on a team, alternately sending the stone across the icy surface. The head man, or captain, was called the "skip." He was stationed at the circles and marked the scores made with a broom, usually twenty-one points in a game. The stones that didn't reach the head line didn't count and the circles each counted higher than the center. It was the players' aim to knock the opposition's stones out of the circle and replace it with his. Curling stones were mushroom-top in shape with a handle, and usually weighed about 40 pounds. It took a pretty strong man to send a stone sailing a hundred feet or more across the ice. (One of the curling stones used at the ice palace remains in Leadville, and is on display at the Healy House Museum.)

Monty Fitzgerald was superintendent of the ice rink and kept the ice in topnotch condition for the skaters. Each morning before the palace opened for the day the rink was swept clear. The ice surface was sprinkled with hot water, allowed to freeze, and was smooth as glass for the crowds of skaters, or skating event. The room temperature of the rink averaged 25°-40°.

Otis Richmond, a Leadville miner, was the skatemaster. He taught ice skating and skate dancing. Richmond also belonged to a Leadville skating team that competed throughout the United States. The team brought many accolades, awards and honors to Leadville as a result of their skating skills.[22]

Graceful figure skaters and ice dance skaters caught the attention of the crowds. Ms. Christensen was noted to be one of the most graceful skaters, and Ms. Allie Murdock was reportedly confidant and sure footed as she moved about the rink. Alex Harvey had the attention of many of the ladies and "fetched the fixed gaze of the dear girls," as he cut his fancy figures and danced upon the ice. John Harvey sported one of the finest pairs of silver plated ice skates.

One of the many humorous carnival stories came out of the ice palace's ice rink and involved two of the girls who worked "down on the line." One evening Laura Evans and

---

[22]Interview with Pat (Mrs. Owen) Hodgell, granddaughter of Otis Richmond.

a girl called "Spuddy" decided to visit the ice palace. They were feeling no pain, having imbibed a little too much liquor. They hired, or borrowed, a horse and sleigh and headed toward Capitol Hill. However, instead of tying the horse outside, they drove straight into the palace. The poor horse, not sure of his footing on the ice, and frightened by the noise of the crowd, broke its traces, tipped the sleigh over, kicked the hell out of it, and sent the frightened ladies flying. In his haste to exit the palace, the panicked animal kicked one of the statues over, sending pieces of it flying into the scattering spectators.

One of the popular jokes being circulated during winter carnival days, "Will you skate with me tonight?" asked he. "I cannot skate, dear John," said she. Then he said as he drew to the maiden's side, "I guess I'll just have to let you slide."

THE BALLROOM & DINING ROOM
Eat, Drink, And Be Merry

Coble & Kerr's contract called for construction completion of the wooden buildings on December 20th. The structure, although not finished, was far enough along to be turned over to the Director General Wood and he could not say enough good about the work these men and their workers accomplished. In spite of the lumber having to be cut and shipped from the lumber camps, and the fact that they did not really begin construction of the buildings until December first, their performance was nothing short of miraculous.

Both the east and west wings of the palace housed reception rooms with polished wooden floors. Lounges provided for the ladies and gentlemen were lavishly furnished with rugs, rich wall hangings, overstuffed sofas and chairs, and ornately framed paintings. The dressing rooms for the ladies and gentlemen had maid and valet services available, their services were included in the price of the admission ticket. These rooms were heated by base-burner coal stoves. The cloak rooms were ornately furnished as well.

Every room, with the exception of the ice skating rink, was heated by coal stoves, furnished by the Dickinson Hardware Company. The ballroom and dining room were each heated by four huge base-burner coal stoves. The exposed exterior walls of the building were calcimined[23] a frosty silver-gray, lending an icy look to blend with the

---

[23]A white or tinted liquid containing zinc oxide, water, glue and coloring matter used as a wash for walls and ceilings. Calcimine was cheaper to use than paint.

outside ice walls. The west wing, in addition to the dining room, contained a multi-purpose room, cloak and supply rooms, the restaurant and a snack bar.

Plans called for a grand ballroom 50 feet by 80 feet in the east wing of the palace. Lumber walled three sides with windows serving as the wall facing the skating rink. The ballroom floor was built of imported Texas pine and the interior wainscoted walls were painted terra cotta on the bottom to lend a feeling of warmth, and a blue-gray color on top to give the walls a frosty look and blend with the ice motif of the rink. The ceiling was painted a steel blue.

The ballroom accommodated 80 couples. Benches were placed in front of the windowed area so dancers and spectators could rest and watch the dancers and skaters if they so desired.

William Youe was head dancemaster of the ballroom. He was assisted by instructors who would glide around the ballroom with their partners, all eager to learn the latest dance steps of the day. The ballroom was filled day and night with couples who enjoyed the music of the bands and orchestras.

One of these instructors was Professor Gustavas Augustus Godat, a dancemaster. He came to Leadville in 1878, the year the town was incorporated. The popular professor had two dance academies; the first one at East Seventh and Poplar Streets, then later moved to the corner of West Fourth and Pine Streets; and he opened the Leadville Dancing Academy in what was then called the New Turner Hall in 1882. This gentleman is credited with bringing social culture to the city of Leadville. He is also the reason this author became interested in the Leadville Ice Palace and its history; this wonderful, talented man is the author's great grandfather.

The dancers swayed to the waltzes, danced the Schottische, skipped to the Heel and Toe Polka and the lively "Ice Palace Quick Step." The less faint of heart danced to the romping gallop. Other popular dances were the Quadrille, the Varsouvienna, the Lancers, the Rage, the Newport and the Virginia Reel.

In an unpublished paper, Mr. Ezra Dickerman told of a beautiful Cherokee Indian woman, Miss Laura Holcomb, who was an excellent dancer and accomplished skater, and was always dressed at the height of fashion. She was very popular with the local bachelors, never wanting for an escort. Her companions made certain she had a very good time at the masquerade balls. At one of the balls, wrote Mr. Dickerman[24], "but at the unmasking hour, they with one accord were found missing." At two of the masked balls she was so well disguised no one knew who she was.

Little *five-year-old* Josephine Poole, a longtime Leadville resident, visited the ice palace with her mother and father and, as youngsters do, became tired and cranky. They lay her down on one of the benches in the ballroom and covered her with a coat to keep her warm. Shortly thereafter, someone came along and covered her with another coat, then someone else with another coat. Because she was buried in the coats and unnoticeable, someone came along and sat on her! But the little lady survived, enjoyed a long life, and passed away in 1985.

---

[24]Stephen Hart Research Library, Colorado History Museum, Denver, Colorado.

The dining room was the same size as the ballroom, 50 by 80 feet, with a floor of grooved, imported Texas pine. The colors were blue-gray and orange. It, too, had a windowed wall facing the skating rink. The west wing of the palace was also used as an auxiliary ballroom and whenever the grand ballroom became too crowded, the overflow was moved into the dining room. A number of the exhibits were displayed in this wing of the ice palace.

John E. Miller, a popular Leadville confectioner and baker, was in charge of the dining room at the palace. He offered all kinds of foods that could be prepared on short notice: soups, stews, sandwiches, pie, coffee, tea and other edibles. In an interview with his daughter, Florence Miller Anderson, she laughingly told me he may have had the first "fast-food" restaurant in the United States at the ice palace. Most of the food for the ice palace diners was prepared in Mr. Miller's bakery at 118 East Sixth Street or his restaurant at 425 Harrison Avenue. The food was then taken to the ice palace where it was kept hot on a coal stove and served from the palace's kitchen. Caterer Miller served elegant meals to the crowds every day and his dining room was not surpassed. Given as little as eight hours notice, he could prepare a banquet for a group that was "fit for a king." Off of the kitchen there was a walk-up/skate-up snack bar. A visitor could order a snack or a full course meal from the kitchen, relax, dine, and watch the skaters in the comfort of heated dining room.

(Florence is quite proud of her father's accomplishments in Leadville, one in particular. Mayor Henry C. Rose declared "Bobby Burns Day" a legal holiday for Leadville to celebrate the poet's birthday, and the resurgence of mining. On that special day, January 25, 1911, Mr. Miller and his staff prepared food at his Star Bakery, and served a banquet for 350 people. This was no ordinary banquet, however; the meal was served underground at the Wolftone Mine on Carbonate Hill.)

(A relative of mine, Milt Thelin, was a real jokester. He told me a story in 1968, of how he had danced in the ballroom at the ice palace. I questioned its authenticity because he was not old enough at that time to have been able to do so. He laughed and said that he had indeed; his mother was very pregnant with him at the time. Milt was born February 20, 1896.)

Miners carved of ice. Note exhibit frozen in ice wall, left background. *Courtesy Fred Smith*

THE CRYSTAL PALACE MUSEUM
The Ice Sculptures

The ice sculptures were kept a deep, dark secret. Director General Wood made sure his ice carver was given the privacy to work; kept under lock and key, so to speak.

Although reporters made many attempts to get in to see the sculptor at work, they were stopped and steered in a different direction. They finally gave up trying, and resigned themselves to seeing the sculptures on opening day.

The museum was heralded as one of the most attractive features of the Crystal Carnival, but had humble beginnings indeed. In early December, Phillip Kelly, described as "a rather seedy-looking Bohemian type," called on Director General Wood and told him he was experienced in carving. Although he was more familiar with clay than ice, Kelly felt his work was good enough that his ice carvings could warrant a place in the ice palace. Wood, dubious of the carver's abilities; nevertheless, gave him an opportunity to prove his skills.

Kelly was given a stable behind the ice palace's construction offices. The carver soon began piling up snow for the figure of a miner. The process he used was to freeze water with the snow and mold it as he worked. Water was then rubbed over the snow to give the finished statue a polished sheen. The onset of warm weather slowed the project considerably, making it difficult for Kelly to obtain the desired details. After the cold weather set in again, the ice sculptor was able to finish his statue. When Kelly has finished, the Director General was more than pleased with the carving of a miner holding an upraised pick. Every detail of the physical features, his posture, clothing worn to a polish, and tools, were perfect.

Kelly was contracted to do the carvings and went on to do many ice statues that were placed throughout the palace as well as the towers and bays. A burro with a bridle, saddle and a miner's pack; a miner staking his claim; and a miner dressed to the nines in top hat and tails, toothpick in his mouth, hands in his pockets depicting a man who had sold his mine for a huge profit, were among them.[25]

The majority of the ice carvings represented the miners and the mining industry. Director General Wood wanted to make sure the Leadville miners, who had brought so much wealth to the community through their hard labors, received the recognition and honor they so justly deserved.

A cross section of a mining shaft with miners at work in a stope[26] was made of snow and showed a mineral vein, all to illustrate the mining process. The miners were carved out of ice with a real mining cage iced over.

When the sculptures were finished, they were kept in cold storage, under guard, until they could be moved to the ice palace.

"LEADVILLE," a 19-foot tall, allegorical, solid ice statue representing the fair maidens of the mining capitol, stood on a 12-foot ice pedestal at the main entrance of the ice palace. She wore an ice crown on her head and her figure was covered with a flowing ice gown. Her right arm

---

[25]Photographs of these ice sculptures were featured in the *Illustrated American Magazine*, page 35, January 11, 1896.

[26]A steplike excavation formed by the removal of ore from around a mine shaft.

pointed to the mines east of the city, the area that had given Leadville her wealth. Over her left arm she held a scroll, embossed with raised pure gold figures, proclaiming $200,000,000, representative of mining revenues produced by the mines of the Carbonate Camp through 1894. (The amount of ores produced since 1879 was $209,768,222.15. It is this author's opinion that the figures were probably rounded off as more pleasing to the eye.)

When the Chinook wind blew into Leadville, the statue was wrapped in layers of gauze to protect her from the sun and wind.

THE RIDING GALLERY
A Merry-Go-Round

During the second week of November the city council was petitioned to grant the use of grounds on 7th Street, starting at a point 125 feet west of Leiter Avenue and running west to a line parallel with the west line of block 54, also known as Maple Street, and beginning at a point 100 feet south of the south side of 7th Street running north to the south side of 8th Street. This addition would accommodate the annex building or Riding Gallery as it became known and was located at approximately 419 West Seventh Street.

Director General Wood, along with Frederic L. Sherwin, F. O. Stead, Thomas Robson, J. W. Smith, D. H. Dougan, Adolph Schayer, Charles Hayden, John E. Miller, George L'Abbe, James W. Newell and others signed the petition, requesting use of the land up to July 1, 1896. The petition was granted.

Mrs. E. S. Moore, 419 West Seventh Street, lodged a complaint with the county commissioners. She stated that two lots leased to the Crystal Carnival Association by her husband were sold for $500. She and her husband had divorced after a short marriage and she stayed in the house. Taxes had not been paid, so the lots reverted back to the county commissioners. She wanted to stay in the house and felt that possession was ten points of the law! (Apparently, she thought the Crystal Carnival Association was going to confiscate her house. Not so! They just used the vacant lots.)

Alex Grant, a foreman at the Arkansas Valley Smelter, operated the merry-go-round in this annex building, independent of the ice palace. Unlike the other concessionaires, Mr. Grant was given the Association's permission to operate without a permit. The expense of building the ice palace's riding gallery was costly for Alex Grant; he had spent $3,000

161

for the entertainment facility. Because of this expense, Director General Wood requested that the permit fee be waived. Permission was granted.

The Riding Gallery was an extension of the ice palace, connected to the ice palace by a 27-foot ice archway that spanned West Seventh Street and served as a walkway from the palace into the gallery. The outside, southern wall was painted a frosty silver-gray to make it appear ice-like. The east and west walls were faced with ice blocks to blend with the ice palace.

The wooden building, 66 feet by 86 feet, was heated by base-burner coal stoves, and housed a full sized merry-go-round for the children. The carousel was mounted with twenty gaily colored horses and some brightly painted double seats. Alex Grant opened his gallery on December 31, 1895 and the concession was popular with young and old alike. The building was crowded with pleasure seekers the entire carnival season.

On January 12, 1896, Mike Riley, a miner at the Ibex, joined in the festivities at the ice palace. He donned a costume, dressed as "Queen Lil." Mike decided to take a turn on the merry-go-round and for whatever reason (dizzy, or too much liquor perhaps?), fell off! He was out like a light for about fifteen minutes. He was taken to jail where jailer Nels Mounson summoned Dr. Lee Kahn, who brought him to and sent him merrily on his way . . . home!

After the ice palace closed, Mr. Grant moved his merry-go-round to the southeast corner of Spruce and West Fifth Streets. At the end of May the city council granted a license renewal to operate his carousel and he ran his merry-go-round business, very successfully, for quite some time at that location.

162

THE PALACE OF LIVING ART AND ILLUSIONS
A Mini-Palace Theater

Director General Wood was granted temporary use of valuable lots on West 7th Street opposite the ice palace. Studebaker Brothers, renowned wagon makers and owners of the property, donated its use free of charge. This property was the site of the Palace of Living Art and Illusions.

Construction of the mini-palace began on December 28, 1895 and the contract awarded to H. C. Dimick.

The theater was 40 feet by 75 feet and had a seating capacity of three hundred. It contained a stage, dressing rooms, and a box office at the entrance. The front and sides of the wooden building were covered with ice blocks and the front entrance was artistically arched with towers at each corner. Decorative battlements gave it the appearance of a small ice palace. An American flag and a Colorado state flag waved from each of the two front towers. An ice-carved burro, carrying a miner's pack, stood on the archway above the entrance way.

W. Sunden of Stockholm & E. A. Covell, originally from London, were the theater's operators. They had exhibited their show in New York and other east coast cities, the Chicago World's Fair and the California Mid-Winter Fair.

Sunden and Covell were also the projectionists for their theater, called the "Pepper Ghost Show." The term was named for the inventor, W. F. Pepper of England. The shows were done by a technique of reflecting light on a canvas screen while live figures moved behind the screen, and appeared to be in mid-air, creating spectacular illusions.

They were also in charge of securing the performers, who were imported from the best theaters in the East. The entertainment consisted of poems and popular features such as "The Miner's Dream." The performers were reproduced in "living pictures," and the classics were shown at all hours of the day. The scenic work was painted by W. H. Blackburn, a reputed "genius with a brush."

The mini-palace, located at approximately 413 West Seventh Street, opened on January 11, 1896. It operated from 2:00 p.m. to 10:00 p.m. daily. Admission was one dollar.

One of the latest features to be introduced was a little child of extraordinary talent who performed difficult and beautifully executed dances.

On Germans Day, February 9th, special features were presented. Visitors were treated to, "Teton and His Model; 'Germania,'" and a German comedy.

The shows were advertised to be of the strictest decorum. However . . . one late night in March of 1896, a show, advertised as what today might be called X-Rated, was nipped in the bud. The theater was raided!

The *Colorado Prospector*, in their March, 1970, edition, reported the following story:

Midnight "Illusions" Prevented By Police

The Palace of Living Art and Illusions proved a disappointment last night to the crowd of midnight visitors who had been attracted there by the announcement that the show would be on very different lines from those that have delighted the audiences during the winter season.

164

At the hour when graveyards yawn, the show was to begin, the maidens who have posed as goddesses, forest and sea nymphs, queens, noble folks and all the other many pictures, were to be presented to the audience 'as was.'

But the show was not given. By order of the Mayor, police officers were present with instructions to stop the performance should it exceed, in any way, the bounds of decency. When the management was informed for what purpose the officers were sent, it was decided not to present the pictures.

The house was well filled when the announcement was made that there would be no show, and though the $1 admission fees were returned at the door, the crowd seemed sadly vexed at the police interference (The *Leadville Herald Democrat*, March 19, 1896).

This author had the delightful opportunity to meet Helen L. Campbell of Denver, who told me a story of her mother, Nellie Droney, and her visit to the ice palace. Miss Droney was living in Salida with her parents at the time. When the ice palace opened Nellie was allowed to travel to Leadville by train with her beau to see this spectacular palace of ice. (Possibly on Salida Day, when they would be chaperoned.) They enjoyed and reveled in the sights and sounds of the ice palace and winter carnival. Before returning home, the couple "just had to visit the House of Illusions." Nellie many years later told her daughter, Helen, of the frightening experience she had there. One of the illusions, a special feature called the "Devil's Razor," showed the figure of a man sliding down a razor's edge, which extended from the ceiling to the floor. As the figure came riding down the razor's edge, arms and legs were flying, his head rolling, and Nellie's hair stood on end. She was so frightened she wouldn't even let her boyfriend hold her hand going home on the train that night! Mrs. Campbell said her mother told of having nightmares of this experience long after the ice palace had melted away.

A DAZZLING TRIBUTE TO LEADVILLE
Description of the Ice Palace

The palaces of St. Paul were described as nothing more than facades, without windows, without roofs, empty and stark. Nothing more than stacks of ice blocks, they were bleak and colorless, and for the most part, useless. Leadville's ice palace was a thing of beauty, alive and welcoming. A playhouse for its citizens and visitors.

The majestic castle was 320 feet wide, 450 feet long, and covered five acres of land. In comparison, it would not have fit in the Denver Mile-Hi (Bronco's) Stadium. This colossal ice palace, although unfinished, opened to the world thirty-six days after the cornerstone was laid.

The outside walls of the palace were 22 inches deep. The ice blocks were 18 inches high and the high walls and walls of the circular towers were of the same width; the tower walls were strengthened by a supplementary wall one foot thick, with an air chamber one foot wide between the two walls.

The main octagonal towers to the north were 90 feet high, 40 feet in diameter, and 126 feet in circumference. The south towers were round and reached a height of 60 feet; they were 30 feet in diameter, and 94 feet in circumference. The east and west circular towers were 45 feet high, 20 feet in diameter, 63 feet in circumference. Buttresses reached midway to the tops of the walls, which were 38 feet high. Turrets with panellings and imitation battlements decorated this beautiful Norman-style structure, which resembled a medieval castle (a popular style for ice castles during that time).

A promenade, twenty feet wide, separated the ice walls from the interior building and was covered by the roof.

167

Ira S. Baker and Charles N. Priddy had the contract for the wiring of the ice palace. Charles A. Fitzsimmons, grandfather of Terry Fitzsimmons, was a lineman for the telephone company, and Mrs. Smiles (Margaret) Doyle's father, Martin J. Cassidy, a Leadville miner, worked on the lighting project. In order to earn extra money, they helped install the wiring and lighting at the ice palace.

After the last ice block had been set in place, the lights were turned on and tested. The ice walls came alive with rose-colored light. The crystal blocks, translucent and brilliant, were an ever changing picture of softness and strength above the city and valley below. At night the ice walls had dark, rich, sea-green and moss agate colors. Inside, the ice had the appearance of cathedral stained glass in places. Where the lights were evenly distributed, the walls resembled opal cubes, deepening to a transparent onyx color.

Charles A. Fitzsimmons   *Courtesy Terry Fitzsimmons*

Tingley S. Wood   *Courtesy Georgina Brown*

Leadville's Ice Palace, 1896.   *Author's Collection*

Charles E. Joy *Courtesy Georgina Brown*

W.W. Coble *Courtesy J.J. Coble*

Frank E. Brown   *Courtesy Doug Brown*

Former Citizens Electric Light Company building at Fifth & Leiter. This utility provided electricity to Leadville's Ice Palace.

TINGLEY S. WOOD, President.
C. T. LIMBERG, Vice-President.
W. L. TEMPLE, Secretary.
F. X. HOGAN, Treasurer.

Souvenir Postcard of Leadville's Ice Palace, Listing Crystal Carnival Association Officers.   *Colorado Historical Society.*

Leadville's Ice Palace Construction. (Note electric light poles in background.)
Denver Public Library, Western History Department

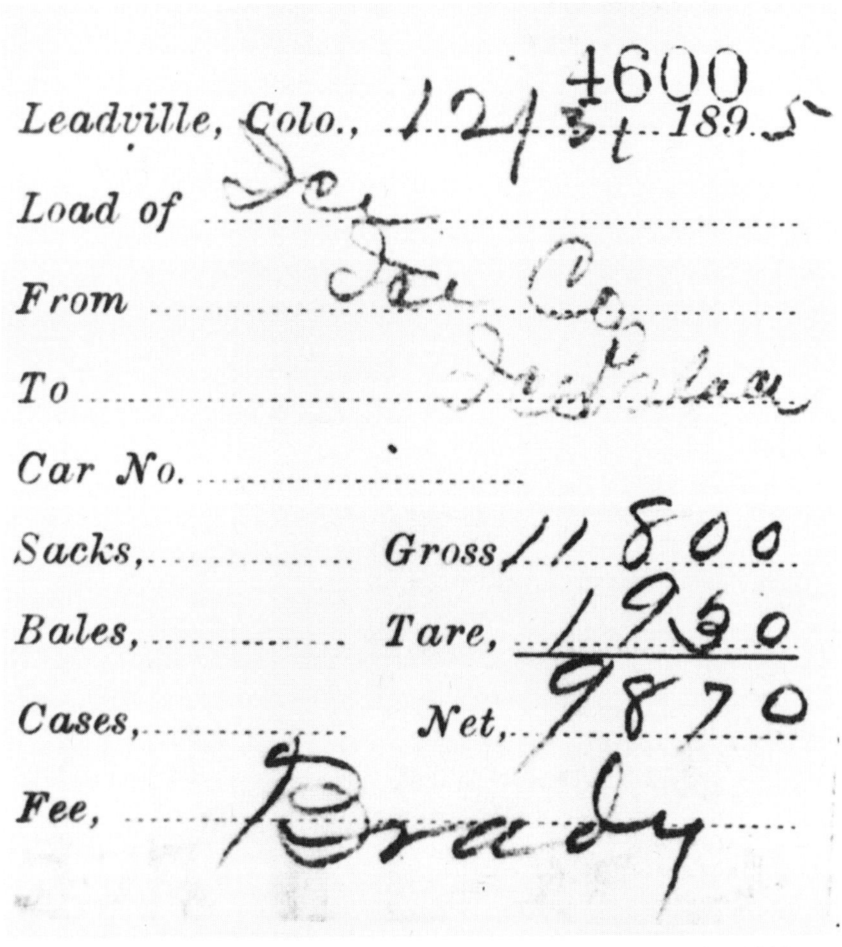

Leadville, Colo., *Dec 31* 189*5*

Load of *Ice*

From *Ice Co.*

To *Ice Palace*

Car No.

Sacks,   Gross *11 800*

Bales,   Tare, *1 930*

Cases,   Net, *9 870*

Fee,   *Brady*

Receipt for last load of ice, hauled to the Ice Palace December 31, 1895.
Courtesy Elvira N. Brown

Northwest View of Leadville's Ice Palace   *Courtesy Jim Tilden*

View of Ice Palace and Riding Gallery Archway Construction. Mini-Palace in Left Foreground.   *Courtesy Francis & Freda Rizzari*

Palace of Living Art and Illusion   *Courtesy Francis & Freda Rizzari*

"Leadville" - Ice Statue At Main Entrance. *Courtesy Eve Cass*

Turnstiles at Main Entrance   *Courtesy Eve Cass*

Interior Archways, Leadville's Ice Palace.
Denver Public Library, Western History Department

Interior Archways, Leadville's Ice Palace.
Denver Public Library, Western History Department

Interior Archways, Leadville's Ice Palace. (Note exhibit frozen in ice blocks at right of archway.)   *Courtesy Eve Cass*

Ice Sculptures, Leadville's Ice Palace   *Courtesy Fred Smith*

Colorado Midland Railroad exhibit at East Entrance (on West Seventh Street.)
Courtesy Fred Smith

Skating Team, Leadville's Ice Palace. Skatemaster Otis Richmond second from left.)
Courtesy Mrs. Owen (Pat) Hodgell

1895 ice skates, a Christmas present purchased at Leadville's Ice Palace and used there. *Courtesy Terry Fitzsimmons*

Orchestra Balcony in ice skating rink, ice statuary, Leadville's Ice Palace.
Courtesy Earl Nordwall

Frozen food exhibits, Conforth Oyster Exhibit on left.   *Courtesy Fred Smith*

Neef Bros. Brewing Co. display. Sign read, "Help Home Industry by Drinking Wierner/Maerzen." *Courtesy Fred Smith*

Stuffed Wolves, Leadville's Ice Palace. (Note frozen exhibits in ice blocks on the left.) *Courtesy Fred Smith*

Ice Palace Repair Crews at Work. (Note men on ladders.) *Author's Collection*

Certificate given to award-winning exhibitors by the
Leadville Crystal Carnival Association.

Militiamen at Camp McIntire, 1896.   *Author's Collection*

THE POETRY
Odes To The Ice Palace

When word was spread that Leadville was going to build an ice palace, poets and poetesses came out of the woodwork. Some were good, some not so good, and some debatable.

The Free Lance printed on November 25, 1895, that anyone writing the words, "beautiful snow," was taken out by the long suffering public and promptly hung from the nearest telegraph pole. *The Lance's* editor seemed to be under the impression that there would be plenty of people in hell with money who would be more anxious to build an ice palace there than in Leadville that winter.

Fundraiser, September 16, 1895.

Yes, Leadville is in it, we hail the device;
the scheme of state is a palace of ice;
and Senior and Junior, and all of the race; will join in
the project—the big ice palace;
and the girls will be there and the boys, I should say;
and night in the palace will be as the day. While
music and laughter and everything nice will be found,
I am sure, in that palace of ice.

It will be slick as ice, for ice it will be
and the state's wondrous industries, too, you will see
exhibited there, as snug as mice,
"friz" up in the walls of that palace of ice.

And the boys will be there and the girls, too, I think;
a spinning around in that beautiful rink. And music

169

and dancing and all that is nice will be found in the
Cloud City's palace of ice.

There will be on exhibit, and grand I am told,
the riches we'll see in silver and gold.
In fruits and in flowers, in game and in fish,
all snugly ensconced in an ice-covered dish.
And fathers and mothers, and sweethearts and beaux,
and everyone else I should rather suppose
will surely be there, and all for one price,
to visit our beautiful palace of ice.

So we'll build our Ice Palace, and when it is
done,'twill be on the basis of sixteen to one,
sixteen of pure silver to one of pure gold,
we'll exhibit its "parity" colors I'm told.
Fair dames will be there, fairer maidens, no doubt
and the "new woman" too will likely get out,
and the girl with the bloomers will take a nice ride,
and can "go it alone" on the toboggan slide.

— Edwin W. Senior

September 17, 1895.

The railroads are "wid us" and will give the cheap rates
and thousands will come from "way back" in the states.
We'll astonish them all with exhibits of ore, our coal
and "pertaters" and fruitage galore.
There'll be music and dancing and beauty and wealth,
and "ozone" sufficient to give one good health.
There'll be plenty to eat, and something to drink,
when you leave the pavilion or tire of the rink.

The Cloud City will give you her warmest and best,
and you'll learn the glad cheer of the wild wooly west.
We'll show you the grandeur of mountains and hills,
white capped with the beautiful, and icicled rills.
And the girls will be there, and the boys will be too,
and you'll swear 'twas rare sport before you get thro'.
You'll go home and be telling 'twas awfully nice,
galavantin' around in the palace of ice.

— Author Unknown

The Free Lance, **November 25, 1895.**

The snow; the snow, the beautiful white snow,
How I wish it could to hades go:
For the devil needs it to cool his feverish brow,
and we'll have plenty to spare between Spring and now.
It blows in the door and chokes up the well;
and t'w'd be lots better cooling off in hell.
For while it makes us shudder and hug close to the fire,
it would cool off hades, so the imps w'd not perspire.
It comes through the cracks and sifts under the sill;
gives a fellow the blues and makes him feel ill.
While down in hell t'w'd be a most welcome thing;
and hailed with delight as we do the flowers in Spring.
But things are not equal in hell and on earth;
here some folks have poverty and a riches of dearth.
Leadville has dead oodles of ice and snow to sell;
while through lack of materials there'll be no ice palace in
hell!

— Author Unknown

171

In honor of the Grand Opening —
January 1, 1896.

There's a sting in the air, and the white on
    the mountains;
like diamond dust gleams 'neath the sun's wintry glow.
Old Jack Frost is chilling the heart of the fountains,
and the earth's buttoned up in an ulster of snow.
For Christmas is here with its halo of pleasure,
Its harvest of presents, its wealth and good cheer;
with its glow of good feelings, that flow
    without measure,
the merriest season of all of the year.
High up on the hills where Leadville is sleeping,
where the giant crags peer through the mist
    that enshrouds;
where the Ice King has taken the world in his keeping,
and the baby peaks tickle the feet of the clouds;
a crystalline mass the bright sky is sweeping,
with turrets and towers of splendid device,
with tall minarets, whence the sunlight is leaping
o'er the pride of the mountains, the palace of ice.
And these bold mountaineers send this plain invitation;
our palace is open and our banners unfurled.
We don't bar a soul in the whole of creation -
come up and look down on the rest of the world.
When cold blow the winds, warm hearts beat the faster;
we love the long winter, and cheer that it sends -
and though among men we acknowledge no master,
we have wide open hands to extend to our friends.
Jim, Leadville sends greeting, and hopes to be meeting
her friends from the valleys as well as the hills.

172

Don't think for a minute that she "isn't in it,"
for when Leadville slops over you can gamble she spills.
By the bills that they throw out they've got a
    big blowout,
A palace that's built out of huge chunks of ice.
They've got dancing and skating, and if half
    they're relating
can be taken for true; they've got everything nice.
They've a swift way of joggin' upon a toboggan;
a mile in a second, or not more than two
From the top to the bottom it's just like they shot 'em.
They give 'em a start, and whiz-ziz! They are through.
Then there's riding and sliding and all kinds of gliding.
With carnivals, parties and masquerade balls;
with flashlights a-flashing and pretty girls 'mashing,
and ice of all colors mixed up in the walls.
Which there's plenty of eating, with desserts
    for completing;
there's icicle pie, and frost ala mode;
snow soup, if you like it, braised ice, if you strike it,
and big frosted cakes just to top off the load.
They've got silver and gold served hot or served cold,
lead, iron and copper; with zinc for a spice,
and mines by the score, with exhibits galore
and fruits from all climates friz into the ice.
That ain't all, but it's plenty and I'll go you a twenty
that they're giving a show that's clear out of sight.
For when Leadville goes mixing with any such fixing,
you can stake your existence that it's pretty near right.
Will you be there? You bet me! That's if the fates
    let me,
and take the old woman and kids for a spell.

When I die there's no knowing just where I am going;
chances are they won't have no ice palace in h—l.
Now don't get excited, for you are invited,
whether peasant in cottage, or king on a throne;
we'll try not to freeze you, but will try to please you;
come up, and fill on our mountain ozone.
Come, you of the Eastland, who deem this the least land
that ever was painted by God's golden sun;
we'll treat you well (and often), and, acquaintance
    to soften,
we will fill you with silver at sixteen to one.
Come, from the northland or southland, from westland
    or drouthland,
from home of magnolia, lilac or rose,
from Maine to the isthmus — come, visit old Christmas
up here in the hills where the Columbine grows.

            —   Frank E. Vaughn
                December, 1895

Storming the Castle

Brave King Carnival marshals his legions;
with high courage, and cunning device.
They march onward through storm-smitten regions,
and dedicate the palace of ice.
On the rock-ribbed mountain we gather,
and near a palace of ice,
and swear by Jehovah above us
we'll defend the palace of ice
We'll fight its battle like heroes,
and defend the castle like men;

174

and for every man that falls bleeding,
in his tracks will rise nine or ten.
Cease thy grumbling; do thy proudest;
Hail!, the Snow King
Shout thy loudest.

— Author unknown

In honor of the Formal Opening —
January 8, 1896.

Ye sturdy boys of Seventy-nine
in carnival array,
welcome, thrice welcome to our gate,
How are you anyway?
In '79 you wore your pants tucked
loosely in your boots;
far different were your costumes
then from these ice palace suits.
No bootblacks pained the mountain
air with their discordant cries,
while patrons of the barber shop
were dudish, in your eyes.
You did not come in palace cars,
with ev'ry want supplied;
but got here any way you could,
full many did not ride.
You rustled when you got here, too,
you did not look for guide;
but simply scattered out and dug
on every mountain side.

175

You always took your whiskey straight,
mixed drinking was a sin;
and he who asked for fancy drinks
would pass his checks right in.
What matter if, at divers times,
you took a drop too much?
Water was very scarce and high,
"One more," don't count in Dutch.
I wonder if each one can tell
where then he laid his head;
or where, when meal time came
around, his hungry stomach fed?
An easy game in Seventy-Nine
was getting money here;
but cigars, whisky, beds and grub
were most almighty dear.
Those who came here from the other
camps to grumble with disdain;
but tenderfeet who met these facts,
of gave old timers pain.
The bravest of the brave were they,
the kindest of the fair;
the noble ladies who came here
to breathe the mountain air.
To suffer in the smelter smoke,
to ward away pneumonia's stroke;
to help their dear ones make a
stake, as this wild mining camp forsake.
To them we owe the highest praise,
and tender care for all their days.
Ye pioneers of Seventy-Nine,
Heavens bless you, every one!

Leadville is proud to greet you
here, each is a "favorite son."
You may be even prodigal,
but we can only laugh;
we do not care for that at all,
we've killed the fatted calf.
We've built a place for you to play,
nor do we greatly care,
so long as you are blessed with
wealth, for silver in your hair.
Leadville is yours, and while you
stay, command us, every one
God Bless you boys of Seventy-Nine!
For them leave naught undone.

> — George P. Wallihan
> February, 1879

Leadville Crystal Carnival Souvenir Booklet

On a massive range, where towering peaks
hold white the font of the river's flow,
we have builded a house from the Frost King's freaks,
and invite all the world to play in the snow.

> — Tingley S. Wood

Written for the Leadville Crystal Carnival "Souvenir"—1896.

On the rock riven ramp of the mountains
with the gleam of a gem of great price
from the deep, frozen heart of the fountains
is builded the Palace of Ice.
Of the beams, from the Northern Lights, shifting,
of the diamonds that sparkle on snow
of the blue that the cloud films sweep, drifting,
of the sunset's incarnadine glow;
Of the rubies that bead the wine chalice,
of the gold-molten rays of the sun,
of the rainbow-is reared the fair palace
damascened with pure silver, frost-spun.
Crystal clear shine its glittering towers,
all effulgent its icicled halls—
frowning over, the icy keep lowers
steel-bright ramparts engirdle the walls.
Brave King Carnival marshals his legions—
with high courage and cunning device
they march onward through storm-smitten regions,
and beleaguer the Palace of Ice.
Through the hall of the barbed front arrows stinging,
to the heart of the stronghold they win—
dancing, shouting, exulting and singing
flushed with triumph, the victors throng in.
Down the snow fields toboggans are sweeping
where the light snow-shoes silently go;
mirth and music their revels are keeping
as the swift skaters glide to and fro.
Merry, dazzling, the pageant of pleasure—

and in joy of the hour will suffice,
as the dancers shall trip a gay measure
in the halls of the Palace of Ice.
For when green-ventured Spring, too long banished,
shall unfetter her close-prisoned streams
we shall mourn our lost palace, then vanished,
to the far sunset land of our dreams.

— Virginia Donaghe McClurg

**In honor of Aspen Day —
January 21, 1896.**

Those Aspen boys, those Aspen boys,
so full of vim and glee
how marched they down on Leadville
town how proudly and how free!
Wide open stood our city's gates,
when Aspen's trumpets blew,
and through them poured the jolly
throng, the pathway well they knew.
All oft had walked on Leadville's
streets, all knew their welcome sure;
'twill grow and strengthen with the
years, that Leadville shall endure.
Let them come early or come late,
come wealthy or come broke;
we'll give them warmest welcome here
as friendship's pipe we smoke.

— George P. Wallihan

Concert at the Ice Palace —
February 7, 1896

See the man going down the street,
What is the man doing?
He seems to be crazy
but why is he pushing his arms
about, as if he were shoving people.
There is no one near him.
But he thinks there is, my child.
But why does he think so"
He has a very vivid imagination, my child.
He thinks he is in a crowd of
Denver people who came up to see the ice palace.
Isn't he a funny man?
Yes, my child, but not half as funny
as the reports in the Denver papers
about the big crowds that will come
to Leadville to see the ice palace.

— Author Unknown

In honor of German Day —
February 9, 1895.

Sing German song the whole day long,
while we join the sweet refrain
and all will say when you go away,
Glueck auf! Auf wiedersehen!

— Frank E. Vaughn

180

In honor of Shriners Day —
February 14, 1896.

The Shriners are coming St. Valentine's day
with their camels and sand quite hot,
and with them their ladies and
band that will play for the novices
who gaily will trot.
O'er the sands of the desert, so
wild and dreary,
with but one well in sight;
to reach this goal refreshes the weary
and makes life's burdens light.

— Author Unknown

In honor of Elks Day —
February 15, 1896.

From night till morn the merry horn
gives forth discordant call,
for "it's day all day" in Leadville
and there is not night at all!
Throw off dull care, and everywhere
let Pleasure have full sway;
the world is bright, our hearts are light—
The Elks are here today!
Our palace grand, at their command
assumes a scarlet hue!
They've boldly said: "we'll paint her red!"
And that is what they'll do.

181

Put on your suit, get out and toot
in carnival array,
for none should weep, and none can sleep,
The Elks are here today!

— Frank E. Vaughn

A trav'ler, arriving in Leadville one day,
was heard to a Leadville old timer to say;
"What city is this, draped in colors so gay,
whose people are robed in such gorgeous array?
The other made answer in proud tone and word;
my friend, is it possible that you have not heard
of Leadville, that lies in the mountains so high,
above the soft, cloudlets, that fleck the blue sky?
Which mountains are stored with rich silver and gold
and constantly yielding up riches untold.
Whose ozone all people and classes entice,
to breath it, and visit our Castle of ice.
You seem quite a stranger, and if it be so,
around o'er the city with you I will go;
and if you desire it, your escort I'll be,
and take you about, that the sights you may see.
The Elks have provided this costly display,
in planning to make this a bright, gala day.
We'll visit the castle, and there we'll remain;
today, at a banquet, the Elks entertain.
More jolly, good fellows, lighthearted and free,
it never had been my good fortune to see;
with goodness, and virtue their badges abound,
from ocean to ocean their praises resound.
Melodious laughter and mirth are abroad,

and light hearts are beating in tuneful accord;
and rich mellow music is wafted aloft,
now rising, now falling in cadences soft.
But see! They are forming a splendid parade!
Let's join it and march to the grand colonnade.
You now see the top of its dazzling arcade,
and soon you'll behold its magnificent facade.
Majestic it rises against mountains so bold,
with clear lights of crimson, of green, and gold,
and delicate tints of most exquisite hue,
and charming reflections of silver and blue.
The stranger, enraptured, looked earnestly where
the turret tops gleamed in the pure ether air;
while silently gazing he spake not a word, yet every
depth of his being was stirred."

As he reposed on his pillow that night,
sweet dreams and fair visions flashed forth on his sight;
A beauteous scene out of dreamland came thrice,
in which he reigned, king, in the castle of ice.
But, 'wakening from slumber, and somewhat surprised,
and looking quite thoughtful, he soliloquized;
an ideal city, I've found here at last,
with beautiful Leadville my fortune I'll cast.
I've traveled afar, in all countries and climes,
In lands of the cypress, and roses and vines;
where flowers ever bloom and the sun ever shines,
but grander than all are these mountains and mines.
I've wandered through Ceylon, the most beautiful gem
in India's fair crown, 'tis a bright diadem,
where murmuring rills are with precious stones purled,
whose jewels, the wonder and pride of the world.

I've visited Italy's sweet, sunny vales,
I've traversed her Alps, and I've roamed through her
    dales,
regaled by soft breezes from meadows of spice,
but never saw there any castle of ice.
No more will I wander, no more will I roam,
but here, in the Rockies, I'll build me a home.
Henceforth and forever my wand'rings shall cease;
and here I will dwell in contentment and peace.
From turmoil and strife, in retirement and rest,
my last days on earth will serenely be blest;
and when the death angel my throbbing heart stills,
I'll die in fond Leadville and sleep 'neath her hills.

—   Mrs. S. E. Lenfest,
February 15, 1896

In honor of Miners Day —
February 24, 1896

Hail, brothers of the brawny arm!
hurrah for the miners bold,
who search the earth for its treasured worth
of silver and of gold.
In the dark and the damp by the flickering lamp,
midst dangers that appall,
they win from its soil by honest toil,
prosperity for all.
True-hearted friends of silver they!
Hurrah for the metal white!
Though justice sleeps, while production weeps,
ye must lead them to the light.

184

Be brave and strong to right this wrong,
ye sturdy mountain lads;
and the world ere long will join the song,
for the dollar of our dads.
Hail Miners' Union!
In your acts be ever kind and true;
let yours be taught by honest thought
with Justice aye in view.
But hand in hand, as brothers stand,
loyal to friend and neighbor,
whenever right, must live by might,
or greed would throttle labor.

> — Frank E. Vaughn, in
> Mining Day Program

In honor of Irish Day —
March 5, 1896

Arise! ye sons of Ireland, who have in slumber lay
and toiled the hill and valley for many a weary day.
One day of recreation is placed at your command, to
view the grandest structure erected in the land.

> — Cornelius Maguire

There is a little spot on earth
that's dear to you and me,
the pride of ev'ry Irish heart,
the green "Isle of the Sea."
Where nature first the shamrock,
so beautiful and green

185

to ne'er be trampled under foot
by England's boasted queen.
Tis Erin, poor old Erin,
the land that gave me birth,
whose people are by England
crushed almost to the earth.
But by and by they'll surely rise,
for slaves they will not be;
and shout aloud to all the earth
that Erin must be free!
Then hand in hand together,
we'll cross the deep blue sea;
with the green flag waving o'er us,
for Erin must be free.
My poor distressful country!
My own, my native place!
don't be ashamed of poverty,
for sure 'tis no disgrace.
Be proud as any nation,
for the bloody flag of red
will be torn down by the Irishmen,
the green shall wave instead.
Oh! let your hearts be full of hope,
Tho' want may close your doors;
for Liberty has got her eye
upon your vernal shores.
She looks from proud America,
across the deep blue sea,
and bids us follow after,
for Erin must be free.
And then when Freedom smiles on you
and joy will bless your land;

then look back at America,
and let her have your hand.
Her Irish sons of freedom
she gave in you the cause
to drive oppression from your doors,
and break up England's laws.
Then Erin, dear old Erin!
Forever change the scene,
your lovely girls and honest lads
be wearing of the green.
And ever let your motto
to other nations be,
the shamrock grows, the green flag
flows, and Erin must be free.

— Author Unknown

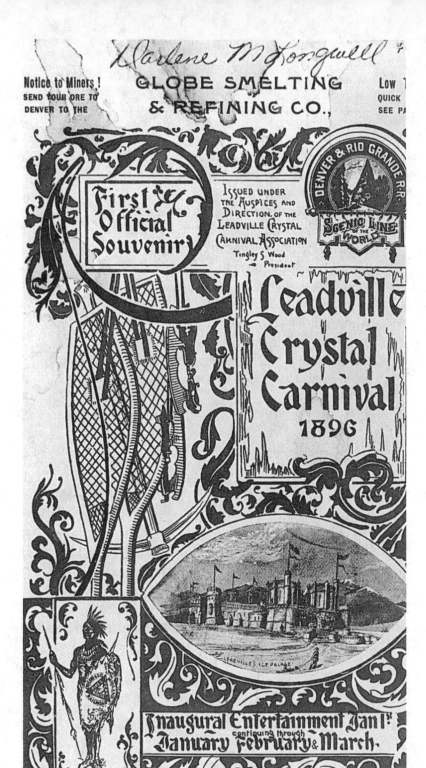

Cover Page from Souvenir Booklet.   *Author's Collection*

LEADVILLE'S CRYSTAL CARNIVAL
A Souvenir Booklet

The first official souvenir booklet was issued in January 1896, under the auspices and direction of the Leadville Crystal Carnival Association. The inaugural entertainment was to begin on January 1, 1896, continuing throughout January, February and March.

The 44-page booklet contained a brief description of the ice palace and the many attractions within its walls. It also carried many advertisements from businesses around the country, (some of which are still in business today.) Many of the ads were elaborate, full-page advertisements. The cover was of an ornate design and white, blue and red in color. The cover plate was made by the Williamson-Haffner Eng. Co., Denver. The book was printed by the Marsh & Carter Printing Company of Denver. "The inks used throughout this book were procured from The Standard Printing Ink Co. Grant C. Snyder & Co., of Denver, are the agents."

In August, 1962, Evelyn Furman, of the Tabor Opera House in Leadville, revived the Souvenir Booklet with reprints from an original copy.

Among those advertisers were: **Denver & Rio Grande Railroad**; The Ph. Zang Brewing Company; **Colorado National Bank**, Denver; First National Bank, Denver; Denver National Bank, The Knight-Campbell Music Company; **The Denver Fire Clay Company**; **Colorado Fuel & Iron Co.(CF&I)**, Pueblo, Denver, Chicago, New York & Salt Lake; **A. E. Meek & Co.**, Denver.[27]

---

[27]Companies still in business today shown in bold.

NEW YEAR'S DAY
The Grand Opening
January 1, 1896

The *Leadville Herald Democrat* of January 1, 1896
printed the following article with headlines of various sizes:

King Carnival Reigns In All His Crystal Splendor
Of Imprisoned Colored Lights

The Great Ice Palace Dedicated
Many Acres of Solid Fun

A Great Pageant of Leadville's Greatest Men
Greet The Ice King's Bride

Miner's Union Grand March
The Tin Bucket Brigade Outnumbers All Other Societies
& Organizations

A Rainbow Rink of Roses
Pillars of Opalescent Hue More Beautiful Than The
World Has Ever Seen Before

Leadville had been outstanding at the Festival of Mountain and Plain in Denver in October of '95. The Cloud City had the best entry in the parade, thanks to the clever abilities of Mrs. John (Nellie) Campion, who had designed it. The float, pulled by a team of beautiful horses, carried a goddess holding a cornucopia from which poured forth the precious metals of Leadville in gold and silver. Best prizes also went to Leadville citizens who competed in all sorts of contests.

Would the Carbonate Camp do any less with their own winter carnival and ice palace? Leadville had a reputation of being second to none and their winter enterprise would be no exception.

The Cloud City, for many years, had been encased in depressing, perpetual cold weather and deep snows. In 1896 the city welcomed the winter with open arms, reveling in the excitement of the ice palace and winter carnival.

The New Year's Day parade was the first of the carnival parades that occurred every day throughout Leadville's Crystal Carnival.

On December 28th a parade committee meeting was held at the Vendome Hotel to finalize parade plans for opening day at the ice palace. The meeting was attended by Captain W. R. Harp, chairman of the reception committee; Mayor S. D. Nicholson, county commissioner Hugh Kelly, E. J. Gaw, Harvey Brown, Carl Nollenberger, Theo Nollenberger, Charles Limberg, Francis X. Hogan, W. B. Sherick, John Ten Eyck, Roland L. Hill, Frank White, W. B. Felker, Jr., Herman Strauss, Adolph Schayer, C. H. S. Whipple, Charles Sands, C. N. Priddy, John A. Milner, Frank W. Hurd, Henry M. Blakely, James McNulty, Charles Bennett, Charles E. Dickinson and George P. Brown.

New Year's Day arrived, cold and cloudy, but the townspeople didn't notice. Harrison Avenue was alive with color. The store and business fronts were decorated with flags, buntings and streamers made of colored cloth. Pictures of the ice palace adorned many of the windows in the business district.

It was Ice Palace Day in Leadville, Colorado. Paraders began lining up at the Armory Hall on East Fifth Street that morning at 10:00.

The excitement of the upcoming parade and anticipation of the ice palace's opening spread a warmth over the city. The crowds began gathering early on Harrison Avenue, although the parade was not scheduled to start until 1:15 p.m. By that time the temperature had reached the high for the day of 20°.

Never were the Leadville citizens so enthusiastic. Everyone, young and old, was thrilled by the color and pageantry. The delightful shrieks of the children could be heard through the crisp mountain air. Little boys ran to the edge of the wooden sidewalks looking for the parade. Little girls frowned and turned their noses in the air at the boys' outlandish behavior. Friends and neighbors laughed and greeted one another as the stood on the Avenue awaiting the starting signal. The viewers stamped their feet to keep warm as they talked about the ice palace, how crowded the streets were, and how good it was to see old friends in Leadville for the winter carnival.

Director General Wood requested owners and managers to close their stores and businesses at noon so their employees could march in the parade, or join the spectators along the parade route. The children were on Christmas holiday from school so they, too, could join in the fun. The miners weren't paid, but that was of little concern that day, because they wanted to be a part of the festivities.

Finally, at 1:15 p.m., Grand Marshal Captain W. R. Harp, mounted on a beautiful white horse decorated with brightly colored tassels, rounded the corner of Fifth Street onto Harrison Avenue.

Heading the procession came Marshal G. W. Burgess, with his "fine flourishing Missouri whiskers," and Police Captain L. F. Long who were followed by the "guardians of the public peace," members of the city's police force.

Next, came the entry that captured the hearts of the parade viewers; a pair of Pug dogs harnessed to a sled carrying their precious cargo, tiny Helen Marechal, "a sweet five-year-old girl of the Rockies." The dog team was driven by her papa[28]. This childhood scene was said to be enough to melt a miner's heart.

Cheers and applause rose from the crowd as the Fort Dodge Cowboy Band filled the air will lively music and stirred the fires of patriotism. The band was followed by a bass drum so enormous, it was carried by four gaily decorated donkeys. The drum was a gift to Leadville from the city of Pueblo.

Chief aide Captain David LaSalle and the Leadville Snowshoe Club were the best costumed in the parade; 82 strong, 44 of whom were women. Next came the Leadville Hockey Club dressed in brightly colored costumes. They wore white, pure as ermine, blanket-cloth coats and trousers piped in red, red stockings, white buckskin moccasins, caps of blue with red tassels and red gloves. Many carried hockey sticks over their shoulders. The Ladies Toboggan Club, dressed in suits of "red hot colors" followed the snowshoers, and contributed a warmth of color to the pageant.

---

[28]Julius Marechal was employed as a candymaker at John E. Miller's confectionery. Source: Interview with Don Griswold.

194

William H. Korn carried his "sweet, dear little daughter," three years old, on his sturdy shoulders. They were two of the most picturesque characters in the parade.

The Leadville Ladies Carnival Club, 23 members strong, followed.

At the Vendome Hotel Director General Wood joined the procession, accompanied by Charles Limberg, A. V. Hunter and Judge Frank W. Owers, whose costume attracted the ladies admiration. It was made of old iron, the color of one of the carnival metals.

Next came Mayor Nicholson and Dr. D. H. Dougan, dressed in colorful carnival attire. The city alderman, dressed in togas and sashes, county commissioners and county officials, and the Carnival Executive Committee followed.

The 2,000-member Miners Union, led by James R. Amburn and Gresham F. North, was the largest entry in the parade.

The Patriotic Sons of America, with their large regalia of Stars and Stripes in great profusion, was one of the favorites.

Then came the uniformed firemen led by Captain Charles Goodfriend, perched atop the ladder wagon, with all the fire equipment colorfully decorated.

Amid a burst of applause, cheers and whistles, came the stars of the parade, the men who had built the ice palace. Their pride and exuberance was unbounded. Some of the workers carried a banner which read, "We Helped Build The Ice Palace," that stretched the width of Harrison Avenue. Workmen had improvised small sleds made of crude, rough boards that carried blocks of ice similar to those used in the ice palace walls. The icemasons carried their tools: saws, axes, clamps, tongs, adzes and every other device used in the construction of the ice palace, each carrying his tool over his shoulder.

Last, but not least, came the citizens of Leadville on foot, on sleds, and in sleighs shouting and waving to the spectators as they moved up the Avenue.

This truly was Leadville's Day at the ice palace. Dignitaries from all over Colorado had been invited to attend the Grand Opening of the Ice Palace. Not one of them attended! Denver's officials were not represented. Regrets were received from the Festival of Mountain and Plain Committee.

(On December 19th Messrs. J. W. Smith and S. K. Hooper, representatives of the Leadville Club of Denver, met with the board of directors of the Festival of Mountain and Plain. This meeting at the Brown Palace Hotel was called for the purpose of personally inviting the Festival officers to Leadville on December 31st. Platte Rogers and Mr. Hooper accepted the invitation on behalf of the members. Agent B. L. Winchell of the Denver & Gulf (South Park) Railroad offered use of a special train to the Cloud City. The board of directors, a short time later, declined the offer. Instead, they opted to come to Leadville on Colorado Press Day, staying over the next day. January 16th was designated special recognition day for the Festival of Mountain and Plain.)

The Fort Dodge Band arrived in Leadville a day early, on December 31st, so they would have a full day to practice in the two-mile-high altitude before marching in the New Year's Day parade.

A reception committee was appointed to be in charge of the ice palace opening day ceremonies. W. R. Harp and nine businessmen served on the parade committee.

196

This was a gala day for Leadville. The people, who the previous year were unhappy and depressed, dived into the pleasures of the Winter Carnival. "It was a glorious, gladsome day, when beautiful women shared the pleasures with the men, and joined in the celebration," reported the *Herald Democrat*.

The Crystal Carnival was an equalizer. The millionaire and the worker, the servant and the socialite danced on the same floor, to the same music. There was no class distinction. Never were the citizens of Leadville so enthusiastic. Every man, woman and child was thrilled by the magnificent ice castle. The carnival overshadowed any Fourth of July event ever held in the city and there were not enough adjectives in the English language to describe the magnitude and beauty of the ice palace.

Entrance was made at the east gate (West Seventh Street) of the palace. The north entrance was yet unfinished and boarded up, and the two main towers had not been completed. Upon arriving at the palace, the admission fees were collected from everyone, and the crowds entered the palace.

The inaugural ceremony was held in the grand ballroom, the most colorfully decorated and most comfortably heated room in the ice palace.

Director General Wood and A. V. Hunter were escorted to the center of the ballroom where they were surrounded by the Snowshoe and Toboggan clubs.

Major George P. Brown gave the signal to call the enthusiasts to order, and the men uncovered their heads.

The (Fort Dodge) Cowboy Band took its place on the elevated platform.

Speeches were made; first by Mayor Nicholson, who spoke of the honor attached to the dedication of the magnificent ice monument, and to the commitment and generosity of the Leadville people. "Mr. Wood and his assistants have crowned, with success, one of greatest achievements. But, there remains a duty for every man, woman and child to perform in the proper reception of the carnival guests."

Dr. D. H. Dougan followed with some aptly chosen words and a few facetious remarks. He concluded by saying, "We now propose to cut ourselves loose and have a good time and inaugurate the Crystal Palace with the right spirit, and enjoy ourselves right royally. The beauty of the palace when the electric lights are turned on at night is beyond the wildest dreams of the Arabian Nights, and it belongs to the people of Leadville. To Director Wood belongs as large a portion of the credit for the erection of this beautiful building." His remarks were followed by salvos of cheers and applause.

Then came Director General Wood. Mr. Wood insisted that speeches be short because he had not built the ice palace for making speeches, but for the enjoyment and entertainment of the people. In his speech, Director General Wood said, "It was time for levity. Now that we have a carnival, let us enjoy it. This is not my Leadville Palace, but yours." Resounding applause echoed through the hall. "It belongs to the people and was built to no one's credit, but for the honor, the glory and the reputation of

198

Leadville. . . . The carnival is now open, enjoy your-
selves."

Following the speeches the carnival began. The crowd
spread to all rooms of the palace. Some to the ice rink,
others to the exhibit hall or concession stands. Many of the
young adults stayed in the ballroom, kicking up their heels
to the "cowpunchers" (the Fort Dodge Cowboy Band). The
ballroom was described to be as beautiful as a garden of
roses in bloom on that day.

The skating rink was opened at 1:30 p.m. and skating
began at 2:00 p.m. Although not completed by opening
day, when finished, the north and south walls contained
beautiful displays in illuminated ice, and was considered
the finest skating rink ever seen in the United States.

From the rink, Grand Marshal W. R. Harp moved outside
to the toboggan slides and the official initiation. Mr. Harp
was joined by his daughter, Anna Harp, Madeleine Nell
Davis and Director General Wood. With some apprehension,
the party seated themselves in the cushioned toboggan and
Mr. Dimick gave the signal. The board was tilted and the
passengers were sent flying down the steep incline. The
heart-stopping ride, whether viewed as dangerous or
exciting, was deemed a tremendous success.

The rush for the toboggans was on! The first few thrill
seekers experienced a rather rough and bumpy ride due to
the scaly condition of ice, but it didn't take long for the
slides to turn smooth and glassy.

Leadville's Winter Carnival had begun!

Serving on the Opening Day Committee were:

Harp, W. R. — Chairman	Nicholson, S. D. — Mayor
Brown, George P.	Higgins, H. I.
Brown, Harvey T.	Nowland, John
Dougan, Dr. D. H.	Sheridan, John
Fahnenstock, K. L.	Starne, Maurice

Serving on the Parade Committee were:

Harp, W. R. — Chairman	Nicholson, S. D. — Mayor
Kelly, Hugh	McNulty, James
Bennett, Charles	Milner, John A.
Brown, George P.	Nollenberger, Carl
Brown, Harvey	Nollenberger, Theo
Blakely, Henry M.	Priddy, C. N.
Dickinson, Charles E.	Sands, Charles
Felker, W. B., Jr.	Schayer, Adolph
Gaw, E. J.	Sherick, W. B.
Hill, Roland L.	Strauss, Herman
Hogan, Francis X.	Ten Eyck, John
Hurd, Frank W.	Whipple, C. H. S.
Limberg, Charles	White, Frank

THE LIGHTING CEREMONY
A Breathtaking Spectacle

On New Year's Day eleven inches of snow covered the ground in Leadville and the temperature hovered around 22° during the evening. This did not keep the thousands of people away from the ice palace with the scene on West Seventh Street ablaze with the glowing electric lights. The carnival people and the city had been very liberal with the additional lighting for the winter carnival. One continual avenue of brilliancy lighted the street from the Vendome Hotel to the Crystal Palace.

At 7:00 p.m. New Year's Day the ice palace site was packed with people. Crowds of visitors and locals lined West Seventh and extended onto West Eighth Streets as well. It was time to turn on the lights at the ice palace.

Mr. H. I. Higgins, a prominent figure in the community and president of the American Smelting Company, was chosen to throw the switch that would light the ice palace.

Amid the music and frivolity of the event, a hush fell over the crowd as an announcement was made that the lighting ceremony was about to begin. When the switch was thrown, Leadville's Ice Palace on Capitol Hill came alive with a spectacular blaze of colored lights. The crowd gasped in wonderment as the breathtaking rainbow of colors lit up the sky. Thunderous applause, shrieks of delight, and gasps from the spectators, all in awe of the beautiful palace, filled the chilly night air.

The ice blocks glowed with a soft rainbow of colors: blues, pinks, yellows and greens radiating from the palace walls in an array of shades of indescribable beauty. The towers were illuminated with shades of purple, pink and green, casting a translucent glow over the entire city and the valley below. The main towers were not finished yet, and remained dark for the grand opening.

Then came the miners, two thousand strong, storming the castle with their shouts and yells scattering the spectator as they all made way for the castle.

"Brave King Carnival marshals his legions;
 with high courage, and cunning device.
They march onward through storm-smitten regions,
 and dedicate the palace of ice."

— Author Unknown

THE RAILROADS
All Aboard For Leadville

When talk of the ice palace was first raised in Leadville, one of the biggest arguments was, who would come to Leadville in the middle of winter to see an ice palace? Bear in mind there were no paved roads, and winter travel by rail was hazardous or non-existent, depending upon the weather. It could be a hair-raising experience in those days. But the Leadville citizens put that argument to rest. Some of these trains had to add extra cars that brought the thousands to see Leadville's beautiful crystal castle.

Special round trip tickets were offered by the Western Passengers Association to make a round trip rate of one fare plus two dollars, from all parts of the Western Passengers Association territory. These tickets were good for one day in January, February or March. The intention of this low fare was to lure visitors from as far away as Kansas City, Omaha, Chicago and St. Louis.

B. L. Winchell of the South Park Railroad; S. K. Hooper, Denver & Rio Grande and W. F. Bailey of the Colorado Midland had obtained 10,000 small posters for advertising purposes and rate schedule information. "The three (rail) roads leading to Denver are spending lots of money advertising novelties for the Ice Palace," the *Denver News* reported. The Rio Grande and Midland multi-colored flyers, each told of the attractions of their respective routes. The South Park's Colonel Winchell had posters in three colors, showing the carnival crowds on skis being pulled toward the Cloud City by a South Park train. Another pictured a scantily clad young woman sitting on a huge cake of ice with the palace as a background.

By mid-December the railroads were anticipating they would be filled to capacity, bringing people to Leadville.

A Denver & Rio Grande ad stated, "In the Ice Palace at Leadville, grandest sight on the great American continent, we want every man, woman and child in Pueblo to see it." Their round trip rates for opening exercises were $5 for December 31 and January 1; Saturday to Monday, $8; and tickets valid for ten days were $13.50, including two admission tickets to the Palace.

Before the opening day of the ice palace was delayed, the railroads were being inundated with reservations to Leadville. Even after the delayed opening was announced, railroad reservations continued to pour in.

In mid-December, freight business for the Colorado Midland had increased to the point that more switch crews were added, bringing the total to three.

By January 2nd, The Colorado Midland, Denver & Rio Grande and South Park railroads had arranged 24 special pullman cars to Leadville. The price for berths for the round trip to Leadville and return, including sleeping accommodations both ways and a berth in Leadville, was $5.

The Camera Club of Denver secured a special train to Leadville. The club was given a special excursion rate on the Denver, South Park line. The excursion was later opened to anyone wanting to make the trip. A round trip rate of $8 was agreed upon, and would be reduced to $5, for special days. The rate that included dinner en route at Como, meals at the Vendome, and sleeper car accommodations, and was $10.50. The ticket permitted sleeper car occupancy for the entire trip.

All fares included two tickets to the ice palace. Sleeper fare was usually $5, meals at the Vendome $1. The round trip fare with no meals or sleeper accommodations was $4.

The excursion train traveled over Kenosha, Boreas, and Fremont Passes, with a thirty-minute stop in Breckenridge. Another stop was planned at Robinson for viewing of the Mount of the Holy Cross, weather permitting. A special conductor was on board to comment on points of interest along the way. Arrangements were made so that all trains would be traveling slowly over the passes, for camera buffs to take pictures, or just enjoy the scenery. Departure time from Denver was 8:00 a.m.

Upon arrival at Leadville the train was met by the Fort Dodge Cowboy Band and the excursionists were escorted to the ice palace. Director General Wood waived all picture taking fees at the palace that day.

The Denver & Rio Grande offered accommodations to Leadville visitors, sidetracking several first class sleepers near their station. The siding was lengthened to hold six cars.

Leadville's South Park depot had two additional electric lights placed at either end of the platform for the safety of the visitors during the carnival. The management team had extra narrow gauge cars of the Colorado Central and South Park overhauled and repaired in anticipation of increased travel to Leadville's Ice Palace.

The Denver & Rio Grande added a number of lights around their depot for the carnival travelers.

Colorado Midland's Agent Bailey arranged a special car for Governor McIntire and his staff, Denver Mayor Thomas S. McMurray and other city and state officials. They were his guests while in Leadville for Colorado Press Day.

For Western Slope Day, February 22nd, round trip tickets from various points in Colorado were offered by the

Denver & Rio Grande, Colorado Midland and the Rio Grande Southern railroads. All fares included two tickets to the ice palace.

Fares for Western Slope Day offered by the railroads were listed as follows: [29]

Grand Junction	$ 6.10
Lake City	6.05
Palisade	5.80
Gunnison	4.20
DeBeque	5.15
Crested Butte	5.00
Parachute	4.75
Durango	11.20
Rifle	4.25
Rico	8.80
Newcastle	3.80
Telluride	8.20
Aspen	3.45
Mancos	10.50
Emma	3.45
Ophir	8.20
Carbondale	3.45
Sapinero	4.95
Glenwood	3.45
Cardiff	3.45
Eagle	3.25
Basalt	3.45
Montrose	6.10

---

[29]*Grand Junction Sentinel*, 2/20/1896.

Gypsum	3.10
Ouray	7.25
Ridgeway	6.85
Delta	6.75

One planned excursion hit the skids when the management of the Rio Grande Southern reneged on a offer to route a group from Telluride to the ice palace via Grand Junction. Three weeks prior to Western Slope Day, the *Telluride Journal* announced tickets would be available for the ice palace trip. Because many had not taken this trip before, more than a hundred people, in addition to the Telluride Cornet Band, planned to make the excursion.

For whatever reason (jealousy had been mentioned) the Rio Grande railroad, by orders from President Jeffery, refused to sell Telluride tickets via Grand Junction to Leadville even though an agreement had been made with S. K. Hooper, General Passenger Agent of the Rio Grande Southern Railroad.

A message was sent by President Jeffery to Agent Atchison the afternoon prior to the trip instructing him to sell tickets to Leadville via Salida. Later than evening another message was sent countermanding the previous order and to proceed with selling tickets via Grand Junction. Because of the late hour, it was impossible to notify the Telluride citizens of the change. As a result, less than a dozen people took advantage of the offer, much to the dismay of Howard Lee and I. W. Bunting, local promoters of Western Slope Day.

The *Telluride Journal* printed an open letter reprimanding the Rio Grande's management, relating they were the losers by the large amount of revenue lost because of their petty actions. Ticket agent Atchison was absolved of any wrong doing in the way the matter was handled; he was only following the orders of his superiors.

(There was a lot of unrest and wars going on among the railroads at that time and may have been the reason for this boondoggle.)

Between 1895 and 1897 Leadville was being served by three railroads. Anthony Sneve was the agent of the Colorado Midland Railway; the local office in the Breene Block at 322 Harrison Avenue and the depot at the corner of West 4th & Spruce Streets.

The Denver & Rio Grande Railroad Company, Sam M. Brown general agent, had a local office at 401 Harrison Avenue, the depot was located between 13th & 16th on Poplar Street.

The Denver, Leadville & Gunnison Railway, (sometimes called the Gulf and South Park, was Leadville's main route from Como to Gunnison). H. D. Milton was the commercial agent, B. L. Winchell was general passenger agent and Mr. Trumble was the receiver agent. Offices at 500 Harrison Avenue.

OUR PALACE IS OPEN TO THE WORLD
Formal Opening of The Ice Palace
January 8, 1896

The *Denver Republican* newspaper reported a huge banner had been hung between the Equitable Building and the Albany Hotel in Denver, pointing out the headquarters of the Leadville Club.

Prior to their visit to Leadville, David May, chairman of the club, estimated 25 pullman sleeper cars and 100 cases of champagne would be needed to transport the party. Howard Chapin, the Leadville Club of Denver liaison in charge of accommodations, estimated 800 visitors would be in attendance. C. H. Morse of Leadville was active in planning the city's end of the excursion and he estimated 1200 people would be attending. However, by the end of December only 350 had signed up to make the excursion.

The Colorado Midland, the Denver & Rio Grande, and the South Park arranged for 24 special pullman cars for January 2nd. The price of berths for the round trip to Leadville and back, including sleeping accommodations both ways, and a berth at Leadville, was $5.

In the very early morning of January 4, 1896 six pullman cars left Denver carrying 1,000 Denver members to the city. Three sections came in on the Colorado Midland, three on the Denver & Rio Grande, with more to follow on the South Park. One of the trains came in two sections. The last section was occupied by men who were not accompanied by ladies. A special Midland train carried the committee appointed by Director General Wood. The official greeters left Leadville for Granite at 6:45 that morning to meet and escort members of the Leadville Club of Denver back to Leadville.

The special train was furnished, free of charge, by the Colorado Midland and the sleeper cars were held over in Leadville during the party's stay.

The Leadville train arrived in Granite shortly before 8:00 a.m., and had a short wait until the train arrived from Denver. Following much cheering upon the train's arrival, Mayor Nicholson gave a short speech, then presented Mr. David May a key to the city. The key, made especially for the occasion, was fashioned of thin iron, two feet long, and covered with golden bronze. Attached to it with a red, white and blue ribbon, was a card bearing the words, "Key to the City of Leadville." Then Dr. Dougan presented Colonel George Cook with a pot of red paint. The doctor was given the assurance that the paint would be used, implying that all the "red spots," saloons, gambling resorts and houses of prostitution would be patronized. The Leadville special was attached to the cars of the Denver train and amid the cheers and hurrahs, the entourage boarded the two trains and headed toward the Cloud City. Many friendships were renewed during the trip and talking about old times passed the time quickly. The Mandolin and Banjo Club of the George Cook Drum Corps entertained with lively music as the train sped toward Leadville.

Upon arrival at the Midland Depot, the group was greeted by hundreds of welcomers. The Leadville Snowshoe Club was decked out in their costumes and the Fort Dodge Cowboy Band filled the air with music as the committee and the Leadville Club alighted. More cheers for Leadville and more cheers for Denver also filled the air. Included among the passengers were several hundred members of the Leadville Pioneer Society.

Immediately, a parade was formed and moved up the street to town and on to the Denver & Rio Grande depot. The Leadville Club members stepped from the train onto the platform amid applause and cheers. The procession was re-formed and headed south toward town. The air was filled by the music of five bands and the carnival clubs in their many colored uniforms added to the festive air of this eventful day. A platoon of police headed the parade, followed by the First Regiment Band members. Mayor Nicholson, and eight of Leadville's ex-mayors followed the First Regiment Band and George Cook's 60-piece band took their places in the middle of the procession.

Little Helen Marechal, pulled on her sled by her Pug dogs, was such an attention-getter in the New Year's Day parade that she and her "Pa" participated again. Then came the Leadville Snowshoe Club, the Leadville Club of Denver, the Fort Dodge Cowboy Band, and the Leadville Toboggan Club, 60 members strong, all wearing colorful costumes of black and brilliant red, with black stockings. The Ladies Toboggan Club members were very attractive in their red costumes, carrying Chinese lanterns. George W. Cook's thirty-six member Zouave Drum Corps band was led by Captain French. The band was made up of 15 stringed instruments, six guitars, five mandolins, three banjos and one violin. A long line of sleighs, from the swankiest to a hand sled pulled by a burro, brought up the rear. The merrymaking paraders then moved on toward the city.

In preparation for the visitors, the three railroads combined forces to host a hospitality center for the Leadville Club of Denver. The center was located in the Patterson & Thomas Block.

All but four of the former Leadville mayors were present for the celebration. One was in California, two were deceased, and H. A. W. Tabor was in Denver. Those in attendance were present Mayor S. D. Nicholson, W. H. James, 1879-80; Dr. D. H. Dougan, 1881-1882, J. J. DuBois, 1883; J. D. Fleming, 1883-84; George W. Cook, and T. W. Jaycox.

H. A. W. Tabor, Leadville's first Mayor 1878-1879, often called the Father of Leadville, did not attend. It may be assumed his absence was due to the fact that Leadville's citizens had not taken kindly to his adulterous affair and marriage to Baby Doe. Leadville regarded Augusta Tabor, the abandoned wife, very highly and did not have much respect for Baby Doe.

During the afternoon the ex-mayors gathered for a photo session. This, indeed, was a rare occasion. The pictures were taken by O'Keefe and Stockdorf, official photographers for the Crystal Carnival Association.

The skating rink did not open until the regularly scheduled time of 1:30 p.m., which allowed the workmen time to continue working without interference from the crowds during the morning hours. There were no special programs or events set for the skating rink that evening but the carnival visitors were free to enjoy skating, dancing or meandering through the ice palace, taking in the sights.

Two concerts were provided by the Cowboy Band in the east Ballroom. Spectators listened to the strains of a

Caprice Heroeque,[30] "The Awakening of the Lion." Captain Cook's musicians, led by Captain S. M. French, livened up the halls with the "Leadville Ice Palace Quickstep," and the "Battle of Gettysburg." The First Regiment Band played a Sousa march, "Directoria Imortellen Waltz."

The Midland Special for the Leadville Club of Denver left the depot, bound for Denver at 11:45 that same night.

Mr. F. H. A. Lyle, general manager and treasurer of the Glenwood Hot Springs Company, traveled to Leadville on January 9th to promote the famous resort and make arrangements for visitors to the ice palace to stop and "take a bath." No doubt some of them took advantage of his offer on their way home.

A special fare of $5 was agreed upon by the city of Glenwood, the Colorado Midland and the Denver & Rio Grande. This fare was good throughout the Crystal Carnival season for trips made Friday or Saturday and returning on Monday.

On January 9, 1896, Hannah Rivers wrote to a "dear little friend," in Ft Wayne. Her letter in part stated:

> I wish you could see our Ice Palac (palace) Leadville is having and ice carnivall (carnival) it will last three months I sapose (suppose) you have seen something about it in the papers. We can see it from my kitchen window and at night . . . it is lit up with differnt (different) collors (colors) of light it is a marval (marvel) of buity (beauty) and a tabogan (toboggan) slide that is a mile long. Well its

---

[30]A loose, irregular type of composition in which the composer continually digresses from his subject. In a live, free, whimsical style.

(it's) lots of fun for the young people. We are having a
mild winter heare (here) not anuf (enough) snow to go
slayhe (sleigh) riding and some days its (it's) so warm that
they hafto (have to) strech (stretch) canvas around the Ice
Palac (Palace) to keep it from melting.

By mid-January the ice palace was the talk of the entire
state, and the thousands of visitors made excursions to
Leadville to see the Crystal Castle. Word of mouth accolades and rave reviews were bringing hordes of people to
the Cloud City.

Committee members for the formal opening were:

Baer, Sherwin A.
Bohn, A. V.
Brown, George P.
Campion, George F.
Cavendar, Charles
Dougan, D. H.
Fahnenstock, K. L.
Foutz, J. E.
Frisbie, George
Harp, W. R.
Harvey, John
Hunter, A. V.
Jaycox, Thomas W.
L'Abbe, George A.
Limberg, C. T.
Maxwell, J. M.
Milner, J. A.

Mudd, S. W.
Niblock, John J.
Nicholson, S. D., Mayor
Nimon, James
Nowland, John
Owers, F. W.
Page, W. F.
Parish, S. F.
Priddy, C. N.
Schayer, A.
Sheridan, J. A.
Smith, J. W.
Sterne, Maurice
Stotesbury, John H.
Taylor, George E.
Weddle, J. H.
Wigginton, James C.

Members of the First Regiment Band of Denver were:

Frank Havil, Manager
Oswald H. Richter, Bandmaster

Baum, J	Meyer, J.
Biele, William	Nordstrom, J.
Bisbee, H. S.	Nutting, F. J.
Bosworth, E. A.	Oliphant, H. A.
Chase, John	Parker, E. W.
Emmons, W. F.	Quirk, T.
Gresecke, P.	Rogers, W. A.
Habert, A. F.	Rose, Frank
Habert, P.	Schiermeyer, L.
Haunchild, R.	Schubert, F.
Hoffman, J.	Smiley, E. J.
Lepold, F. J.	Tate, D. W. W.
McIntyre, F. S.	Wells, J.

Helen Marechal, a "little sweetheart of the Rockies," and friends.
Courtesy Jim Tilden

IT WON'T BE CLOSED
Lies! All Lies!

As early as January 10th, newspapers throughout the state were driving nails into the ice palace's coffin. On January 12th the *Leadville Herald Democrat* put silence to the ridiculous reports.

It is certainly time to call a halt to the absurd and silly rumors which have been set afloat during the past few days with reference to the ice palace. It must be very candidly stated that some of these rumors were set afloat in Denver, and by Denver people, who ought to know better, but who must have been inspired by the most unworthy motives when they placed them in circulation. We propose to nail these one by one.

Lie No. 1 — The Ice Palace is melting.

This is simply one of those absurd statements set afloat by people who imagine a few hours of sunshine can make a perceptible impression on 6,000 tons of solid ice. They think because the weather is pleasant and sunshiny that necessarily the palace must at once melt down. In the first place, it is very much colder on the hill. The walls are amply protected by canvas, and the sun simply doesn't make an impression on them to amount to anything. The south wall is necessarily whitened, but go up and see if there is any damage.

Lie No. 2 — The walls are falling.

This is one of the silliest of the lies about the Crystal Castle, and one of course, an off-shoot of Lie No. 1. Let it be known that when a block of ice is laid, it is frozen to

217

the block beneath it, and the mass, when completed, is like a wall of granite. However, that there may be no possibility of danger, the workmen are constantly employed at night, making repairs on the walls, in places that seem to have been, in any manner, affected by the sun. Director General Wood, very pointedly, stated that there can be no danger of damage on this score. Anyone who will take the trouble to examine will soon see that the walls are sound and solid, and would last like granite if cold weather continued.

Lie No. 3 — The Ice Palace won't be completed.

The ice palace is practically completed now. By Monday (January 13th) the entrance will be through the north portal, and it should be stated right here, that all has been stated concerning the great structure, is not overdrawn, not overstated. The grand palace is one of the most beautiful and artistic structures ever conceived and completed by mortal man, and the people who are trying to belittle it, who are making disparaging remarks concerning it, to say the least, ought to be ashamed of themselves.

Lie No. 4 — People who come here can't get enough to eat.

If they can't, they must have appetites like boa constrictors after a winter's fast.

Lie No. 5 — The town is infested with hold-ups and robbers.

Since the inception of the ice palace, there hasn't been a single holdup. W. K. Burchinell, it was said, was robbed.

218

The fact is, that Burchinell was not robbed, nor anyone else. A young man named Dalton said he lost a diamond stud, and probably did. But even he wasn't sure that the loss was through pickpockets. The fact is, that considering the crowds who have come here, and the temptations for the thieving element to operate, there has been remarkably little stealing of any kind during the carnival season. The average criminal has a wholesome fear of Leadville, and doesn't flock here in very big numbers.

Contrary to reports from the Denver newspapers that on March 4, 1986, the ice palace would close, the Crystal Carnival Association, by way of the *Herald Democrat*, assured its readers that the ice palace was to remain open the entire month of March. An article in the *Aspen Tribune* reported that Denver had never shown support for Leadville's Ice Palace, and:

> The seemingly jealous feeling which the capital city has manifested toward the Carbonate Camp's glacial wonder, the fact remains the same that the dazzling palace of ice and the names of its enterprising promoters will appear on the pages of the state's history in bold faced type when some of Denver's money grabbing schemes, which she pleases to term enterprises, will be fortunate to find a place in lower case agate.

The *Cripple Creek Times*, however, reported on March 6, 1896, "The time left for seeing the Leadville Ice Palace is growing very short, and those who fail to see the beautiful structure will always regret it."

PROCLAMATION
Colorado Press Day
January 15, 1896

Hearken all Ye People!

Give ear unto the words of the Lord High Mayor of the city of Leadville.

Know then that I, Samuel D. Nicholson, the exalted potentate of the City of the Crystal Castle, do send word unto the people of the land, from Carbonate Hill even unto the uttermost parts of Malta, and to all inhabitants thereof, to obey and submit themselves to the will of the King Carnival, who will enter the gates of the Ice Castle on the 15th Day of the month known as January.

I ordain and decree, by the power vested in me by the Mystic Council of Seven, that on the day of arrival of the August King Carnival, ye shall not appear on the highways and byways of the city, between the hours of 2 o'clock in the afternoon and 10 o'clock at night, unless the face be covered by a masque. Nor shall ye enter unto the castle walls unless clothed in fantastic dress suitable to the majesty of his royal icicles, King Carnival.

And to him who fails to obey the decree will be meted out the lightnings and thunders of the royal anger.

The officers of the law and all the wearers of the king's regalia are hereby charged to lay hands on all who disobey the decree and hasten with them into the dungeon known as Jebel el Calaboose, that they may be given over to the torturers, who will freeze them in blocks of ice to be placed in the great wall of the Crystal Castle, that all men may see who hath dared to disobey the word and decree of

221

the mighty King Carnival, by his Grand Janizary, the Lord High Mayor.

And it shall be also ordained that all the inhabitants of the city, both male and female, shall provide themselves with a musical instrument with which to make a joyful noise on the day of the entrance of the Lord of the Ice Castle. They may be instruments of brass or of tin, or tinkling cymbals or stringed instruments that will sound with the merry strain when King Carnival enters our gates.

And be it known unto all men that the great gold, silver, lead, iron and copper, sixteen to one, key of the city will be delivered over unto the High Priest of the Ancient Order of Pen Pushers who will especially honor King Carnival by their presence in the city above the clouds.

And unto all the men of the Ancient and Noble Order of Pen Pushers shall be granted, without money and without price, the freedom of the hills. And all keepers of places of refreshment shall give unto them of their abundance of the juice of the corn and the rye and the barley, even of the juice that is fermented or distilled and costeth 15 cents a glass.

And, lastly, let there be rejoicing throughout the length and breadth of the city on the day of the coming of the great king. Let the door of the shopkeeper close, and the sound of the hammer be not heard within the walls for the space of ten hours. Let all with the price enter into the palace that hath prepared for them and whoop 'er up for the glory of the Mighty King Carnival.

And in testimony whereof I have affixed the great tin seal of the City, dyed this proclamation with red paint, that all the people of the state and the inhabitants thereof may

222

know that it goes, and that all, from Chalk Ranch even unto Granite, may know that King Carnival reigns and we are his subjects, and bow loyally to his will.

ss: Samuel D. Nicholson
Lord High Mayor, Grand Janizary of King Carnival and Keeper of the Key.

```
┌─────────┐
│         │
│  SEAL   │
│         │
└─────────┘
```

Attest: John H. Goodman, City Clerk.

COLORADO PRESS DAY
Official Opening Of The Ice Palace
January 15, 1896

The two previous opening days had to yield to Press Day for attendance and color. On January 15, 1896, Leadville's citizens, guests, and excursionists were celebrating the actual completion of the ice palace.

The visitors did not pour into the city as was expected. Members of the Crystal Carnival Association and the businessmen took the position that once the ladies and gentlemen of the press began reporting the magnificence of the ice palace and winter carnival, there was no doubt Leadville and the ice palace would be packed with excursionists.

Press Day dawned bright and beautiful in the Cloud City. The air was crisp and chilly that morning as trains rolled into the city. The Denver & Rio Grande was the first to arrive with a load of newspaper reporters, representatives, and dignitaries. They came from Denver, Colorado Springs and points in the southern part of the state. Later, the Colorado Midland arrived with a trainload. The excursionists were met by the Press Club committee and escorted to the hotels.

Buffalo Bill Cody was invited to attend Press Club Day. A. S. Patterson, corresponding secretary of the Leadville Press Club, sent a special personal invitation. Regretfully, the famous Cody was unable to attend. He was on his way from North Platte, Nebraska to New York. Dignitaries in the city for the day included: Governor McIntire and his staff; Lt. Governor Brush and other state officers. Denver Mayor Thomas S. McMurray and other city officials;

225

General Wheaton, directors of the Festival of Mountain and Plain; prominent railroad managers and Mayor J. C. Plume of Colorado Springs were among those who made the excursion.

During the morning they toured the Little Jonny Mine, hosted by John Campion and Mr. Kenneth Fahnenstock. Upon reaching the mine's surface following the tour, the governor complained of "weak knees," a result of climbing up and down the steep mine ladders. The entourage then paid a visit to the Carbonate National Bank to view the gold brick display—$150,000 in pure gold bars from the Little Jonny Mine. Later in the day the governor took the opportunity to clamp on a pair of ice skates and cut a fancy swath on the ice palace's skating rink.

The ice palace was closed during the morning hours of Press Day, but the visitors found plenty of things to do: shopping, sightseeing, or enjoying the magnificent scenery and the climate. The cool air was tempered by warm sunshine, which made for pleasant strolling along the Avenue.

The Press Club doors swung both ways during the day. The Leadville newspaper hosts provided warm hospitality, refreshment and entertainment for the travel-weary pen-pushers. The Fort Dodge Cowboy Band serenaded the Press Club visitors. The crowd then marched to the ice palace, where the Editorial Association convened.

A committee on resolutions was appointed, then reported the following resolutions, suggested by Charles S. Sprague of Colorado Springs. The resolutions were unanimously adopted:

Whereas, the spirited and enterprising citizens of Leadville have, at the expense of not less than $40,000, erected an ice palace, which in beauty brilliancy, design and proportions, surpasses any similar structure ever erected on this or any other continent: be it

Resolved, By the Colorado State Editorial Association, in regular meeting assembled, that the Leadville Ice Palace had rivaled the most fervid expectations of our members; that it is an enterprise worthy the recognition and patronage of every citizen of this state, as in addition to its beauty and attractiveness, it is an advertisment for the state of the greatest value and in its conception as an advertisement equaled by no other city in Colorado; be it further

Resolved, That the ice palace should be heartily supported by the citizens of the various sections of the state; and to further this end, we recommend that the railroad make especially low rates, not exceeding $5 for the round trip, from any point in the state, and that the rate be made to cover a period of not fewer than four days; we beg to suggest that these low rates be made at least every Friday, in order that visitors may spend Saturday and Sunday in visiting the Cloud City and its resplendent attractions: Be it further

Resolved, That the members of this association are under obligations to the rail for courtesies extended, and to the good people of Leadville and to the management of the Ice Palace, and especially the Leadville Press Club for their generous hospitality. The members of the Editors Association of Colorado are under lasting obligations to Leadville, which we will try to discharge in our individual capacity and with hearty unanimity.

(Signed) Charles S. Sprague, Chairman
K. G. Cooper
C. E. McSheehy,
Committee on Resolutions.

During the meeting, Secretary Halsey Rhoads read the report of the secretary and a number of applications were acted upon. Many new members were inducted into the Association that day at the ice palace. Following the election of officers and the installation ceremonies, the meeting adjourned at 4:00 p.m.

It should be noted here that C. C. Davis, owner of the *Leadville Herald Democrat* and *Evening Chronicle*, was not present or publicly mentioned. He was in a Denver hospital, seriously ill and was not expected to live. His daughter, affectionately called Miss Nellie, had taken his place and was praised for her poise and the manner in which she handled the situation.

During the afternoon the streets were jammed with people and the merriment grew fast and furious. A parade brought King Carnival to town, accompanied by his attendants, pages and clowns, soldiers, sailors, imps, devils, whirling dervishes, policemen, mercenaries, wild Indians and badmen from Borneo. The tooting of horns, blowing the kazoos, rolling the drums and blares of the trumpets attracted a crowd that packed Harrison Avenue.

Among the newspapermen in Leadville for Press Day as reported by the *Leadville Herald Democrat*, were:

A. W. Armstrong, editor of the *Bud*, Morrison, Colorado who was said to have registered with a steady hand.

W. C. Calhoun of the *Rocky Mountain Herald*, was prominent among the Denver editors.

Frank M. Gray, proprietor of the *Evening Call*, Pueblo, was described as "a host among the newspaper fraternity."

Mr. Charles Silvey Sprague, Manager of the *Evening Telegram*, Colorado Springs, was a distinguished guest.

Another stalwart representative of western journalism was C. E. McSheehy, president of the Western Editorial Federation, Trans-Mississippi States, president of the Arapahoe Press Association, and editor of the *Rocky Mountain Herald*.

J. O. Stewart and Will J. Matthews "care for the interests of the *Evening News* and *United Press Association* in splendid style."

J. A. Sheely, proprietor of the *Silver Wheel*, Platteville, was a jolly visitor of the pen craft.

Howard T. Lee ably represented the *Daily Sentinel* of Grand Junction.

F. C. Hitchcock, who has been booming the Crystal Palace through the *Mosca Herald*, was a welcome guest of the Leadville Press Club.

Chief among the Colorado newspaper men was Halsey M. Rhoads, secretary of the Editors' Association.

George A. Scibird of the *San Juan Prospector* was an early arrival.

M. Beshoar, second vice president of the Colorado Editors' Association and editor of the *Daily Advertiser*, Trinidad, was present.

C. H. Frowine, president of the *Manitou Journal*, who was one of the prominent newsmen in the state, was present with Mrs. Frowine, one of the most delightful of women.

Hon. A. L. Beardsley, in the absence of C. A. Henrie, represented the *New Castle News*, and his presence was doubly appreciated.

The local boys were proud to shake the hand of T. M. Howell, proprietor of the *Morning Times* of Cripple Creek.

He conceded that next to Cripple Creek, Leadville showed up best.

F. M. A. Randall of the *Rifle Reveille* was present.

Ezra Nuckles of the *Commercial Tribune Herald* was among the visiting members of the craft.

H. A. Wildhack of the *Meeker Herald* was the best fancy skater among the pen pushers.

A. J. Saint of the *Glenwood Springs Ledger* was among the Colorado pen slingers.

S. Homer Hill was the competent representative of the *Salida Mail*.

L. F. Willoughby of the Denver type foundry was among the press gang, and well supplied.

H. E. Corser, editor of the *Chaffee County Republican*, was registered on the Press Club's big book.

A. D. Bishop of the *Denver Physician* danced with the fairest.

R. E. Pierce and wife of the *A.O.U.W. Record* were among the pleasant people from the Orient.

Charles S. Sprague of the *Colorado Springs Gazette* was one of the social lions of the day.

A. R. Logan of the *Colorado Farmer*, accompanied by his wife and his sister, was among the guests.

Miss Clarina Cooper of the *Denver Republican* was one of the visiting ladies who enjoyed the toboggan.

A. H. Lacey of the *Wet Mountain Journal* was the driest fish in the puddle.

J. D. Dillenback, editor of the *Mining Industry and Review*, was one of the best posted writers on mining in the state.

K. G. Cooper of the *Denver Republican* business department was one of the best known newspaper men in the state.

Frank I. White, editor of the *Rocky Mountain Editor*, had full swing of the news gang.

J. R. Melrose of the *Colorado Odd Fellow*, was prominent among the fraternity men.

Miss Maud Miller of the *Globeville News* was one of the most brilliant women writers in the state.

Mrs. Luke Turnbull was one of the ablest journalists in the state. She is on the staff of the *Denver Saturday Afternoon*.

J. W. Swisher of the *Summit County Journal*, sat down with the snow goddess and thawed out.

W. C. Wyncoop and F. M. Shopoel of the *Mining Industry* were at the head of the mining editors of the state.

The *Daily Sentinel*, Grand Junction, was represented by a pair of hustlers; I. W. Bunting and Howard T. Lee.

W. H. McGuire, proprietor of the *Denver Globe*, was among the best of the visiting editors.

E. J. Miller of the *Elyria Journal* was a loyal devotee of the Shrine of the Ice King's bride.

George Daniels was the welcome representative of the *Denver Illustrated Weekly*.

A. A. Hopkins, of the *Rocky Mountain World*, waved the carnival colors over the crystal walls.

Will J. Orange of the *Silvercliff Rustler* was a popular representative of the state press.

John G. Garrison, of the *Denver Eye*, came on strong.

Dr. Nicola Gigliotti, the venerable editor of the *Roma*, Denver, was accompanied by Mrs. Gigliotti.

Newspaper representatives from Utah arrived at 12:20 p.m. on the Midland, via the Rio Grande Western. They were accompanied by W. J. Raid, traveling passenger agent of the "Little Giant."

The Utah party consisted of R. G. Taysum, telegraph editor of the *Salt Lake Herald*, and associate Fred Keller; Ray Raymond of the Herald, D. P. Felt of the *Springville Independent*, accompanied by his mother and his wife; E. A. Gregory also of the *Springville Independent*; Charley Johnson, the official photographer; A. N. Rosenbaum, of *Men and Women*; and E. M. West of the *Ogden Standard*.

Mr. Taysum told a *Leadville Herald Democrat* reporter:

> Leadville has a good reason to be proud of her ice palace and of the men who conceived and executed the idea. The enterprise was one that would do credit to a town ten times larger than Leadville. We, of course, expected to see something worth seeing, otherwise we would not have come so far, but the palace is certainly far beyond our most sanguine expectations. Its immensity, its dominating influence, its artistic beauty, must ever live in the minds of those who have ever seen it.

He expressed regret that the invitation to Leadville had not reached them earlier; at least a hundred more would have come.

For those who did not attend the Press Day conference, afternoon skating competitions were held on the ice rink for their entertainment. The boys' races began shortly after the arrival of the Press Club crowd.

The little boys' one-mile race brought laughter to the spectators. The youngsters were skating furiously in their

232

attempt to win the race. The entries were: Ed McCool, Ed Miller, John Lowrey, James Welsh, John Armstrong and George Lanphier.

First prize, a suit of clothes from C. Hayden, Jr., was awarded to Ed McCool and Eddy Miller won second honors, a pair of shoes.

Older boys' one-mile race entries were: Bert Jackson, Johnny Knapp, Bert Hall, Val Jackson and Jules Ernest.

First prize was a boys suit of clothes and a pair of skates provided by Herman Strauss, won by John Knapp.

Second prize was a boy's hat furnished by C. Hayden, Jr., won by Jules Ernest.

Mrs Swanson took the prize for lady in best fancy costume, a $15 hat, compliments of Miss M. J. Frantz.

The prize for best impersonation of Grover Cleveland was a fishing pole, donated by C. H. S. Whipple, and was awarded to George W. Whyte.

Prize for best clown, a hat by Famous, was won by Emil Cundy.

Prize for best Trilby, an elegant belt from W. B. Felker, went to Ben Cohn.

The prize for the best lady's costume of Carnival colors, a season ticket was won by Miss Maggie Potts.

The prize for best gentleman's costume of Carnival colors, a season ticket, was awarded to Dr. B. S. Galloway.

Prize for the best costume representing the *Leadville Herald Democrat*, a dress pattern from J. W. Smith, went to Miss Isabel Colby.

Emily Fernley walked off with the prize for best costume representing the *Leadville News Reporter*; a dress pattern from the Chicago Bazaar.

Carl Killiam, William Pitts and George Cox won prizes for the best farmer's costumes.

As night fell on the city, the streets were crowded with visitors and citizens alike. Harrison Avenue was packed with spectators watching the antics of the hundreds of carnival revelers. Burros were covered with ornate rainbow colors, Chinese lanterns, and decorations of every kind imaginable. The patient little beasts of burden were then hitched to carts and wagons, and coaxed along by outlandishly costumed drivers.

Promptly at 7:30 p.m., Grand Marshal of the parade, David LaSalle, let out a war whoop. With a roll of drums and the lighting of torches, the evening parade marched from the New Armory Hall to the ice palace. The crisp night air was filled with a simultaneous salvo of technicolored meteors, flashes and a shower of stars. The pyrotechnics display lit the Avenue from one end to the other. The rocket fire continued, endlessly, until the parade reached the ice palace. The glistening frosted walls were bombarded with fireworks that spit and hissed toward the icy fortress. But to no avail; as soon as they struck the palace walls, they fizzled out and fell to the ground. King Carnival had pushed the onslaught back, and beckoned the merrymakers to enter.

The ice palace was finally completed, and the massive towers at the main entrance were lighted for the first time that evening. The gleaming spires were ablaze with colored light. The ice blocks resembled beautiful jewels: rubies, emeralds, sapphires and brilliant diamonds.

The evening brought the largest crowd of people yet assembled to the ice palace. A spectacular reception had been prepared for the visitors, and the palace was filled to

234

overflowing. By early evening the ballroom and skating rink were crowded with masqueraders. Men, women and children were dressed in dazzling costumes. The rich colors of their clothing rivaled the splendor of the lighted ice columns, arches and walls.

The ballroom, dining room, skating rink and every corridor and promenade were packed with spectators and participants. The ballroom was so crowded there was scarcely room for the hundreds of entrants of the many contests to model their costumes. Two hundred couples participated in the grand march, which was led by Alex Thomson, dressed as a sailor, and Miss Edith Lazenby, who was dressed as Queen of the Press, representing the *Denver Republican* tabloid. Her dress was made of the New Year's Day and daily editions of the *Republican* with gold and silver lettering, and trimmed in white fur. A golden crown adorned her hair.

Little ladies Buena Alverson and Theo Austin represented the *Leadville Herald Democrat* and the *Evening Chronicle*, respectively. The girls were dressed alike, with the exception of their "sugar loaf" hats; one hat bore the name of the *Herald*, the other, the *Chronicle*. Their dresses were made of the lithograph cover page of the "Ice Palace Edition," with colors of the Leadville Press Club's comical lithograph invitation to Press Day. Four other young ladies wore costumes made from the *Herald Democrat*. The *Leadville News Reporter*, *Pay Streak* and other local papers were also represented.

Nearly every nationality was represented that night. Some of the costumes worn were artistically designed in beautiful patterns. Others were described as comical or grotesque to the extreme. Spanish attire was the favorite.

235

Beautiful colored silk and silver embroidery graced the flowing gowns of the Japanese-clad ladies. On the skating rink, the sable and white fox cloaks and hats, representing the dress of Russian nobility stood out. Two young ladies whose costumes and skating attracted much attention were Ida and Addie Jones. Merrymakers were dressed in costumes representing the countries of Israel, Ireland, Italy, China, Germany, the Netherlands, Sweden, Scotland, England, and Turkey. The American Indian, Uncle Sam and other fellow Americans were well represented.

The most competitive skating contests of the winter carnival were held that night. Wagers had been placed all over the city, and the races had been the talk of the town for a week or more. Out-of-town interest had built up and it was reported that several of the reputed state champions planned to enter the race.

A full and exciting program awaited the anxious spectators. The men's one-mile competition began at 8:00 p.m. Matt Stiffler was first; Willard Riggs, second.

At 8:15 p.m. two teams took to the ice for the Hockey Club championship. The referee was W. A. Moore, and the umpires were Harvey Leonard and George P. Brown.

The Military Athletic Association Club took the championship by a score of 2-0. They were awarded a silver cup from the American Jewelry Company.

At 9:00 p.m., the masquerade Grand March was delayed a few minutes, but was worth the wait of the spectators. The costumes were dazzling as the marchers circled the ballroom.

Because of the delay, the five-mile race did not start until 9:40 p.m., forcing cancellation of the free-style figure skating competition and judging of some of the costumes.

236

A local speed-skating record was established that night. Matt Stiffler, Otis Richmond and Ernest Whitney lined up for the one-mile race. Stiffler took first place with a time of 3:18 minutes, the fastest time yet recorded on the rink; Whitney placed second with 3:24 and Richmond came in third, clocking 3:27 minutes.

Entrants for the two and one-half mile race were: Ernest Whitney, George Blatt, Matt Stiffler and Otis Richmond. Matt Stiffler was declared the winner of race with a time of 8:40 minutes, Stiffler won the $50 first prize and the time prize money was twenty-five percent of the gross receipts, which netted him over $100. Ernest Whitney and Otis Richmond tied with a time of 8:54 minutes.

Finally came the long-awaited and most important sporting event of the carnival season, the State Skating Championship Men's Race. The entrants lined up on the ice were: Sandy Cosseboom, Otis Richmond, Willard Riggs, Matt Stiffler, Ernest Whitney, and George Venable of Denver. As Stiffler approached the finish line, waving his handkerchief in triumph, he dropped to the ice in a dead faint (from exhaustion). He did not cross the finish line; the grueling five-mile race, in addition to the other races he had competed in that evening, had taken their toll. The judges awarded him the second place prize and Willard Riggs won first prize, a diamond and gold medal valued at $100.

John Ten Eyck offered a wager of one to three hundred dollars to anyone who could beat Stiffler in a one to ten mile race. There were no takers.

At 11:00 p.m. the now weary partyers were seated for a late night supper. Two tables, extending the full length of dining room, were set for two hundred pressmen, their ladies and guests. The banquet was catered by John Miller, famous for his lavish, delicious meals.

Dinner was served at 11:30 p.m. Nothing was overlooked in providing for the wants and needs of the visiting diners. Major A. V. Bohn, serving as toastmaster, was seated at the head of the first table. To his right was Halsey M. Rhoads, secretary of the Colorado State Editorial Association and on his left, C. S. Sprague, newly elected president of the Association. Major Bohn delivered a short speech, in which he welcomed the visiting editors. Will J. Orange, *Silver Cliff Rustler*; Tom Howell, *Cripple Creek Times*; C. E. McSheehy of the *Denver World* and Charles S. Sprague, *Colorado Springs Telegraph*, were toasted as their names were called. Brief messages were delivered by Mayor Nicholson and Dr. Dougan. George P. Brown recited Gene Field's poem, "Casey's Table d' Hote." Mr. Sprague proposed a toast to the memory of Poet Field, which was downed in silence. At 1:30 a.m. the partygoers adjourned to have drinks in the Leadville Press Club rooms, followed by an early morning ride on the toboggans.

"I have been treated better in Leadville than anywhere else," were the parting words of Governor McIntire. "The Crystal Palace is a rare gem . . . unless they (the state's residents) embrace the opportunity of seeing this magnificent structure, they will be sorry for it." He reiterated his praise of the Leadville people and their ice palace, promising to return before the carnival was over. The governor's party boarded the Denver and Rio Grande in the wee hours of the morning to return to Denver.

A newspaperman from Colorado Springs, speaking of the ice palace, reportedly remarked, "To be perfectly frank with you, I had an idea that the ice palace was what we would term a fake. To say that I am agreeably disappointed would not express my sentiments. I am simply astounded. The magnitude of the undertaking is almost awe-inspiring. I shall return home, but you'll see me back again, and with as big a crowd from our town as can crowd the trains."

Inducted to the Colorado Press Association on January 15, 1896 were:

Bishop, A. D., *Pythian*, Denver
Bunting, I. W, *Daily Sentinel*, Grand Junction
Calhoun, W. C., *Rocky Mountain Herald*, Denver
Campbell, R. C., *News*, Denver
Daniels, George, *Illustrated Weekly*, Denver
Davis, Madeleine Nell, *Herald Democrat*, Leadville
Gray, Frank M., *Evening Call*, Pueblo
Gigliotti, Nicola, *Roma*, Denver
Hitchcock, F. C., *Herald*, Durango
Lacey, A. H., *Tribune*, Westcliffe
Lee, Howard T., *Daily Sentinel*, Grand Junction
Mathews, W. J., Colorado Springs
Mingay, H. M., *Clipper*, Canon City
Stewart, J. O., *Evening News*, Colorado Springs
Swisher, J. W., *Summit County Journal*, Breckenridge
White, Frank I., *Rocky Mountain Editor*, Denver
Williams, George Wallace, *Herald Democrat*, Leadville
Wyncoop, W. C., *Mining Industry*, Denver

Colorado Press Association officers elected were:

President: Charles S. Sprague, *Telegraph*, Colorado Springs
First Vice President: C. E. McSheehy, *World*, Denver

Second Vice President: Miss Madeleine N. Davis,
 Herald Democrat.
Secretary: Halsey M. Rhoads, *Rocky Mountain Herald*,
 Denver.
Treasurer: R. H. Tilney, Cripple Creek.
Executive Committee: K. G. Cooper, *Republican*, Denver;
 W. J. Orange, *Rustler*, Silver Cliff; and Dr. M. Beshoar,
 Advertiser, Trinidad.

The Hockey Club Championship teams were:

Military Athletic Association:
C. H. MacNutt, Captain

Robinson, Arthur   Stevens, Eugene
Glaser, Richard   Bloss, D.
Jones, William   Harvey, Alex

Tomkins-LaSalle Invincibles:
David LaSalle, Captain

Riggs, Willard   Colman, Samuel
Cummings, Richard   Houghton, Douglass
Baisinger, Oram   Lumsden, Arthur

A HORSESHOW IN THE ICE PALACE

● ● ●

A Unique Attraction!

● ● ●

Sunday, January 19

★ ★ ★ Two Performances ★ ★ ★

2:30 Matinee   Evening at 8:30

● ● ●

THE BEST IN THE WORLD
The D. M. BRISTOL
Equescurriculum!

The Finest School of Educated Horses
Known to Exhibitors

Horses That Can Solve Questions in Arithmetic
Add, Subtract, Multiply and Divide!

No Advance in Prices
ADMISSION, 50 Cts.

These were the headlines that heralded the spectacular
Bristol Horse Show.

Parents were urged to bring their children to experience the intelligence of the beautiful beasts of burden. "Only a monster would dare strike one of the lovely animals!" reported the *Herald Democrat*.

The show was advertised as the most astonishing and wonderful exhibition, and the only one of superior excellence in the world. The entire troupe of horses, thirty in all, were without harness or bridle. They entertained the fascinated crowd for two and one-half hours and the massive animals performed the grand march with an indescribable beauty, grace and precision.

Prior to the horses appearing at the ice palace, the horse show played at the Weston Opera House for three nights and a Saturday matinee, which began on Thursday, January 16th. Seats for the evening shows were priced at $.50 and $.75. The matinee seats were $.35 and $.50; children were admitted to the matinee for $.25. Reserved seats were available for all of the shows at the Weston.

ASPENITES INVADE THE CITY

Several Hundred of Her Good Citizens
Visited the Palace and
Made Merry With Us

BROUGHT THE BAND WITH THEM

The Gates of the Carnival Swing Wide Open
Some Fancy Skaters Came Over
Overwhelmed With Delight

Aspen Day
January 21, 1896

These bold headlines in the *Leadville Herald Democrat* announced Aspen's Day at the ice palace. Among the promoters of Aspen Day were prominent mining engineer, Dr. D. W. Brunton and wife; S. L. Malaby and James L. Riland. Two trains brought the visitors to Leadville, with the Denver & Rio Grande train the first to arrive. The entourage, headed up by the 18-member Knights of Pythias Band, marched to the Colorado Midland depot. From there the late arrivals were escorted to town. It was estimated that the combined forces numbered close to 500. The Aspenites were escorted to the Vendome Hotel by Mayor S. D. Nicholson, W. R. Harp, Harry True, Dr. Bradford S. Galloway and others.

The paraders carried banners bearing mottos that evoked laughter and cheers from the spectators. "We Broke Bread

243

With You in '79," and, "Here You Are! The Leadville
Chronicle All About the Shipwreck on Mosquito Pass."
Upon arrival at the Vendome Hotel, the parade disbanded,
and the visitors went inside to register.

After lunch the revelers formed another parade led by
the stirring music of the Knights of Pythias and Fort Dodge
Cowboy Bands, and climbed the hill to the ice palace.

The beauty and majesty of the ice palace, and the view
of the city and mountains from the top of Capitol Hill,
visibly affected many of the excursionists.

Some of the afternoon visitors took advantage of the
skating rink. Many of the old timers tried on the "newfan-
gled" skates, but grumped for the good old standbys.

The evening brought the partyers back to the palace for
a hockey match. Captain Harp tried to encourage the
Aspenites to get a hockey team together for a match, but
was unsuccessful in his attempt. The match ended up being
between the two Leadville teams. Some of the visiting male
spectators railed against the new rules. They were happier
when the game was a skull-crushing, shin-smashing battle
they fought as youngsters.

Facing off in the competition were:

Military Athletics	Harp's Team
C. H. MacNutt, Capt.	A. V. Bohn,
Capt. Robinson, A.	Coleman, S.
Jones, Warren	Harp, W. R.
Bloss, Alva	Hall, Gus
Harvey, Alex	Dickerman, Ezra
Glaser, R.	Niblock, W.

The game was evenly matched and exciting while it lasted. It was finally called on a 1-1 tie.

After the match the skating rink was opened to the public and among the skating Aspenites, John Forbes caught the attention of many viewers. Forbes was a champion one-miler and a state-renowned figure skater.

Charles O. Johnson captured the limelight that evening with his figure skating and skate dancing. A veteran skater and teacher, he was scheduled to come back to Leadville in February to give a figure skating exhibition.

The Aspen Uniformed Rank of Knights of Pythias Band received glowing compliments and accolades for their musical performance. All of the band members belonged to the K. of P. and were so talented that they were booked to play at the Grand Lodge Session in June in Salt Lake City; the Supreme Lodge Session in Minneapolis in August; and the Grand Lodge Session in Durango during September.

Among the visitors to Leadville for Aspen Day were: J. W. Chatfield, Jacob Sands, J. D. Bransford, and C. H. Allen.

PROMOTING THE ICE PALACE
A Whirlwind Tour

To promote Leadville's Ice Palace, members of two of the carnival clubs took to the rails. On the night of January 22nd members of the Snowshoe and Toboggan clubs left the city to spread the word and advertise Miners Exchange Day and Wheelmen's Day.

Harvey D. Leonard of the American National Bank coordinated the excursion, and accommodations were provided for thirty-five members of the Snowshoe Club and fifteen Toboggan Club members.

Director General Tingley S. Wood had successfully negotiated with the railroads to provide free transportation for the clubs. Anyone who accepted a free ride had to be attired in carnival costume or uniform, and participate in all of the parades. A number of wheelmen rode their bicycles, decorated in carnival colors, in the processions.

Ten thousand brochures listing the itinerary were printed and distributed along the parade routes in the various cities and towns.

The entourage left Leadville at 10:05 p.m. on the Colorado Midland, arriving in Colorado Springs at 4:10 a.m. on Thursday. They breakfasted at the Antlers Hotel at 7:15 a.m., then lined up to parade from the hotel at 8:00 a.m.

Their itinerary took them from Colorado Springs on the Denver & Rio Grande at 9:43 a.m., arriving in Denver at 12:20 p.m. They paraded from Union Depot to the Albany Hotel for lunch and promotional work. At 5:00 p.m. the revelers left the Albany and paraded to the Brown Palace Hotel for dinner at 6:30 p.m. Following dinner, they paraded the streets with fireworks and torches. Later that evening they attended the 8:30 performance of "The Widow Jones," starring May Irwin.

247

At 11:30 p.m. they departed the city on the Colorado Midland, reaching Victor at 7:05 a.m. on Friday. They had breakfast at the Victor Hotel, then formed a parade through the streets, heralding the beauty of the ice palace and the special days scheduled.

The snowshoers and tobogganers left Victor at 11:15 a.m., arriving in Cripple Creek at 12:15 p.m. They paraded from the depot to the Palace Hotel for lunch at 1:00 p.m. At 2:00 p.m. they left the hotel to tour the mines until 6:00 p.m. A night parade was held that evening at 7:30 p.m, featuring fireworks.

The bedraggled crew left Cripple Creek at 9:20 p.m via the Florence and Cripple Creek, and then on to Leadville via the Denver & Rio Grande, arriving in Leadville at 6:00 a.m. Saturday morning.

Their grueling trip proved to be successful—wheelmen and miners came to Leadville by the hundreds.

BULLS AND BEARS STORM THE PALACE

Two Million Shares of Stock Transferred
At The Big Call At The
Night Session

BIG BLOCKS CHANGE HANDS

Nearly A Thousand People From Mountain
And Plain Enjoy A Rare
And Unrivaled Pleasure

**Stock Exchange Day
January 25, 1896**

On December 21, 1895, a telegram was sent to General Agent Anthony Sneve in Leadville which stated:

> During the excursion to Cripple Creek at the time of opening Midland broad gauge facilities into that city, it was unanimously resolved by the seven mining exchanges represented to accept the kind invitation of the Director General of the Ice Palace Carnival, extended through Mr. W. F. Bailey, to meet within the walls of the Ice Palace on the last Saturday in January and hold a joint call of Colorado stocks.

The Leadville Mining Exchange was organized on January 9th, with offices at 613 Harrison Avenue; just in time for Colorado's Stock Exchange Day at the ice palace. There were

249

50 seats on the exchange, and each sold for $10. The membership of seventy-five was shortly increased to one hundred, and the membership fee was increased to $25. A hundred applications were received for the twenty-five newly created memberships.

Charles H. Brown was appointed official caller for the exchange, with their first call to be held at the Leadville Ice Palace on January 15th. There were sufficient stocks ready to be listed and more were to be secured.

Brown, James Glynn and R. R. Ripley were appointed committeemen to prepare and had a pamphlet printed containing information about Leadville, its mining district, the Mining Exchange, and other pertinent facts. Five thousand pamphlets were circulated throughout the country to all stock exchanges, boards of trade and commercial bodies in all of the cities.

The Leadville members hosted, what they hoped to be, the biggest event of the carnival season. They combined business with pleasure, with business being secondary. Mr. Brown was appointed chairman of the committee in charge of arrangements for Stock Exchange Day. The reception committee included: Maurice Starne, T. S. Wood, W. R. Harp, T. C. Wood, Sam Brown, W. B. Sherick, Harvey Brown, James Nelson, George L'Abbe, R. R. Ripley, L. C. Rucker, J. H. Snell, C. H. MacNutt and other members of the Exchange.

Six hundred rooms had been secured for the out-of-town guests. Between eight hundred and a thousand visitors flocked into Leadville for this special event. Approximately two hundred of them were stock brokers, who came to town for this special call. Large delegations came from Denver, Cripple Creek, Victor and Colorado Springs and brokers from throughout Colorado traveled to Leadville to participate.

250

The morning dawned bright and crisp over the snowy peaks of Leadville, and brokers, some with their families, arrived in the city on the early trains. The excited visitors then left the depots and headed for the ice palace which for the first time, opened to the public before 1:30 p.m.

The Fort Dodge Cowboy Band paraded around the outside of the massive castle, followed by the visitors, who were in awe of the beauty and size of the magnificent ice structure. After the parade ended, the crowd poured into the ice palace.

A giant blackboard had been mounted and covered one wall of east ballroom. A private telegraph line had been installed, and quotations were received over it. Stock trading and bone fide sales were conducted within the walls of the Crystal Castle, and a total of 235 stocks amounting to more than two million shares changed hands that day.

The first call was scheduled for 10:30 a.m. The east room was crowded with the gathering of bulls, bears and lambs.

Director General Wood climbed to the podium, greeted by a rousing burst of applause, his address was brief and informal. He welcomed the brokers to Leadville, and the ice palace. The Director General urged the bulls and bears to "bury the lambs with as much decency as possible." Colonel Brown of Cripple Creek, in his short speech, called Leadville the pride of Colorado. W. B. Root, president of the Denver Stock Exchange, commented on the outstanding business records of the many exchanges. Major Gowdy of Colorado Springs, Milton Irwin of Cripple Creek and Colonel John Curley offered their commentaries.

Then the calls began. Harry Bannigan, of Bannigan & Riley of Denver, took the floor to call for the first fifteen minutes, followed by J. M. Schrote of Cripple Creek, Berger of Colorado Springs and Howell of the Consolidated Exchange of Cripple Creek.

Sales were slow and trading was very light. The brokers seemed to be more interested in their surroundings than the business at hand. The result of the morning transactions was as follows:

STOCK	PRICE	SHARES
Atlas	$.09½	1,000
Argentum J	.59	1,000
Banker	.19⅝	1,000
Bob Lee	.02⅝	2,000
B & M.H.*	10.00	5,000
Cripple Creek Con	.21	200
Copper-Gold Mountain	.02½	1,000
Cripple Creek & Chicago	.03¾	7,000
Eagle Bold	.02	3,000
Gold Bar	4.75	10,000
Hamilton	.03½	1,000
Ontario	10.00	1,000
Orphan Bell	.03	10,000
President	14.50	7,000

*Price per 1,000 shares.

The afternoon was sunny, with a temperature of 35° and the Avenue was bustling with locals and visitors. The restaurant and saloon employees were hustling to fill the needs of the thirsty and hungry customers (most, more thirsty than hungry). The liverymen and expressmen did a lively business, taxiing sightseers to Capitol Hill.

The second call of the day was held at the Leadville Exchange on Harrison Avenue. This was the also the first call held in the newly founded Leadville Stock Exchange quarters. The sales increased from transactions at the ice palace morning trade. The traders crowded into the small space behind the railing. The call began at 3:00 p.m. and lasted half an hour. The curious onlookers, both ladies and gentlemen, were unaccustomed to seeing the brokers in action and thought them to be a bunch of raving maniacs. The spectators found it hard to believe that business was actually being transacted. There were 275,000 shares of stock sold at the call; perhaps a preface to the call which would take place later that evening back at the ice palace.

The third, and last, call began in the east ballroom at 8:00 p.m. Crack callers from around the state were put into service: Mr. Riley, caller for the Gettysburg and Charles R. Burger, president of Gettysburg in Denver; J. L. Howell of Cripple Creek and J. M. Shrote of the Victor Exchange. Anxious buyers and sellers tossed shares around in hundred, thousand, and hundred-thousand blocks. Furious trading abounded as the shares changed hands.

One of the largest traders was C. R. Burgermeyer, representing the G. Morgan Brokerage Company of Colorado Springs. "Burgey" acquired 125,000 shares of C. C. Southern. William Dean of Victor bought and sold 100,000 shares. He grabbed up President, Chicago and

Cripple Creek stocks. John R. Curley exchanged 123,000 shares. Clemens, a broker from Cripple Creek, acquired 70,000 shares of President and Aurum. George B. Bartholomew transacted for 150,000 shares. Tom Morris of Victor, Ed Brown of Cripple Creek, N. Leipheimer and Ed Arkell of Colorado Springs, were successful with their bids and sales. Newcomers, Charley Brown and Ed Little of Leadville, plunged in to dump or acquire blocks of stock as well. Chairman A. V. Hunter announced a new stock was being offered. In honor of the ice palace, the Leadville and Cripple Creek Ice Palace Gold and Mining Stock was listed on the board and Mr. Andrews, who implemented the idea for the stock, started off with a $100 bid.

Neither the bears nor the bulls prevailed. Bankers' and Bob Lee stock went up a little, Aetna appeared to be a favorite, Gold and Globe was sought after and went in a hurry. Blocks of C. C. & M and Anchorage changed hands. This was one of the liveliest calls in the history of the mining exchanges in Colorado, and a record breaker. More than two million shares were exchanged.

The following was the record of the evening's calls:

STOCK	PRICE	SHARES
C. C. & Chicago	$ .06¾	10,000
Vallejo	.07¼	5,000
Aurum	15.00	11,000
Gold Bar	4.50	3,000
Big Bull	.02⅝	125,000
President	.16	10,000
Blackhawk	.08½	45,000
C. C. & Chicago	.06⅞	75,000

Record of the evening's calls, continued:

STOCK	PRICE	SHARES
Defender	.01⅝	10,000
New Year	18.00	30,000
Gold Reserve	.20	30,000
Congress*	10.00	15,000
Alex Pectoris	3.00	1,000
Aurum*	15.00	50,000
C. C. & Chicago	.08⅞	30,000
Vallejo	.07	5,000
Congress*	10.00	30,000
Silver Leaf*	17.00	20,000
Merry Gold*	10.00	10,000
Blackhawk	.07½	25,000
First National	.05	83,000
President	.16	20,000
Senate*	10.00	20,000
Modock*	8.50	10,000
West Aspen*	4.50	40,000
Gold Bar*	4.00	25,000
C. C. Con	.21	10,000
Gould	.16½	8,000
Aetna	.02¼	3,000
Gold & Globe	.22	15,000
C. C. & M	.07¾	18,000
Union	.40	20,000
Alamo	.08¾	33,000
T.F.T.	.03⅞	16,000
Aetna	.02⅞	50,000
Anders	.01⅞	20,000

Record of the evening's calls, continued:

STOCK	PRICE	SHARES
Scranton	.01⅝	32,000
Portland	1.90	2,300
Anchoria L.	2.85	2,000
Marion Gold	.01⅝	30,000
Sacramento	.08¾	6,000
Brother Jno	.04	25,000
Big Six	.08	10,000
Jack Pot	.12¾	18,000
Doctor*	5.50	28,000
Bob Lee	.02⅞	19,000
Buckhorn	.07¼	8,000
Fanny Rawlins**	.09⅛	6,000
Pharmacist	.16⅝	22,000
Apache	.01¼	100,000
Ben Hur	.09¼	9,000
Arapahoe	.03⅛	50,000
Addie E.	.01	48,000
*Kangaroo	3.50	16,000
Monarch	.06⅞	14,000
C. C. Southern	.01	125,000
Colorado C&M	.07⅞	20,000
Jack Pot	.12½	18,000

*Price per 1,000 shares.

**A Leadville favorite

BIKERS WHEEL INTO THE ICE PALACE

Wheelmen of the State Will Have
A Big Day January 25

Wheelmen's Day
January 25, 1896

On January 22nd, members of the Leadville Bicycle Club, dressed in carnival costumes, traveled statewide to advertise Wheelmen's Day, at the ice palace. Director General Wood successfully arranged free transportation for members of the Snowshoe and Toboggan Clubs to promote the ice palace and winter carnival. They visited Denver, Colorado Springs, Pueblo and other Colorado cities and towns. The wheelers took their bicycles with them so they could parade the streets, and whoop it up for Leadville's Winter Carnival.

Invitations had been sent to all of the bicycle clubs in the state, urging the members to attend the carnival. Personal invitations were mailed to the League of American Wheelmen[31] board.

The L.A.W. was honored on January 25th. Harvey D. Leonard, president of the Leadville Bicycle Club, was in charge of program arrangements and clubs from all over

---

[31]The League of American Wheelmen is still active in the United States today, with national headquarters in Baltimore, Maryland.

257

Colorado were in Leadville that day. George L. McCarthy, chief consul of the Colorado Division of L.A.W., and P. J. Aldrich, chairman of the press committee were among those who arrived for the celebration. Other members came too, but because they were not in uniform the local committee was unable to identify them. The Wheelmen were urged to visit the club room at the new Armory Hall to introduce themselves, and register. Members of the local club were available to provide information and assistance.

On Saturday evening, nearly a thousand revelers marched up Harrison Avenue in this special parade. Five hundred members of the local and visiting bicycle clubs carried torches. Many of the honorees were dressed in costumes or uniforms; the carnival clubs took part as well and a fireworks display was provided, courtesy of Director General Wood.

In honor of their visit to the ice palace, bicycles decorated in carnival colors were displayed over one of the archways above the ice rink and the letters "L.A.W." hung suspended from the cantilever.

A bicycle track was built around the ice rink for the cycling sports that took place. Bicycles on snowshoes were featured, as well as others that ranged from comical, to weird, or grotesque to the extreme. The ballroom and skating rink were available for the enjoyment of the visitors. On Sunday morning the ice palace was opened so the Wheelmen's executive board could meet.

All railroads offered a special round trip rate of $5 to the Wheelmen from Friday through Monday. The Denver and Colorado Springs delegations took advantage of this opportunity and a number of them came in on Friday, affording them a long weekend in Leadville.

The Wheelmen shared the honors that Saturday with the Colorado stockbrokers.

Prior to Stock Exchange Day and Wheelmen's Day, Alderman C. C. Joy proposed a motion at the city council meeting on January 21st, which was passed; and the street supervisor was instructed to nail slats on the sidewalk on West Seventh Street to prevent people from falling as they trekked to or from the ice palace.

HORSE SHOW

—IN THE—

Ice Palace.

✳✳✳✳✳✳✳✳✳

Most Unique Attraction Ever Presented!

TO

D

Headlines from The Herald Democrat, February 19, 1896.

OTHER SPECIAL DAYS AT THE ICE PALACE
Contests/Awards

Director General Wood planned a series of fete (recognition) days during the carnival season. Special events were held for the cities and towns throughout Colorado, ethnic groups, fraternal organizations and societies, schools and businesses. The Director's purpose was not only to give recognition to the visiting guests, but to regulate and increase the attendance as well. The observances would alleviate overcrowding of the palace and the city, and he emphasized the importance of being able to provide ample food and lodging for the visitors; to ensure the carnival guests were properly entertained.

Ballroom dance competitions; free style, dance and other skating contests and races; a State Championship Speed contest; World Championship Rock-Drilling competitions; a potato race, and a greased-pig contest were featured events. Prizes were awarded for floats, costumes and impersonators. A $10,000 prize was offered to the group, organization, city or town having the largest attendance in a day.

On the days there were no special events featured, the visitors to the ice palace enjoyed skating, dancing, and concerts and a variety of other entertaining programs.

The Director General's plan entailed having local lodges take charge of events on the day their lodge would be honored. The Association allowed them a small percentage of the receipts for expense money to arrange entertainment for the visiting members and any profits they made benefitted the local lodges. Large numbers of club members visited the ice palace during Leadville's winter carnival.

261

The Odd Fellows Lodge was the first to take advantage of the offer. Odd Fellow Lodge members from around the state came to Leadville to be honored on that occasion and enjoyed a day at the ice palace. (There were five Odd Fellows Lodges in Leadville during that time.)

January 14th was another of the non-event days. The skating rink was in topnotch condition and an exciting musical program was provided by the famous Fort Dodge Cowboy Band. The concert hall was full of spectators at both performances with the afternoon concert beginning at 2 o'clock and the evening performance at 8 o'clock.

♪ **AFTERNOON** ♪

March	— *"Semper Fidelis"*	*Sousa*
Selection	— *"Gaiety Girls"*	*Jones*
Overture	— *"Barber of Seville"*	*Rossini*
Chileandanaces	— *"Manana"*	*Missaud*
Selection	— *"Ione"*	*Verdi*
Potpourri	— *"Musical Tour Through Europe"* . .	*Couradi*

♪ **EVENING** ♪

Caprice Heroique	— *"Awakening of the Lion"*	*Koutski*
Polonaise	— *"Concert"*	*Von Clarens*
Overture	— *"Semiramide"*	*Rossini*
Song and Dance	— *"Kentucky Jubilee"*	*Beebe*
Grand Fantasia	— *"Bohemian Girl"*	*Balfe*
Grand Galop	— *"Militaire"*	*Schomberg*

The Colorado Education Association was given recognition at the winter carnival on January 16th.

A five-mile skating competition took place on January 18th. A $25 first prize was offered, and the second place winner received a pass to the ice palace for the remainder of the carnival season. Entrants were: Matt Stiffler, Willard Riggs, Otis Richmond, Sandy Cosseboom and George Venable.

The figure skating competition that had been postponed on Press Day was on the evening's program.

A two-mile skating competition entertained visitors on January 21st. Contestants were Otis Richmond, George S. Blatt, and Harry Newcomb. The first prize winner was awarded $75, the second place award $25. Tingley C. Wood was assisted by Kenneth Fahnenstock, Charles H. MacNutt, W. T. Perkins, George L'Abbe and Mr. Martin as judges, scorers and timekeepers.

The fancy skating contest entrants were: Otis Richmond, Alex Harvey, and Merritt P. Walley. The gentlemen executed their programs with varying degrees of success. Some of the exercises were described as, "real feats of skatesmanship." Richmond appeared better trained and more at ease than his competitors, although Walley's turns were gracefully executed. Alex Harvey was not at his best; he was experiencing difficulty executing the figures. The contestants were required to do a full program with no intermission, which proved to be too much for Harvey's weak ankles. The first place award went to Otis Richmond.

Local gamblers and some members of the Leadville Mining Exchange offered a $100 purse to the winner of a race between Matt Stiffler and Willard Riggs.

During the winter carnival contests and prizes were awarded almost every day. Following are examples of some of the contest categories, and the prizes that were awarded for them.

Best lady fancy skater, first place, a $7.50 opera hat, Hanley & Kringen.

Second place, a celluloid glove box. G. A. Eldredge & Co.

Best fancy dress made from newspapers, $60 gold medal.

Best lady's costume of carnival colors, season ticket.

Best gentleman fancy skater, first prize, a box of cigars, Harvey T. Brown; second place, one-half dozen handkerchiefs, Beggs Dry Goods Company.

Best gentleman's costume of carnival colors, carnival season ticket.

Best boy fancy skater, first prize, a pair of skates, Beman, Dickinson & Co.

Lady in best fancy costume, first prize, a $15 hat, Miss M. J. Frantz.

Best German maid (one award), Barny & Berry skates, Leadville Hardware Company.

Best Irish biddy (one award), a pair of $5 skates, Tomkins-LaSalle Hardware Company.

Best costume representing the *News Reporter*, dress pattern, Chicago Bazaar.

Best costume representing the *Herald Democrat*, dress pattern, J. W. Smith.

Best impersonation of President Grover Cleveland, a fishing pole, compliments of C. H. S. Whipple.

Best clown (one award) a hat, by Famous.

Best Trilby (one award) elegant belt, W. B. Felker.

Best French maid — pair of skates, Beman, Dickinson & Company.

Prize — Winner Fat Man's race — sweater. (No competitors)

Best typical miner, 100-pound sack of flour, E. J. Van Camp and a $10 gold piece.

Best tramp, 100-pound sack of flour, J. W. Hall.

There were many contest categories planned, however, some did not have prizes awarded. Whether there were no contestants, or the winners were unreported can only be assumed.

On Thursday evening, January 23rd, an Old Men's race was scheduled at the palace. George Lancaster and Mr. Follett were among the oldies who could still whiz around the ice. A Fat Men's race was on tap for the evening's program.

January 25th was special recognition day of the Caledonians, a Scots society. That day was poet Robert Burns' birthday and it was fitting that the poet and the Scotsmen should be honored. Between forty and fifty members in full dress uniforms marched to the ice palace. A concert was provided, featuring renowned piper Colin Allen who was reputed to be the best Scottish piper in Colorado. Allen spent the entire winter in Leadville.

A masquerade ball, costume competition and skating contests were scheduled for the evening of January 29th. It was ruled that costumes worn at the Press Day carnival were ineligible to compete, and if you came without a costume . . . no admittance to the skating rink or ballroom.

Sunday, February 2nd, the World Christian Endeavor Society observed the fifteenth anniversary of their founding. The day was observed at the Leadville Ice Palace on February 1st, and members poured into Leadville. The first annual convention of the Young Peoples Society for

265

Christian Endeavor of the Northwestern District of Colorado was held in the Cloud City, and Saturday afternoon and evening were spent visiting the ice palace. On Sunday, the Endeavorers held a rally in palace's multi-purpose room. Nationally renowned speakers were in the city for the landmark event.

The Commercial Travelers (traveling salesmen) prepared to paint the ice palace a blazing red on Monday, February 3rd, "and they were the men who knew how to do it."

There was a lull in the frenzied winter carnival schedule on February 7th. The crowd was on its own. A concert in the east pavilion was provided for the entertainment of the palace visitors and Professor Howell's orchestra played. David E. Fisher, a violin teacher at the Denver Conservatory of Music, captivated the audience with a violin solo by Handel.

The ice palace was turned over to the children from the public schools on February 8th. More than a thousand children invaded the ice castle for a day of fun. In a little over two hours, the youngsters on the ice rink had ground up enough ice to cover their shoetops. There was no music provided, or needed. The delightful shrieks and laughter of the children would have drowned any music the orchestra attempted, no matter how loudly they would have played. The teachers were there to chaperon the energetic youngsters, wipe away the tears, and tend the scrapes and scratches. George D. Greenfield, Secretary of the Board of Education, called, "Daddy Greenfield" by the children, was an observer. Charles Limberg, John Nowland and John Milner were among members of the Crystal Carnival Association in attendance. This outing almost equaled

266

Sunday School Day, when approximately 1,200 protestant and parochial school youngsters, "owned the ice palace."

On February 16th, in addition to having an open day at the ice palace, at 8:30 p.m. the visitors were entertained with a special evening concert. The Leadville Drum Corps performed a stirring exhibition on the skating rink.

The Colored People were honored on February 24th. They were recognized and admired for their tenacity and ability to, "live, thrive and prosper at an altitude that tries the endurance of the white man." Colored Troops presented an exciting exhibition for the visitors.

On March 8th there was no public special event or recognition day at the ice palace. The entertainment that evening was provided by Mr. J. Williams Macy and Company and attracted a number of visitors who enjoyed an evening of musical and literary diversion.

Souvenir Postcard   Colorado Historical Society

GERMANS TAKE THE CASTLE

A Grand Pageant of Magnificent Proportions
Inaugurates the Most Successful Feat Day
of the Winter Carnival

Turn Vereins[32] day
February 9, 1896

A special invitation from the city fathers was sent to Salt Lake City. Mayor James Glendenning was recipient of correspondence extolling the grand pageant that would be the finest of the carnival season and the letter invited citizens from that city to Leadville's German Day. Leadville was expected to host the biggest outside attendance since the ice palace opened. Visitors from throughout Colorado and surrounding states poured into the city.

The morning was cold as the town awoke to a temperature of 11°. By parade time the sun was shining, but the air was cold and the temperature hovered around 33°. The parade was certainly the longest one of the carnival season. When the head of the procession reached the ice palace entrance, the rear guard had not yet left Turner Hall at 206-208 East Third Street. It was so long that when the head of the parade reached the ice palace, the rest of the

---

[32]Turner — one who engages in gymnastics; a gymnast, tumbler. verein — German for an association, union. Thus Turn Verein, a German gymnasts association.

269

parade came to a halt on the corner of West Eighth Street on the Avenue and extended all the way down Leadville's main thoroughfare to Third Street and around the corner. The parade, in order, consisted of:

A police battalion
City and County Officials
Ice Palace Band
Leadville Snowshoe Club
Cloud City Skating Club
All Carnival Costumed citizens
B.P.O. Elks
Ancient Order of Hibernians
Caledonian Club
Silver Camp No. 12, Woodmen of the World
Junior Order of American Mechanics
Miners Union
Drum Corps.
Court Star, Foresters of America
Court Skandia, Foresters of America
Patriotic Sons of America
Leadville Lodge de Harugari, No. 591
Denver Turn Verein
Vorwaerts Turn Verein, Denver
Central City Turn Verein
Schwaben Verein, Denver
Harmonia Gesang Verein, Pueblo
Float, Girls' Class Turn Verein, Leadville
Boys' Class Turn Verein, Leadville
Leadville Turn Verein
Floats
Fire Department
Citizens in Vehicles

The German Day parade also featured five mounted cavaliers, dressed in rich old German costumes, escorting a lady in a carriage.

The prize-winning Leadville float that had been entered in the Festival of Mountain and Plain in Denver in '95 was placed on exhibit at the ice palace for the visitors viewing.

Upon arrival at the ice palace, Mayor Nicholson welcomed the Turn Vereins to Leadville on behalf of the city. Phillip Kleinschmidt, in charge of the key to the city, turned the key over to the Marshal of the Day. The key was huge; approximately five feet in length and weighed just under a ton. Marshal of the Day, Tony Heichemer, accepted the key on behalf of the German honorees.

An outstanding program had been arranged by the Leadville Turn Verein for the visitors' entertainment and Mayor Nicholson paid high compliments to the German citizens for the amount of work that went into the program's preparation.

The citizens were not only entertained, but came away with a deeper appreciation of the physical accomplishments and capabilities of the superb athletes.

The proficient gymnasts who were in Leadville turned the ice palace rink into a winter circus and trapeze artists electrified the spectators with their performances.

A portable stage had been built for events such as this. The gymnastic equipment was placed on the elevated platform, providing the spectators a good view of their performances. The platform could be removed from the ice rink very quickly when not in use.

The afternoon was filled with exhibitions by the East Denver, West Denver, and Leadville Turn Vereins. The Denver clubs proved to be expert gymnasts, equal to the best, and their prowess on the parallel bars and in pyramid exhibitions was unexcelled.

The first demonstration was given by the Leadville boys' team captained by John Lindsay. Their execution of exercises with the Indian clubs brought cheers and applause from the audience. The team uniforms were white sweaters, with gray breeches and red belts.

Next came the Leadville seventeen-member girls team. The graceful movements in executing their calisthenics program drew raves from the crowd, and the fancy step drill was applauded. The team was captained by Rupel Vonderfehr. She was described as having remarkable muscular strength and ability, and her dexterity in handling the Indian clubs and ability to maneuver the clubs without any noticeable body movement brought the house down. The team's mascot was Coach A. E. Schmidt's little three year old daughter, Alma, whose antics filled the rink with laughter.

A special performance, and a rare treat, was given by Professor Otto Wendleburg's Ladies Indian Club Team. The team was part of the East Denver Turn Verein and their skill and dexterity left no doubt they were experts. The elite, award winning class included: Kate Schaefer, Lena Wagner, Lizzie Beckert, Rose Mahlinger, Mary Mahlinger, May Mahlinger and Minnie West.

The Denver East Side men's team captured the crowd's attention with their pyramid performances. Their cat-like movements captivated the audience.

Denver's West Side Turn Verein team was represented by some of the top athletes in the country. Charles Seitz, the team's captain, executed his program with skill and grace that gave him recognition as a superior gymnast.

Alfred Graeber, a member of the Denver Fire Department, was outstanding on the parallel bars. He had set national records as an all-around gymnast, and was the recipient of a number of medals in national competitions. He had also been awarded a medal of honor, not as a gymnast, but as a result of saving a woman and three young girls in Kaskaskia, Illinois on August 4, 1893. The four ventured into a river beyond their depth and were caught in a whirlpool.

Other members of the West Side team were: Adolph Ott, Jr., Albert Josepeit, Gustav Winter, George Eyser, William Meuser, and William Rett. Professor Jacob Schmidt was their coach. This team captured first prize in a competition held in Kansas City in 1895.

The Leadville Turn Verein men's team, although not as well-trained as their Denver competitors, gave the Denverites a run for their money, and outperformed them in some of their pyramid exercises.

The Leadville team included: Captain Fred Rust, Fred Robinson, Fred Stockdorf, Anton Clemens, Harry McDonald, Robert Liestner, Victor Murdock, Gustav Schleffer, F. Fitzgerald, Herb Roechen, Tom O'Neil, Robert Ball, John O'Neil, Thomas Cahill, Max Hahnewald, Daniel Field and Edward Boyle. Their coach was Alvin Schmitt, reportedly one of the best gymnastics coaches in the western part of the country.

There were no prizes awarded for the exhibitions. The Denver West Side team did not want to compete with the East Side Turn Vereins, and both teams graciously declined "taking the medals from Leadville."

The musical program was recognized as a cultural experience. The competition drew a number of spectators

273

to the east ballroom. Members of the Mannerchor and Harmonic societies were entertaining as well as competitive. The groups provided a program filled with rousing selections of the German culture. Their presentations demonstrated to the ice palace audience, the dramatic power and musical range of the performers. The choirs sang their first song fairly well, but both groups failed to execute the intricacies of the second selection. The first prize, a silver cup, was awarded to the Leadville Mannerchor. The second prize was awarded to Pueblo's Harmonia Society. The choir's leader was presented with a handsome baton. Judges for the competition were Professor Carl Moritz, Denver; Professor Marx Schware of Pueblo and Professor John Volkert of Leadville.

The ice palace visitors enjoyed a concert presented by Professor James Ross, who directed the Ice Palace Band. The program featured:

March	— *German National*	*Boettger*
Overture	— *Gems of Germany*	*Kuhner*
Waltz	— *Wein Weth und Gesang*	*Strauss*
Selection	— *Der Freischutz*	*Weber*
Overture	— *Caliph of Bagdad*	*Beiedieu*
Fantasia	— *Atilla*	*Verdi*
Waltz	— *Tausend und Eine Nachlit*	*Strauss*
Galop	— *Silverus*	*Zimmerman*

After the musical awards and concert were over some of the spectators stayed in the ballroom to dance, while others strolled to the restaurant to enjoy refreshments provided by Caterer Miller.

During the evening a number of the out-of-town guests and others visited Turner Hall for liquid refreshment and a buffet. At 1:00 a.m. the next morning, Grand Marshal Heichemer gave the Key to the City to Prince Peter Freiderick, a representative of Zang's Brewery. The key was taken back to Denver to be stored in the archives of the Denver Turn Verein, as a souvenir of their visit to the Cloud City's ice palace.

> *Sing German song the whole day long,*
> *while we join the sweet refrain*
> *and all will say when you go away,*
> *Glueck auf! Auf wiedersehen!*

So sang the ice palace poet laureate, Frank Vaughn, as the citizens of Leadville bade goodbye to the visitors.

WOODMEN OF THE WORLD

It Is Zero Weather But The Air Is
Sultry With The Ice Palace
Excitement

WOODMEN'S ROYAL TURNOUT

Woodmen of the World/Red Men's Day
February 12, 1896

The Crystal Carnival was thrown open to the Woodmen of the World and the Red Men organizations on February 12th.

Prior to the visitors trip to Leadville, J. P. Wright and his committee of D. D. Escher, F. J. Ballinger and Joseph Belken, traveled to Pueblo and talked to one hundred fifteen members of Valley Camp #29, the largest in the state with W. H. Doherty as its commander, extending invitations to Leadville's Ice Palace. Shortly thereafter, Wright, L. Frank Brown, E. T. Boyd, D. D. Escher and William Earl traveled to Denver. They visited with three hundred twenty eight Woodmen members, promoting Leadville and its Winter Carnival. Five hundred souvenir badges were purchased and distributed to the lodges, statewide.

Only one member of the Denver Woodmens Lodge traveled to Leadville. When C. A. Whitcarver and his family arrived, it was such a surprise that George E.

Taylor presented him with a gold and silver medal. It was suggested that he be given a gold brick from the Carbonate National Bank. Director General Wood directed the Ice Palace Band to escort him and his family to the depot when they were ready to depart.

The parade committee was headed up by E. J. McCarty. Charles Grabert served as his chief of staff, assisted by John O'Rourke, George B. Harker and Joe McDonald.

At 7:00 p.m., the procession lined up. A foghorn caught the crowds' attention as did the children's kazoo band, made up of street urchins. The parade was led by Marshal of the Day, E. J. McCarty, followed by the police band, the mayor, and city and county officials. Then came the guests of honor, Woodmen of the World members, the James A. Garfield Post No. 8, Grand Army of the Republic, the Miners Union, Patriotic Sons of America, Navajo tribe, #9 Red Men, Junior Order of American Mechanics, eighty members of Lodges 5 & 40, the Scottish Order of Caledonians in colorful kilts (and bare legs), the Turn Verein, the Ancient Order of United Workmen. The Ladies of the Violet Grove (Woodmen of the World Auxiliary) rode in sleighs, followed by the carnival clubs, and last, but not least, the Leadville Drum Corps.

The Leadville Snowshoe Club fired Roman candles along the main thoroughfare sending them skyward over the building tops. The parade began at 7:45 p.m. and headed south on Harrison Avenue to Second Street then countermarched back up the Avenue to West 8th Street, then west up the hill to the Palace.

A fireworks display greeted the visitors as they reached the main entrance to the Crystal Castle. There were no special events at the skating rink that evening, but the visitors crowded the ice rink to skate or dance in the ballroom. Others strolled through the exhibit halls or enjoyed refreshments in the dining room.

The Ladies of Violet Grove hostessed an open house from 10:00 a.m. to 5:00 p.m.

"Idealized Love Heart," souvenir Leadville's Ice Palace.
Author's Collection

Silver candy dish, souvenir from Leadville's Ice Palace.
Author's Collection

SISTERS HOSPITAL CHARITY BENEFIT

AN EXCITING POTATO RACE

The Benefit Not A
Big One, But A Pleasant Time

A charity benefit and ball for Sisters Hospital was held at the ice palace on Monday evening, February 13th. All tickets were fifty cents, and no season passes were honored for this event. The new managers of the toboggan concession gave everyone who purchased a fifty-cent ticket a free ride on the toboggans, and would-be toboggan ticket sales proceeds went to the hospital charity.

The benefit did not fill the ice palace's halls to capacity, but the spectators were entertained by contestants who entered the ice skating competition for little boys, and a potato race. There were no prizes and the skaters had volunteered to participate.

The half-mile boys race started with six entries, but one of them dropped out on the first lap. The winners were Frank Hale, first; Arnet Goodsir, second, and Zan Shaeffer won third place.

The competitors for the potato contest were: Matt Stiffler, W. L. Temple, Harry Newcomb, Otis Richmond, Hugh Harney, (?) Fitzgerald and George Blatt. Six rows of potatoes were set on the ice near the north end of the skating rink, ten in a row, about a foot apart. Six skaters at the south end of the rink were to gather the potatoes, one at a time, carry them back to the north end of the rink, and place them in their assigned boxes. Ten trips were required and the first man to fill his box was declared the winner. Stiffler and Newcomb tied for first place. To break the tie, they competed in a race. Stiffler won.

A free style skating exhibition by Otis Richmond, Temple, Newcomb and Alex Harvey completed the evening's entertainment.

WHERE ARE THE CAMELS?
Shriners Day
February 14, 1896

The Shriners are coming St. Valentine's Day
with their camels and sand quite hot,
and with them their ladies, and band that will play
for the novices who gaily will trot.
O'er the sands of the desert, go wild and dreary,
with but one well in sight,
to reach this goal refreshes the weary,
and makes life's burdens bright.

— Author unknown

The Shriners came skating in on their camels on St. Valentine's Day, February 14th. It was predicted that February 15th would be a banner day at the ice palace since they were expected to be so fascinated by the beauty of the Crystal Castle and its many attractions, that they would remain overnight and attend the Elks Day festivities the next day. Thus, with the combined attendance of the two organizations, they would win the $10,000 prize for the largest attendance in one day.

Shriners from throughout Colorado, Wyoming, Kansas, and Texas traveled to Leadville for this special event. An invitation was extended to the mayor, aldermen and city officials of Salt Lake City by Leadville's city council and two special trains, carrying Shriners came in from Utah—four cars from Salt Lake City, three from Ogden, Park City and Fort Douglas. Special trains left Denver's Union Station on February 13th, at 11:00 p.m.

It was suggested that if you were married to take your wife and if not, heaven help you! — 1896 was Leap Year.

It was a great day in Leadville when the Shriners arrived. The caravan of merrymakers brought a carload of specially painted scenery, among which was a backdrop with Leadville's toboggan slide. It made the local tobogganers green with envy.

A crew of repairmen were called in to work on the chutes and the toboggan runs were put in tip-top shape so they would run smoothly for the Shriners. It was reported that there would not be much ice left on the runs once the Shriners got through.

A rollicking parade began the celebration. The uniforms worn by the fun-loving merrymakers were impressive and their full dress suits and red fez's, with gold stars and crescents, were a colorful sight as the hundreds marched up Harrison Avenue to the ice palace.

A Ceremonial Session was held at the ice palace that St. Valentine's Day. The special event was under the direct charge of the El Jebel Temple of Denver. The temple, at that time, was one of the largest and wealthiest in the country and had a membership of 750, of which Leadville proudly boasted 75 members. Officers of the Denver El Jebel Temple were: A. J. Vickroy, potentate; A. Vickers, recorder; D. A. Barton, director and Frederick C. Smutzer. Leadville's Dr. D. H. Dougan was named second official in charge, an honor conferred on him that day by the Order. Thirty members were installed on the grand occasion with Leadville being the second city in the state to have the honor of this impressive ritual.

A dance in the ballroom was just one of many activities planned for the visiting "Fez-heads."

The *Herald Democrat* reported, "The great fun makers, the Shriners, propose to leave all competition in the cold when it comes to turning their camels loose on skates, and burning the sheiks on an ice pile."

Souvenir medals were designed and worn by the Shriners in honor of the occasion. They sported souvenir medals in the shape of a burro with a scimitar in his pack. The burro also had a can of red paint tied around his neck, implying that the wearer of those medals intended to paint the town red. Another of the souvenir badges was a gold colored brass toboggan pin attached to a gold ribbon which stated, "The Mystic Shrine, El Jebel Temple, Caravan To The Crystal Carnival, FEB. 14th 1896." The ribbon was attached at the bottom to a clear square of glass resembling an ice block.

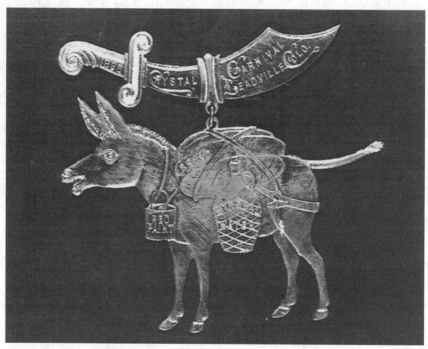

Shriner's Souvenir Badge *Author's Collection*

THE ELKS OWNED ALL

B.P.O.E. Stampede The Palace

THE PARADE WAS A STUNNER

Grand Masque Ball at the Palace Closes
a Day That Will Be Remembered
in the Carnival Annals

"Perhaps one of the biggest and most unique sensations of the carnival occurred on Elks Day, February 15th," reported the *Herald Democrat*.

Dennis Taylor of Aspen, came to Leadville a few days before to meet with officers of the Elks Club and arrange a program at the ice palace in conjunction with the special day. A *Herald Democrat* newspaper reporter wrote a flowery, tongue-in-cheek, article about Mr. Taylor "being a member of the Callithumpians[33], a Royal Benzonion of The Ancient Aristocrat and Only Genuine Order, founded in 972 1/2 B.C. in Zerabbabel Belicosaris of Tatterdmalionia, a city on the Ganges River."

The Leadville Elks Lodge went to great expense to bring Taylor's novel circus menagerie to Leadville.

---

[33]Shivaree — a noisy demonstration or celebration. Mock music with kettles, horns, bells, etc.

The parade was scheduled to start at 2:00 p.m., but because some unruly burros, jacks and jennies refused to line up, the parade was delayed until 2:45 that afternoon. The procession formed and the parade began at the Elks Lodge on the corner of 8th and Harrison.

The visiting lodges were escorted by some of Leadville's finest. First in the lineup was the Ice Palace Band. Directly behind was parade organizer, Lew Cummings, and Alderman C. C. Joy. A unit of the police force came next, followed by city and county officials and the Leadville Snowshoe Club. The Cripple Creek Lodge was represented by 52 members, and came with the only band made up entirely of Elks members. Then marched the Aspen Elks accompanied by the First Regiment Uniformed Rank and the Knights of Pythias Band, bedecked in handsome blue uniforms.

Members of The Grand Army of the Republic and Ancient Order of United Workmen joined in to swell the parade ranks.

And last, but not least, came the highlight of the parade, a sight never seen in Leadville: the menagerie of trained animals, five hundred strong, "imported from China," which astounded and amazed the spectators. The parade included seventeen Hippogriffs, (winged horses), twenty-nine dragons, fourteen mastodons and a flying sea serpent. The tribe of Zoo-Zoos, near relatives of the Yori-Yori tribe in Ceylon, and the original Callithumpian band, court musicians and one hundred other features. Little boys along the way fell in line and marched to the ice palace behind them. The parade, for all its fantasy, was one of the biggest drawing cards of the season.

The masquerade ball, skating competition and costume judging were also highlights of the day and the events drew some of the largest attended during the carnival. At 8:00 p.m. the crowd moved to the skating rink for the prize awards. The judges selected were J. M. Lyon of Denver, and Harry Phillips and Will Youe of Leadville. A $10 cash prize was awarded to Miss Jennie Windsor for the best designed costume. Her gown had an elk's head painted on the front of her pink satin skirt. Best costume representing Leadville went to Miss Edith Lazenby, who wore a snow white gown decorated in silver and gold. There was no costume deigned worthy of a prize for the most comical character so the judges awarded $5 to Miss Laura Holcomb. Other prizes included best lady's and gent's costumes in carnival colors — season tickets; best male and female Shakespearean characters — $5 cash; best costumed Elk and Shriner member — $5 cash; a prize for lady & gent's costume with most carnival badges; Jack Frost — $5 cash; best monkey — $5 cash; best Follies girl — $5 cash; best Gypsy girl — $5 cash.

Competitors for the men's 2 1/2 mile race went begging. When the contestants found out that Matt Stiffler was entered, they refused to compete so Stiffler skated the necessary laps and claimed the prize.

Competition was stiff between the Cripple Creek and Aspen Lodges. An elk's head, valued at $100, was awarded to Cripple Creek Lodge #316 for the largest number of members represented, fifty-two. A silver service was presented to the Aspen Elks Lodge, attendance runner-up.

The Cripple Creek Lodge was known throughout the state as "the babies." It was the youngest lodge in Colorado at that time and they boasted a membership of 160, and it boasted as being the most financially sound. Cripple Creek's lodge ranked second only to Denver in number of members.

They traveled to Leadville in style for Elks Day, having chartered a train of three Pullman cars, two coach cars and a lounge car. The party left Cripple Creek at midnight, boasting that every member was sober . . . at the time. Porters and attendants were at their beck and call with the mere push of a button.

Aspen Elks showed a strong turnout even though some of the members had been in Leadville earlier for Aspen Day. Two bands came along: the First Regiment Uniformed Rank, Knights of Pythias and the First Regiment Band of Denver. The Aspen band members were: James Williams, conductor; Art Shelladay, drum major; and Charley Ball, Henry Wright, William Moorhead, Charles Thomas, Charley Allen, George Hunt, Louis Brien, Otto Gutting, R. M. Wright, H. Fergeson, William Young, Charles Berryman, Denny McIlwell, William Thomas, C. N. Crowder and George Manly.

The Aspen Elks reportedly paid as they went, "putting nothing across the bar less than a $5 bill."

Park and Summit Counties were represented at the ice palace. Special trains left early, arriving in Leadville at 10:00 a.m. Low rates were offered from Jefferson, Como, Alma, Fairplay, Breckenridge, Dillon, Kokomo and Robinson.

Breckenridge was a contender for the $10,000 attendance award. The town had the largest number of visitors, per capita, in Leadville for Elks Day. At the time, Breckenridge's population was 2,000. There were 143 South Park railroad tickets sold, and it was estimated their attendance was in the running for the big money.

J. W. Swisher, editor of the *Breckenridge Journal*, Mayor Kaiser and enterprising merchant, Frank Payton, were credited with making the excursion a success. It was reported that if Breckenridge did get the prize, her citizens would use the money to build an ice palace the following winter. With favorable weather, and donated labor, their ice palace would match Leadville's.

DOCTORS, DENTISTS, DRUGGISTS DAY
February 19, 1896

D.D.D. DAY

Doctors, Dentists, Druggists Visit

The Death Rate Takes A Sneak Out the Back Door While the Sawbones Were Here

---

Stiffler Can Skate But He Cannot Get Over The Hurdles
McKenzie Gets Away With the Amateur Medals

An impressive parade and torchlight procession by the Leadville Snowshoe Club preceded the evenings events and upon arrival at the ice palace, fireworks bombarded the castle. Following the dazzling pyrotechnics display, the revelers stormed through the portals for the evening's program. The Doctors, Dentists, Druggists Day committee was comprised of Dr. Sol Kahn, Dr. E. M. Conrad and Harvey T. Brown.

Beautifully costumed women and polished gentlemen filled the archways of the skating rink awaiting the lineup of the competitors and to cheer their favorite racers on. Excitement and anticipation filled the air as the contestants took to the ice and interest in the races held at the ice palace that evening were second only to those held on Press Day.

A speed skating contest was the first program on the agenda that evening. The race was open exclusively to doctors, dentists and druggists. Dr. Sol Kahn was favored to win the race. He created quite a stir when he entered, stripped to his white sweater and white woolen knee britches. Other contestants included: George Nicolai, Harvey Brown and Charlie McKenzie. Dr. Kahn jumped in front of the pack immediately, Harvey Brown slipped on a curve and was airborne for a spell, losing one of his skates. His mishap caused great disappointment to a bevy of young female fans, who had bet perfume cases on his winning the race. The Kahn supporters, urged him on with noise from their noisemakers, but he lost out. Charley McKenzie sped past him to take first prize, a $25 medal. Kahn placed second.

There were three entries in the young men's one-mile speed contest: Jules Ernest, David O'Neill and Leonard Jackson. Although Ernest was the smallest of the competitors, he was also the fastest and won first prize of $12.50. Dave O'Neill was second place winner, claiming the $7.50 cash award.

The main event of the evening was the hurdle race, reportedly one of the most exciting races yet seen at the ice palace. There were five entries: Willard Riggs, Matt Stiffler, Otis Richmond, Leonard Jackson and Burt Frey. The race was several laps in length and it was difficult for even the best skaters to keep from skimming the tops of the hurdles. Stiffler was deemed the fastest skater, but as a jumper he was no match for Riggs. Riggs cleared the last hurdles and won the race in 1:57 minutes. He was awarded the $30 cash prize. Attempts were made to promote a race between Stiffler and Riggs, but Riggs refused the offer.

Many prominent druggists were in Leadville for the day. They included: Professor C. M. Ford, a lecturer at the Denver School of Pharmacy; John Anglum, a Colorado pioneer druggist and a Denver pharmacist for 25 years; Fred Schultz, reputedly the most prominent retail druggist in the state; S. T. Kostich, a former Leadvillite came with his wife and children. It was reported that the retired pioneer came back to Leadville to encourage and thank the men who helped him make his fortune, which he had reinvested it in the Carbonate Camp.

F. H. Arcularius, president of the Colorado Pharmaceutical Association, his wife, two daughters and two granddaughters were in town for the day's festivities. Mr. Arcularius was a former Leadvillite. Before moving to Denver, he had a pharmacy at 414 Harrison Avenue for fourteen years.

Fred Luedke, for the first time in twenty-two years, put on a pair of skates and tested the ice rink that evening. Reputedly, as a young man, he was one of the best skaters in Minnesota.

Undertaker James Nelson drew a lot of attention, and laughter, to his establishment that day. The banner that decorated the front of his mortuary at 717-719 Harrison Avenue read, "Welcome to My Friends."

Reduced rates were offered by the railroads and a round trip fare, including two tickets to the ice palace, was $5 from Denver, Colorado Springs and Pueblo.

Souvenir Postcards, Leadville's Ice Palace   Author's Collection

WESTERN SLOPE DAY
February 22, 1896

West Meets East At The Ice Palace

The Largest, Jolliest and Most Appreciative
Crowd of Visitors It Has Had

WESTERN SLOPERS WERE "IN IT"

THE GEM OF THE ROCKIES
Salida Joins In

Western Slope Day was also American Day and Salida Day at the ice palace. In celebration of Washington's birthday, the three were combined. This was a red-letter day for Leadville and the ice palace, with attendance, fireworks and a brilliant parade exceeding any carnival event prior to it.

Held on Saturday, February 22, 1896, this event was long in preparation by the people of Grand Junction. As early as mid-January considerable talk of arranging an excursion to Leadville's ice palace was heard throughout the city. Perhaps as many as one hundred, or a conservative number of fifty would represent Grand Junction.

Prior to American day, February 22nd, a letter directed to Director General Wood on January 11, from the Grand Army of the Republic, (G.A.R.) stated the following:

297

Sir — I am instructed By J. A. Garfield Post, G.A.R., to inform you that under existing circumstances, this post does not feel at liberty to assume any responsibility in connection with G.A.R. Day at the palace. While this post fully appreciates your kind suggestions in that regard, we have been unable to make such arrangements as were first confident could be made to secure the holding of the department encampment at this place. In that event, a large number of old soldiers would have visited Leadville, making success of our efforts, since neither Leadville nor Garfield post have ever asked for or received like consideration from the department, most favorable terms had been promised us from the several railroads centering at this point. But how surprised we were at a late date when advised that the executive officers of the department, as well as a majority of the council of administration, manifested marked hostility to our wishes, and have since fixed both time and place of holding the department encampment, thereby rendering all hope of such a visit to Leadville by any considerable numbers of our comrades practically impossible. Thanking you and your associates for the kind disposition you have shown toward our Order and especially toward our Post. I have the honor to remain Very respectfully yours, E. W. Smith, adjutant.

On January 24th, Howard Lee of the *Grand Junction Sentinel* traveled to Leadville to discuss plans for Western Slope Day with Director General Wood, who agreed to pay expenses and transportation for the Silver Crescent Band from Grand Junction to Leadville for the special day. Lee also met with Anthony Sneve of the Colorado Midland to negotiate a special rate for Western Slope excursionists. Sneve thought that a rate of one cent per mile would be granted. (The rate did not go through.)

The *Grand Junction Daily Sentinel* suggested that a special day be requested of Leadville and set aside as "Western Slope Day" or "Western Colorado Day" with the privilege of extending the day into one week, if necessary. The extension would enable all residents west of the Continental Divide within the boundaries of Colorado to take Leadville by storm, especially on that designated day. Following publication of the article, the *Sentinel* was bombarded with letters pledging individual support to make their special day a success. Active negotiations for a special train fare rate and the special day caught the attention of many Western Slope newspapers.

Other Western Slope towns and cities lent support and enthusiasm to the forthcoming event.

Eagle County Examiner — " . . . we allow this side of the range from mountain and valley towns and country go together and enjoy a holiday at the Cloud City. There is a suggestion worthy of our consideration, and if carried out, will have the *Examiner's* support and attendance."

The *Glenwood Avalanche* stated, "Glenwood Springs would do her share if such a day were put on. Leadville should think over the proposition."

Glenwood Springs Ledger — "The suggestion made by the *Grand Junction Sentinel*, copied in another column, is a good one, and Glenwood should do everything possible to aid the 'Western Slope Day' at Leadville. There's not a town in the state that can profit more by excursions than Glenwood and reciprocity is always a good thing anyhow."

New Castle News — "The *News* heartily endorses the *Grand Junction Sentinel's* idea for a 'Western Slope Day' at Leadville's Crystal Palace. Many special days have been arranged for the other side of the Continental Divide, but our own country, so far, has been neglected. With a day devoted to Western Colorado and equitable railway rates, Leadville will be given a jubilee long to be remembered. New Castle will send at least fifty people."

The *DeBeque Wild West* reported, "The suggestion is good. No doubt such a programme would insure a very large attendance from Grand Valley."

The *Gunnison News* — "We firmly believe that a Western Slope Day would bring more people to Leadville than any other feature. The Western Slope will turn out liberally."

Plateau Valley Herald — Western Slope Day — "An effort is being made to have Western Slope Day at the Leadville ice palace with a good show of success. The fare will be one-cent a mile, or about $3.75 for a round trip from Grand Junction. The date is fixed for Monday, February 17."

The *Meeker Herald*, without hesitation, endorsed the *Sentinel's* suggestion of a Western Slope Day and, "and bespeak a good delegation from Rio Blanco when the time comes."

Ridgeway Populist — "We would like to see a day set apart by the management of the ice palace to be known as 'Western Slope Day,' and that the railroads would make rates, say one cent a mile from all points to Leadville and returning tickets to be good for at least one week. This would enable many of our people to go and we have not doubt that southwestern Colorado would send a large delegation as it did to the Denver carnival. We are in favor of the trip. What money we spend would be spent in Colorado anyway, and no one need spend more than he can spare."

Pueblo Opinion — This gadfly caustically reported, "The *Grand Junction Sentinel* is bubbling over with a scheme to take all of western Colorado on an excursion to see the ice palace. It strikes the *Opinion* that Leadville is herself to blame for the small attendance. First, the railroad rates are too high, and secondly the palace is not well advertised. So far as we know the newspapers of Pueblo have not received a line of reading matter from the ice palace management and judging from our exchanges the papers throughout Colorado are in the same fix. The *Opinion* would have been glad to have printed something of its beauties, but what could we say, knowing nothing about it? Leadville has catered to Denver so long that they actually believe Denver is Colorado. There are other towns in the state. Properly managed, Pueblo could have sent up to 5000 visitors. As it is, not 100 will probably go. The *Sentinel* will find the same condition of things on the Western Slope."

Telluride Journal — "We heartily approve the efforts of the *Grand Junction Sentinel* to make Western Slope Day at the Leadville ice palace a success. It is hoped that the people will take advantage of the low railroad rates and go to Leadville en masse on February 22, which is the date decided upon."

Salida Mail — "The *Grand Junction Sentinel* is making a move to celebrate a 'Western Slope Day' at Leadville. The plan is enthusiastically seconded by the press of that section and the railroads have made a liberal reduced rate. The date has been fixed for Saturday, February 22. This will afford people of this vicinity a splendid opportunity to meet friends of the western slope and spend a very pleasant day."

Denver News — "The *Grand Junction Sentinel* suggests a 'Western Slope Day' at the Leadville ice palace, and promised to bring everybody to the great crystal castle from the man who raises a pick to the man who raises pumpkins, and picks gooseberries. Western Slope Day should be a go."

Rocky Mountain News — "The suggestion of the *Grand Junction Sentinel* that a Western Slope Day be celebrated at the Leadville Ice Palace was so enthusiastically approved by the press of that section of the state that arrangements have been perfected for the event. The date has been fixed for Monday, February 17th (changed to the 22nd) and the Rio Grande and Midland have made a special rate which will assure a large attendance, and place the trip within the reach of every resident of western Colorado. A programme for the day is yet to be arranged and announced. The Western Slope Day is certain to be one of the largest and most interesting in the crystal carnival series. It will bring together the residents of Grand Junction, Delta, Montrose, Ouray, Telluride, Glenwood and New Castle and the numerous small towns on the western slope of the range. There exists among them an intense local pride and a loyalty to their section unexcelled in any other portion of the state, and it will be their ambition to render the day set apart for them the most memorable in the history of the palace. In this connection it may be added that winter is passing and that the days on which the ice palace is at its best are numbered. The coming month is full of festival days and special events at the palace, and these should be liberally patronized by the people of the state. The ice palace is an enterprise illustrative of the enthusiasm of the Leadville people. No community could have done more to

302

render it a success than have the residents of the Carbonate Camp and their efforts should be cordially and substantially sustained by the people of the state."

Three hundred visitors came from Grand Junction, and other towns and cities along the way added another hundred. In addition to the special excursion trains, the regular trains brought another hundred or more. The Silver Crescent Band from Grand Junction accompanied the Grand Junction excursionists. The band was one of the best in the state at that time and Mr. I. W. Bunting of the *Grand Junction Sentinel*, was regarded as the "father of the band." Among the many honors they had captured throughout Colorado, was the top prize at the Festival of Mountain and Plain in Denver in 1895. The 28-member band was under the direction of S. M. Boyer.

At 12:30 p.m., the excursion train from Salida, with standing room at a premium, pulled into Leadville. Mr. Smith, editor of the *Salida Mail* and Mr. Kilgore were congratulated for their fine efforts in coordinating this successful excursion to Leadville. Three hundred twenty Salida excursionists, along with the 20-member Salida Band, one hundred from Buena Vista, and half of Red Cliff's population, twenty-four, disembarked from the four-coach train. The band directed by S. J. Kilgore, superintendent of Chaffee County schools, led the parade toward town to join in the festivities. The paraders wore ribboned badges declaring Salida, "The Gem of the Rockies."

The parade was the afternoon feature. Throngs of visitors crowded the sidewalks of Harrison Avenue and an estimated 7,000 Western Slopers and Leadville citizens lined the streets to watch the pageant. The town was wrapped in red, white and blue and the Ice Palace Band filled the air with their patriotic music while the crowd on the sidelines kept time to the rousing marches. The regal uniforms of the Patriotic Order of the Sons of America, with silver stars on a deep blue background and red and white striped epaulets, filled the crowd with patriotic pride. Only their hats, with a black and white feather, were out of uniform. A police squadron fell into line, followed by the city and county officials, dressed in street clothes. The Miners Union was sparsely represented due to the fact that they were not able to get off work in the middle of the day. The young boys of the Turn Verein drew applause along the way. The G.A.R., flying Old Glory and battle torn flags were carried by many of the veterans. Uncle Sam was represented by Will McLeod who stood 6'6", and did not go unnoticed in his colorful striped trousers, spike-tailed coat and snow white top hat. Youngsters along the way were in awe of this gentle giant with his smiling face and friendly greetings. The Junior Order of Mechanics (tradesmen) made a good showing.

Next came the members of the school board, in a carriage. The Little Red Schoolhouse, mounted on a wagon, was filled with school children who entertained the spectators with patriotic songs. Four other lavishly decorated floats carried more of the school children, waving to the crowds, laughing, cheering and making plenty of noise with their horns and bells. One of the floats carried the Goddess of Liberty surrounded by more children.

The most beautiful float in the parade was decorated by the Women's Relief Corp, Grand Army of the Republic. Three young women represented the links of the order: "Fraternity," represented by Mrs. P. W. Mullen, "Charity," represented by Mrs. John E. Sherman; and "Loyalty," by Mrs. A. Salts. They were portrayed as rescuing a distressed little orphan girl, disheveled, and shabbily dressed. The scene was very impressive. The colors and designs of the costumes drew applause and acclamations along the parade route.

Next came the Ladies of the James G. Blaine Circle, No. 7. Their costumes brought compliments from the spectators.

The fire department was decked out, and the equipment colorfully decorated with patriotic colors. The hose reels had been turned into floats and the ladder wagon was covered with flags and streamers. Captain Goodfriend reportedly "looked more handsome than ever, if that was possible."

Last in the line of parade was a burro, decorated in American colors. The prospector's faithful little friend was given the applause and cheers, so justly deserved.

The procession marched up Harrison Avenue, then turned on West Eighth Street to the ice palace where the marchers disbanded and entered the castle for an afternoon of sightseeing, dancing and skating. There was no planned program during the day.

The Colorado Midland train bringing the Western Slopers to Leadville was late because it was so loaded with passengers the train was not able to travel as fast as it normally would. The Crystal Carnival Association delayed the parade as long as it could. When the train finally arrived the parade was already underway and the excursionists were not allowed to participate. Nevertheless, with the Silver Crescent Band in the lead, the Western Slope citizens formed their own parade and marched to the Vendome Hotel where they were greeted by Director

General Wood. The band gave a mini-concert of two selections in front of the hotel, then, at the invitation of Director General Wood, marched to the ice palace where they were treated to lunch as guests of the Carnival Association.

Later that afternoon the band gave a concert in the palace ballroom, which was thoroughly enjoyed by the carnival visitors. Those who did not attend the concert spent time wandering through the ice palace, viewing the exhibits, dancing and skating.

The Silver Crescent Band concert was enjoyed by so many people that afternoon at the ice palace, that the band was requested to give another concert that evening. Following dinner at the Vendome Hotel, the band entertained with another concert in the hotel's rotunda.

Everyone in Leadville, along with visitors to the city, were invited to attend the carnival's evening events. They were encouraged to come dressed in costumes of the George and Martha Washington era. That evening an elegant colonial ball was held in the east ballroom and it was touted as the dressiest affair of the carnival season. A number of participants were dressed in 18th century costumes.

Two of Caterer John Miller's little children, a son, 4 and a daughter, 5, walked off with a prize. Their mother had sewn costumes for them and escorted them to the ball, dressed as George and Martha Washington. Mrs. Kate Larson was awarded the grand prize, a $25 dress pattern. She wore a quilted petticoat dress with bodice and pantaloons, and powdered hair. She truly looked like a colonial dame. Fred Arnold won the prize for best costume representative of the "Father of His Country," George Washing-

306

ton. His majestic height and dignified bearing greatly enhanced his costume.

A fireworks display was set off in front of the Patriotic Order, Sons of America headquarters and filled the air with technicolored hues of light. Smoke and flame rose above the porch tops of the Vendome Hotel and Harrison Avenue was alive with color, booming with explosives. Rockets and Roman candles streaked skyward, while firecrackers blew up on the streets.

The day was an epoch in the history of the Crystal Carnival as Leadville celebrated Washington's birthday.

The visitors came away in awe of the majestic ice castle. Western Slope Day was declared an unqualified success. The people that traveled to Leadville reportedly never regretted making the journey.

Some of the Western Slope visitors took the midnight excursion train back to Grand Junction, but a number of them stayed over for another day.

Following a long day of sightseeing, visiting the ice palace, and partying, the train loaded with the tired Salida visitors departed for that city at 11:00 p.m.

Grand Junction's Silver Crescent band included:

- Fritz Welking, piccolo
- James D. Roberts, J. C. Boyer, E Flat clarinet
- J. C. Meyers, C. G. Sumner, Louis Zieman, A. C. Peterson, clarinet
- C. H. Mayo and C. L. Currier, solo coronet
- E. M. Sumner, first coronet
- S. J. Scovil, third coronet

- Ed Walsh, coronet
- M. O. Whitehead, soprano saxophone
- W. P. Reeder, alto saxophone
- H. G. Bedwell, tenor saxophone
- Mr. Thompson, first alto
- C. E. Wood, second alto
- W. G. Struthers, Leo Allison, Bert Collins, and Percy Cogswell, trombone
- J. B. Boyer, baritone
- C. A. Woodmanse, Frank LaSalle, basso
- Mr. Haskell, drums
- Gus Orren, side drum
- John Allison, property manager
- Charles Knowles, banner man

MINING EXCHANGE DAYS
February 24-25, 1896

LEADVILLE'S POPULATION DOUBLES

Grand and Imposing Demonstration
by the Miners of Leadville

THOUSANDS WERE IN LINE

Underground Workers Crowd the Palace
to Enjoy the Rare Sport

IN ONE BLAZE OF GLORY

A Grand Outburst of Excitement and Red
Fire Culminates the Festivities

PARADE OF DAZZLING BEAUTY

An Entire City Aflame With the Unequalled Display of
Magnificent Fireworks

WORLD'S RECORDS BROKEN

The Mighty Burns Brothers Overcome the
Giants of Montana in a Closely
Contested Struggle

Some of these bold headlines were published in the *Herald Democrat* of February 25, 1896.

On February 18th, the city council passed a resolution, drawn up by City Attorney McLeod:

Whereas, The miners of this city have arranged to celebrate the 24th instant as Mining Day; and

Whereas, it is our proudest boast that Leadville is the greatest mining camp on earth and we gratefully acknowledge the miners to be the actual producers of our wealth, and the mines to be the source of our prosperity; now, therefore, be it

Resolved, By the city council of the city of Leadville that, as aldermen and citizens, we do all in our power to make this day the most notable holiday in the carnival season, and that we, with all the city officers, including the fire and police forces, join in the parade.

Resolved, That we call upon all good and spirited citizens to close their places of business at noon and join with our hardy miners in their celebration.

Miners Day was really a big event, with ten thousand people arriving in Leadville to spend the day at the ice palace. The main event was the rock drilling contest and to the winners, the Miners Union offered a $600 purse for double drilling. George L'Abbe contributed an additional $100, bringing the grand prize to $700. The second place winner received $300, and the third place winner was awarded $100.

Once again the Lord High Mayor, S. D. Nicholson, issued an official proclamation. It was declared that Monday, February 24th, from noon to midnight, the city belonged to the miners and everyone was directed to let go and enjoy themselves. The mine managers had recognized the day as a legal holiday. With the exception of enough

310

men to keep the boilers fired and the water pumped, all other employees were free to participate in the day's activities. Because there were so many events scheduled, Miners Day was extended to February 25th.

Father James Brown, pastor of Annunciation Church, donated a four-ton rock of Gunnison granite which was placed on display at the Knights of Labor Hall. Gunnison granite was noted for its uniformity and hardness and this was the same granite that was used in the State Capitol building.

For those who had not entered the rock-drilling contest, the teams were directed to the Miners Hall or the Association's headquarters to sign up.

Twenty rock drilling contestants from Leadville were entered, including six double teams. Victor and Cripple Creek were represented by seven double teams, Creede, Telluride, and drillers from Montana were other entrants.

James R. Amburn, president of the Miners Union, and Ewen DeWar, secretary, were in charge of this drawing card.

Newspapers reported every special day and event as having surpassed every other and Miners Day was no exception. In all of the seventeen years of Leadville's history there had been none to exceed the number of visitors and the exuberance of the crowds.

On February 18th, Mike Burns, a crack driller from Butte, Montana, arrived in Leadville to prepare for the rock drilling contests. He and his brother, Joe, began intensive training at Adelaide Park.

Miners began pouring into the city on Sunday, the 22nd, and more trains on Monday brought scattered representatives. By the 24th the population of Leadville had nearly

311

doubled, more than 10,000 people were in the city for the World Championship Rock Drilling competitions.

The Miners Union headquarters in the Court Exchange building was jammed with visitors seeking information about the parade and schedule of events.

For the evening parade on the 24th, only, Mayor Nicholson, Marshal of the Day, ordered a change from the normal parade route. The parade started at the corner of Eighth Street on Harrison Avenue, moved down Harrison to the corner of Third Street, went west on Third Street to Pine, south on Pine to Chestnut, east on Chestnut back to Harrison Avenue, north on Harrison Avenue to West Eighth Street and on to the ice palace.

Expressmen offered their wagons, free of charge, for the day parade and invitations were extended to the women and children to ride along and be a part of it.

It was estimated that there were 3,200 miners in the parade, and enough other trade unions to bring the total to 4,000 men. Harrison Avenue wasn't long enough to hold half the men in the parade that day. Old Glory was the only flag carried, along with a banner bearing the miners motto, "16 to 1[34] or nothing." Other banners bore abbreviated stories, "California Gulch, 1857"; "We Crossed the Plains in '49"; "We Are The Wealth Producers of The State." There were no displays, no fancy suits, glitter or glamour, and the only parade float was sponsored by D. D. Sullivan, representing the mining industry. The float carried two miners drilling into a rock, while an attendant stood to the side. The float, tastefully decorated with steamers and

---

[34]Sixteen ounces of silver to one ounce of gold.

312

flags, was drawn by six horses, each wearing a banner with the words "16 to 1."

The miners wore their work clothes and marched proudly in their simple attire, their humble clothing and proud bearing making a tremendous impression on the spectators. As plain as the parade was, it demonstrated the silent strength of the ore diggers.

These hard working men were given credit for the wealth Leadville and Colorado had so long enjoyed. The *Herald Democrat* stated:

> After all, the city owes its prosperity, its strong and substantial character as a mountain business center, to these men. Toiling silently, as they do, underground; working in a most unattractive occupation, dangerous in extreme, they are sometimes overlooked in the calculations concerning the general business condition of the camp. But such a demonstration as was seen yesterday certainly impressed even the most impassive with a sense of strength and solidarity of the workers of the mines, of their real importance and influence in the camp.

The contests drew an immense crowd to the ice palace that afternoon. Cash prizes of $1,000 were to be awarded.

The first rock drilling contest began at 2:00 p.m. on the ice palace's skating rink. The block of Gunnison granite was brought to the center of the rink and a raised platform was placed around it. This elevated the drillers into the view of the spectators in all parts of the building. The contest entrants were listed as follows, and drilled in that order:

1 — Con O'Neal and Mike Sullivan, Leadville
2 — Anton Echer and Ben Pretty, Leadville

3 — Jack McKee and Tim Sullivan, Leadville
4 — Landers and Roubideaux, Gilman
5 — W. C. Bradley and George Hill, Silver Cliff
6 — James Driver and Thomas Keegar, Leadville
7 — Mike Burns and Joe Burns, Leadville
8 — Tony Laughenbaugh and Sandy Stewart, Leadville

In fifteen minutes, O'Neal and Sullivan had hand drilled a hole 32 1/16 inches into the granite. They were changing drills every minute, and on the eleventh change of drills, the drill broke, costing them precious time.

Anton Eicher and Ben Pretty drilled for seven minutes, five seconds, and reached a depth of 10 1/2 inches. Their drills kept breaking and they finally had to drop out.

Jack McKee and Tim Sullivan were favored to win this contest with Sullivan the first to swing. With every swing of the hammer the drill was heard cutting into the stubborn granite block. They drilled without a single mishap and when time was called they had drilled a hole 36 5/16 inches deep. This record would be challenged that evening.

Landers and Roubideaux scored 31 13/16 inches.

Bradley and Hill came in with 27 1/8 inches.

Timekeepers were Frank Wolfe of Cripple Creek and Gus North of Leadville. Charles McClellan served as Master of Ceremonies.

The remaining contests were scheduled for 7:30 that evening.

The night parade on Miners Day was a record breaker in every sense of the word. Grand Marshal of the parade was "Hizzoner," Mayor S. D. Nicholson, mounted on a high spirited stallion. The mayor was ably assisted by Field Marshal Edward J. McCarty, who dispensed orders to the

314

marchers along the parade route. A police squad marched behind the Grand Marshal, then the city and county officials, followed by the Ice Palace Band. The Leadville Snowshoe Club released dozens of Roman candles along the parade route and the fire and sparks from the Roman candles faded into a soft glow, gradually vanishing as the rockets sped through the clouds of smoke into the nighttime sky. Then came the Grand Army of the Republic veterans in colorful regalia. Next marched the Ancient Order of Hibernians more than a hundred strong in their official, handsomely decorated uniforms. Two hundred members of the Ancient Order of Foresters, were impressive as they marched. The Junior Order of Mechanics (craftsmen) were followed by the Woodmen of the World, accompanied by the Finlanders Band.

Young boys, representing the miners of pioneer days, carried a banner which read, "We Discovered What You Now Enjoy!" A special feature of the parade was the "Ancient Miners." They were dressed as early day ore seekers, leading burros with packs on their backs. The four young men were J. J. Dooley, Michael McGlynn, Charley Driscoll and Charles Larsen. Dennis Taylor was the organizer of this attention-getting group.

Drum Major Rogers led the Leadville Drum Corps which was followed by a second unit of the Snowshoe Club. These reveling paraders let loose with another display of pyrotechnics that streaked skyward, lighting the Avenue for the Caledonians and United Workmen. Then came the mass of printers and the shoemakers in leather aprons. The Miners Union and the Carpenters and Blacksmiths Alliances all fell in step. Floats of every size and description brought up the rear.

Upon arrival at the palace, the procession was greeted by the bombardment of parachute rockets that lifted above the towers and walls of the ice castle. They fell back to earth as inverted umbrellas of breathtaking colors, splashing the battlements along their downward spiral, then falling to the snow covered ground in a rainbow of color. Fiery dragons were unfurled and leapt toward the heavens in a multitude of brilliant rays.

Excitement and anticipation of the long-awaited drilling contests were immeasurable and the largest crowd to attend the ice palace was there that evening. The east and west pavilions were packed. The ice surface was covered with people, waiting to see if the afternoon records could be matched or beaten. The record set in the afternoon by Jack McKee and Tim Sullivan was out of reach. Their drilling was perfect. There were no misses and McKee's change of drills was flawless. The record of 35-5/16 inches, set at the Festival of Mountain and Plain, had been broken that afternoon. The first contestants, from Butte, Montana, mounted the platform. The strength they showed as they drove their hammers to the steel brought yells from the crowd and those who had wagered earlier, that the afternoon record would not be broken, began to question their judgement. The "big men from Butte" made the steel dance against the granite. But for some reason the steel did not seem tempered to the rock and the blows danced away, not sinking into it. When the last drill was drawn and the gauge was sunk into the hole, applause filled the air. Then a hush fell over the crowd as the judges announced the results. The Butte team had drilled 34-9/16 inches, 1-3/4 inches less than McKee and Sullivan. The applause was deafening and cheer upon cheer resounded through the palace. The Leadville record held!

The bettors breathed a sigh of relief and the crowd grew silent again. There were other men of steel of the Carbonate Camp to be heard from.

James Driver and Tom Keegar fell short of the grand prize. Their drilling attempt measured 33-9/16 inches.

Next came the Burns brothers, Mike and Joe. When they climbed onto the wooden platform their friends believed they would capture second place, besting the Montana team since they were top-notch drillers. They took their places and begun drilling. They had not used a half dozen drills when they realized they were ahead of their steel. They had driven the steel so far into the granite, they could not retrieve it. Word spread like wildfire that they had skipped a drill. A time of thirteen minutes was announced, and they were on their last drill. A declaration circulated through the crowd, and it was evident they had beaten the time of McKee and Sullivan. The excitement was intense and even the judges were nervous as they measured the hole. Marshal George W. Burgess, who was stationed at the platform to keep the crowds back, was craning his neck to see what the tape measured. Judge S. J. Sullivan projected an outward calm amid the uproar as he announced that Burns and Burns had drilled 37-1/16 inches. Hysteria, bordering on pandemonium, filled the halls. Leadville had not beaten Montana once, but twice! The wins sent the Butte team to third place. No one that night anticipated such a triumph.

Tony Laughenbaugh and Sandy Stewart came within a fraction of winning the third place money. Their results were 34-1/3 inches.

317

The Victor team, supported by the Cripple Creek visitors, were the last to drill. Joe Carboneau wielded the hammer along with Thomas Donovan. They drilled 32-5/8 inches, and the contest was over.

There was some quibbling when the winners were announced. It was argued that Leadville did not have the right to claim the World Championship because Mike Burns lived in Montana. The disagreement was settled and put to rest. Mike Burns had made his home in Leadville for a number of years, and announced that it would be his home again.

The people of Leadville were ecstatic. By winning first and second places the Carbonate Camp vindicated itself, and proved that Leadville's miners were the best in the world.

Contest Results
The Number of Inches Drilled
By Each Team

Mike Burns and Joe Burns, Leadville	*37-1/16"*
Jack McKee and Tim Sullivan, Leadville	*36-5/16"*
John Campbell and Joe Freety, Butte, Montana	*34-9/16"*
Tony Laughenbaugh and Sandy Steward, Leadville	*34-1/8"*
James Driver and Tom Kreegar, Leadville	*33-9/16"*
Joe Carboneau and Thomas Donovan, Victor	*32-5/8"*
Con O'Neill and Mike Sullivan, Leadville	*32-1/16"*
	(broke 13th drill)
Landry and Roubideaux, Gilman	*31-13/16"*
Antoine Echer and Ben Pretty, Leadville	*10-1/2"*
(in seven minutes, 5 seconds, when drill broke.)	

Frank Wolfe and Gus North were the timekeepers.

The previous record set in Gunnison granite was 35-5/8 inches drilled by John McKee and Billy Dwyer. This was made in 1895 at the Knights of Labor Hall. The next best performance in this rock was made by Con O'Neill and Mike Sullivan at the Festival of Mountain and Plain in October of 1895. They brought home a Silver Bucket, the first prize trophy. Their drill hole that day measured 35-5/16 inches.

The Burns brothers grew up in Cletcormoor, England, of Irish ancestry. It is interesting to note that the two brothers were not too big in size. Joe weighed 153 pounds and Mike tipped the scales at 195.

Ice archways near main entrance. Denver Public Library,
Western History Department.

WORKERS UNITE AT THE ICE PALACE
Ancient Order of United Workmen
February 29, 1896

Circulars were sent out to Ancient Order of United Workmen lodges within the jurisdiction: Colorado, New Mexico and Arizona. Every lodge returned an affirmative reply.

Valuable prizes were offered to the visiting lodges sending the biggest number of representatives. It read:

Brothers — We, the members of A.O.U.W. located in Leadville, send you greeting, and most cordially welcome you to participate with us in celebrating A.O.U.W. day at the Leadville Ice Palace on February 29, 1896.

We have in our city at present the greatest wonder on earth, namely, a castle built entirely of ice. This castle, besides being the most magnificent ever constructed, contains the largest skating rink in America, snow statuary, exhibits frozen in solid cakes of ice, grand ball rooms, fine bands and orchestras, great toboggan slides over 2000 feet long, and many other attractions too numerous to mention.

Especially at night when illuminated by electricity, the beauties of this wonderful castle are indescribable. Among the many fete days allotted to the different organizations, fraternal and otherwise, the above mentioned day, has been selected by the Ancient Order of United Workmen as their day.

The grand lodge officers will be present. In the evening there will be a grand torch light parade.

Governor McIntire and staff will be present. All the military companies of the state, together with the uniform, secret and labor societies will take part and storm the castle with pyrotechnics. It is the intention that A.O.U.W. day shall overshadow and eclipse anything that has or will be attempted in this line during the carnival season.

321

Brothers, we want you to join us in this grand reunion, and make this a banner gathering in the history of the A.O.U.W. of this jurisdiction, and we can assure you that it will do the Order, in general, a world of good. All the railroads have agreed to make special low rates on this occasion. Organize a club in your city and get the benefit. We can assure you a warm welcome and an entertainment that will cause you to take back a pleasant remembrance of having spent the most enjoyable day of your lives. Kindly write and let us know how many brothers will come to see us. Yours in C. H. and T., ss: E. J. McCarty, Chairman; F. F. Gilden, Secretary."

The parade on February 29th, combined the forces of the workmen and military and was headed by the entire police force. Next came Marshal Charles Grabert, followed by the Ice Palace Band. Proud and tall marched Denver's crack company which was followed by the Colorado National Guard; followed by two of Leadville's companies, and the Chaffee Light Artillery of Denver and the Cripple Creek aggregation. The Select Knights were inspiring in their colorful uniforms and were given an arousing round of applause. The Ancient Order of Hibernians, whose handsome regalia reflected brilliantly in the blazing fireworks, were out in force. The Miners Union members bearing picks and shovels, swelled the parade force and created excitement as they marched. Next, in step, came the Blacksmiths and Tailors Alliances in large numbers. Following the brilliantly red-clad Leadville Drum Corps, came the Grand Army of the Republic, uniformed in blue and the Patriotic Order Sons of America were there in full force. Their marching, military bearing and uniforms created an enthusiastic response from the crowds along the parade route. The

Knights of Pythias Band from Aspen filled the air with their stirring, toe-tapping music. A large number of Woodmen of the World marched along Harrison Avenue, followed by the 5 & 40 Ancient Order of United Workmen, every member present. Then came the mysterious, but noble order of Mogullians (men in donkey or burro costumes with, burro heads.) Their weird costumes and crazy movements drew laughter and cheers from the spectators. Al Lynch, in his "sacred" robes, led the unruly animals.

A float was filled with ladies representing the A. E. Pierce Lodge. It was decorated in red, white and blue, brightly lit with colored lights and was pulled by four majestic horses. Next came the solemn, inspiring float of the Silver Camp No. 12 Degree of Honor, representative of the principles of the lodge; Charity, Mrs. Boyle; Hope, "the widow," and Protection, Mr. Sullivan. Beautifully costumed women atop the float, waved to the masses as it passed along the Avenue. The Leadville Fire Department, a mainstay of almost every parade during the carnival, came with their flag and banner-clad equipment. Chinese lanterns adorned the brilliantly decorated fire wagons and fireworks released by the firemen, splashed against the nighttime sky filling the air with red flame.

Last, but certainly not least, came Dennis Taylor and his "Holy Order of Hogsheads." The brigade was made up of little boys in decorated barrels, who created an atmosphere of fun and laughter with their antics.

All along the parade route, brilliant displays of fireworks continuously lit the heavens with technicolored swishes, booms and blasts. The cheers of the thousands of spectators, the stirring music presented by the bands, the blare of

323

the trumpets, created one of the finest parades yet seen in the Carbonate Camp.

Leadville hosted the Chaffee Light Artillery of Denver. This was the first time the expert militia group had visited the Cloud City although they were well-known to the citizens. Some of the crack team's members made their home in Leadville.

After the parade a large crowd of spectators, both visitors and citizens, lined the sidewalks to witness an exhibition performed by the militia. The skilled team presented an artillery drill in front of the courthouse on Harrison Avenue, with their maneuvers being executed in snap military fashion, quick, and double-quick time. Two guns on exhibition were manned by two corporals; one, the gunner, the other, the caisson. Six other militiamen assisted. Lieutenant Libby, the company's commanding officer, was in charge of the drill. Captains Kavanaugh and Kincade, Major Borstadt, Lieutenant Hooper, and members of the staff stood in review. The Gatling gun used by the company was capable of firing 650 shots a minute and capability could be increased to 1,000, and up to 1200 shots per minute but during the display the speed was approximately 800. The precision drill, which normally took four to five minutes, was executed in 20 minutes since the snow and ice on the streets impeded the team's maneuvers and ability to move the cannons. No child's play here to move the artillery around and Leadville's high altitude winded the men in no time, slowing their performance.

Company K of Denver, attached to the First Regiment, Colorado National Guard, presented an exhibition drill on the ice rink and presentation of the new regulation drill drew applause and admiration from the many spectators.

Major Brooks complimented the team on their fine appearance and mastery of the drill. The Trumpet Drill was another first seen by the Leadville people. In this novel method the commands were given to the trumpeter by the commanding officer from a place of shelter and were reportedly valuable during heavy artillery fire when the commander's voice was drowned out.

During the afternoon, the crowds were entertained at the ice palace with various races. A half-mile boys' race on the ice rink was first. The seven-lap race entrants were James Gardner, John Antonich, Pete Swanson, Frank Quigley, John Dawson, P. Hearne, Dominick Pearo, Jno Knapp, Val Jackson and Pat Simmons. Each boy was given a number and lined up, five to a side, at opposite ends of the rink. Quigley got a quick start, running on his skates to the corner, giving him a good lead. Val Jackson moved on him quickly and took the lead. Jno Knapp trailed him and appeared stronger as Jackson became winded. Knapp, however, hung back, not wanting to take the lead at that time, intending to pass Jackson on the home stretch. His decision cost him the race. Jackson regained his wind and raced to the finish line, capturing first place. Knapp was awarded the prize for second place. Third place winner should have been Pat Simmons, but because of confusion on the part of the judges, the prize was awarded to someone else.

The Wheelbarrow Race was a riot of laughter as the entrants were blindfolded. The race was open to visitors only. Prizes were awarded to those driving their wheelbarrows closest to the finish line, a flag placed at the north end of the rink. The contestants were: H. Bullock of Aspen Lodge No, 12; Ed Scanlon of Aspen Lodge, No. 43; W.

G. Rutherford, of Canon City Lodge No. 7; C. Sanders of Aspen Lodge No. 21; Ben Strathers, of Aspen Lodge No. 23 and A. Parry of Aspen Lodge No. 21.

To begin, the racers were whirled around in place to confuse them. Some started wheeling toward the sides of the rink, bringing hoots of laughter. It appeared that only one man kept his sense of direction. H. Bullock won first place. C. Sanders was the second to reach the flag and A. Parry was awarded third place.

As night fell, this special recognition day brought one of the largest crowds to Leadville's Ice Palace. The turnstiles spun quickly as the multitudes passed through.

The evening's program kept the committee bustling, to ensure that the contests were started on time.

The first event was an egg race. Winners were: Billy Epps, first place; William Smallwood, second prize, and Mr. Gibbons was awarded third place.

There were only two entrants in the Hurdles Race; Billy Epps and Burt Frey. The winning prize went to Burt Frey. Epps lost out because he cut one of the corners which disqualified him.

A Pairs Race was won by Burt Frey and Miss Nellie Tobin. George Blatt and Miss Newcombe were awarded the second place money.

The main event was a Tug-of-War on the ice rink with a team of Scotsmen pitted against a select team of Miners Union members. The Scots team members were: Captain, W. T. Thompson, James McDonald, David Holden, Archie Holden, Matt McIntosh, Lewis S. Murray, Will Rich, A. Kidd, and N. McKenzie. The Miners Union was represented by Jim Doner, Mr. Wince, Mr. Hardten, Mr. Nelson, Pat Connors, T. Randall, Pat Bowen, Ed Cassady, D.

McDonell and A. K. McDonell. The teams were coached by Mike Timmons and John Hearne.

The Scotsmen got the jump on the miners and were able to get the rope to their side of the line. By stiffening up and digging their heels in, they held their ground despite the tugs and pulls, and grunts and groans of the miners. The Scots were awarded the $25 first prize.

Otis Richmond won first prize for the One-Legged Race, with Alex Harvey coming in a close second.

A Greased-Pig Contest was won by Mike Lane. The award was a $10 cash prize.

Architect C. E. Joy and H. B. Hardt were delegated to find a "genuine razor-back shoat" and clip its toenails so it could run on the ice. Joy scouted the country around Mosquito Pass for about a month to no avail, so he bought a pig from one of the local butchers and Joy told the Director General about his find. General Wood asked if Joy "had tried him out," to which Joy replied, "Why, if I turn him loose on the ice we never could catch him." Joy was then instructed to get a gallon of axle grease and have one of the men rub the hog until it was so full of grease that if one of the contestants did catch it, he wouldn't be able to hold on. The mission was accomplished, but proved to be a disaster because the hog had so much of its own fat it could hardly walk.

Carpenters had been instructed to build a fence, extra high and extra close to the ice so the pig could not get away from its pursuers.

A large crowd encircled the enclosure to watch the contest. While they were bringing the hog onto the ice, the Ice Palace Band played a prelude in Symphony B, entitled,

"The Fate of the Pig," or, "Wild Boer of the German Strasse."

The pig was brought in with much pomp and pageantry, accompanied by grooms, valets, and other attendants. He had been placed in a secured box and carried out by the attendants. A rope was fastened around his front legs to prevent him from getting away. The box was placed in the wooden ring and the latch was sprung, but the pig didn't spring. He fell flat on the ice, belly down. Despite pulling and pinching by the grooms and his effort to get up, the pig spread his legs and laid down. The attendants then braced him up by gently prodding him with sticks, but he went belly down again, much to the chagrin of the aids and backers. He was then lifted to his feet by "gentle and loving hands," but wouldn't stand up. After several efforts, he was given a boot, and the signal was given to start the contest. A dozen skaters pounced on the hog who by this time was hugging the ice, too frightened to move.

The Association, keeping its word, insisted that a prize be given to the man who caught the hog, even though the hog simply fell down. Mike Lane was the first to reach the poor animal and was awarded the prize.

First prize for the best parade float was awarded to the ladies of the Degree of Honor, No. 12. The second place prize was awarded to the Degree of Honor, No. 21, and third place was captured by the fire department for the most artistically decorated float.

The Waltz competition delighted the crowd of spectators. Miss Ella Reed and Jim Glenn took first place; Miss Puttkamer and James Gibbons won the second place award; and Miss Wilmotte and Arthur Jones of Aspen were third place prize recipients.

Award for the best A.O.U.W. costume was given to Miss Lena Eckert. There were no other prizes awarded in this category, but had there been, Mrs. Charles Schrader would have been second place winner. Other costumes deserving of recognition were Miss Ella Curley, representing the Leadville Drum Corps, and Miss Bean, a Grecian Lady.

The first prize for the largest number of Colorado A.O.U.W. lodge members in attendance went to Aspen Lodge No. 21, and second place winner was Aspen Lodge No. 23, Colorado City Lodge No. 24 went home with the third place award.

COLLECTI

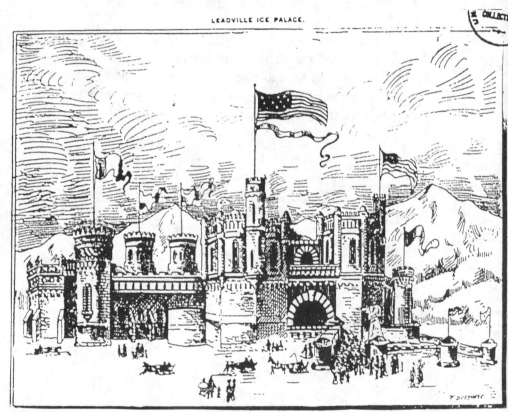

LEADVILLE ICE PALACE

A GREAT DAY FOR THE IRISH
No Blarney Here

March 5, 1896 was designated Irish Day at the ice palace and what a day it must have been. Headlines in the *Leadville Herald Democrat* boomed the grand occasion:

Is Erin's Own

―――

The Sons & Daughters of The Hibernia
Make Merry at the Crystal Palace

―――

Cead Mille Failte

―――

A Day of Unalloyed Enjoyment and Genuine Celtic
Fun and Revelry

―――

Wearing of the Green

Arise! ye sons of Ireland, who have in slumber lay
and toiled the hill and valley for many a weary day.
One day of recreation is placed at your command, to
view the grandest structure erected in the land.

― *Cornelius Maguire*

Leadville's store fronts were decorated in Irish colors, green flags were everywhere. The city was handed over to the Irish at an early hour and freedom of the streets was given to the Ancient Order of Hibernians, dressed in their

331

finest bibs and tuckers. Citizens and visitors were treated to one of the finest parades of the winter carnival on that day.

The sons of Erin fell in line, followed by the Knights of Robert Emmett, a thousand strong, and their noble banners brought stirring applause from the spectators. The floats were the most beautiful and colorful of any in the ice palace parades, resembling those of the Mardi Gras pageants. One float carried 18 ladies of the Drill Corps, another carried the Maid of Erin, Miss Fitzharris, representing the Patron Saint. This beautiful float had represented Leadville at the Festival of Mountain and Plain and had received glowing reviews in the Denver newspapers.

An authentic Irish jaunting cart with seats facing sideways, carried richly costumed passengers.

Many of the floats carried school children. The wee ones were clad in sashes of Irish colors with caps to match.

An Irish washerwoman, bent over a washtub, rode the next float.

Sullivan's house was a typical Irish float, resembling a tented wagon covered with green serge. "The Harp that Hung in Tara's Hall," read the banner.

Irish carts with Irish peddlers came selling their wares. One such peddler was Patrick J. McGeeney sporting whiskers, and real corduroy breeches. He held a short pipe between his teeth and carried a pack on his back.

The rear guard, Taylor's Loyal Celtic Ice Castle Brigade, was afoot and mounted on horses or mules.

Visitors to the palace that day were entertained by Irish piper, Colin Allen, who played the "sweetest" melodies from the Emerald Isle.

Judge Royal of Pueblo delivered the opening address, speaking of the distinguished men of science and letters that made the Irish so renowned. The judge paid a glowing tribute to Leadville's Crystal Palace, extolling its grandeur and magnificence beyond description; that the Leadville people had done themselves proud, and it was regrettable that the entire world could not see it. He complimented the Irishmen on the impression the marching Knights of Robert Emmett had made. He spoke of the past conflict and tyranny in Ireland and said, "The Irish are here today to celebrate the birthday of one of Ireland's most illustrious sons, one who had given his young life as a sacrifice for the rights of liberty and freedom, and to relieve the downtrodden and oppressed." His comments was met with a resounding round of applause. The eloquent speech was followed by the children representing the counties of Ireland singing, "Erin Must Be Free."

The Irish piper accompanied William O'Keefe and Charlotte Fitzharris as they danced the hornpipe reel and slip-jig, to the delight of the spectators.

Professor John Volkert's girls then sang, "The Harp That Once Through Tara's Hall."

At the north end of the ice palace hall a large streamer was draped with the words near and dear to every Irishman, "Caed Mille Failte" (a hundred thousand welcomes).

The thermometer hovered around zero that evening but Harrison Avenue was jam-packed from one end to the other. The night parade was, in many respects, the finest to be seen during the carnival season. Shortly after 8:00 p.m., Marshal of the Day, E. J. McCarty, mounted on a fiery snow-white charger, started up Leadville's main street accompanied by aides: John H. Dunn, Patrick F. Gildey, William Gleason and Michael W. O'Connell, also mounted. The Ice Palace Band followed, filling the air with Irish music. The Grand Army of the Republic veterans were out in force, followed by the United Workmen and Woodmen: the Tailors and Blacksmiths Alliances and the Catholic Knights in their handsome uniforms. The Caledonians were particularly impressive. Fire Chief Greenfield, in his Scottish costume and eagle feathers, led the boys of Scotland. (This was an erroneous report. Charles Good-friend was the Fire Chief and George D. Greenfield was the Police Magistrate.) They were accompanied by the bearded pipers who filled the air with military songs and followed by the Leadville Drum Corps. Then came the Ancient Order of Hibernians and the Knights of Robert Emmett, a thousand strong. Prominent among the marchers was Dennis Nelson, bearing his grandfather's pike. Standing over six feet tall, he held the pike aloft with "manly pride," since the ancient weapon no doubt had sent many a Britisher to his rest. The sight of the weapon created excitement along the parade route.

Next came the floats, with red and green fire flashing, beautiful beyond description. The first float was filled with the Daughters of Hibernia. Another carried the Sisters of Charity and Mercy. The nuns smiled broadly beneath their habits, their black dresses in vivid contrast to the brilliant colors that surrounded them. A burro laden with fishing creels followed, creating laughter and cheers along the way. On the next float came the beautiful Maid of Erin, seated on a pyramid of silver, guarded by four stalwart knights in shining armor. The float, lighted with red fire, was electrifying and drew enthusiastic applause from the crowd. An amusing float, featuring a genuine "Irish washerwoman," busied herself over a tub, while her daughter hung the clothes on the line. Ed Kelly in his

334

jaunting car created laughter along the parade route. Always loyal to the Crystal Carnival, came the fire laddies and their gaily decorated equipment. Dennis Taylor's Loyal Celtic Ice Castle Brigade brought up the end. His aggregation of Celtic curiosities brought roars of laughter and rounds of applause. The brigade was afoot, on horseback, mules and burros, while the Irish tinker, (the real McCoy), created endless fun.

The Day of the Irish did not gather steam until the evening. The paraders poured into the entrances, pushing their way through the turnstiles. The crowded halls and walkways made it almost impossible to move from one place to another.

After many failed attempts to get the program started in the ballroom, for lack of space, J. J. Quinn, master of ceremonies, moved into the skating rink. With the help of the entire police force and the marshals of the day, the crowd was forced back far enough to permit the young ladies of the Drill Corps to form a line across the ice. The precision with which they executed their turns on command were compared to and, according to the "experts," equaled the maneuvers performed by the Denver soldiers. Their uniforms were attractive and tasteful; white skirts, trimmed with a red band at the hemline and a form-fitting top (basque) of emerald green. Square green sailor hats completed the ensembles. Their drills created a frenzy of applause and glowing compliments.

The corps members were directed by Captain Mary Ellen Dooley, "a typical Irish beauty," and Sergeant Nettie Briardy. Members were: Misses Lizzie McMahon, Maggie Vaughn, Jo Corbett, Esther Briardy, Mame McKee, Mary Hopkins, Anna Hopkins, Florence Fearnley, Anna O'Malia,

Katie Hart, Anna McKeon, Mary McMahon, Sadie McMahon, Stella Jones and Mary McAndrews.

The spectators were entertained with a dance exhibition in the ballroom. Martin Rooney and Miss Fitzharris; John Murphy and Mrs. Keough; Patrick Flatley and Mrs. M. A. Welsh; Barney Sloan and Mrs. Keating, and Andrew Flatley and his unnamed partner performed a rollicking eight-hand reel. Mrs. Walsh and Martin Rooney were noted as exceptionally graceful in their execution of the dance steps.

The crowd was then treated to a song and dance by Patrick "Paddy" Flatley, "as fine an Irishman as any in Dublin town."

Over in the corner, Mayor Nicholson, Judge James Glynn and Fen G. Barker performed a jig. The mayor's fancy shindigs caught the admiration of the ladies and Judge Glynn's mastery of the jig delighted the spectators.

Many handsome costumes were worn and admired. Irish laddies: John O'Rourke as King of Munster; Henry M. Jennings, King of Connaught and Patrick J. Quade were three worthy of mention.

The dancing continued until 1:00 a.m. since Director General Wood donated the orchestra to play for an extra hour as a compliment to the Irish honorees.

THE AWARDS BANQUET
Exhibitors Are Honored

Informal invitations were sent by Director General Wood and H. B. Hardt to each of the representatives of companies who had placed exhibits in the ice palace. The cards were notifying them that announcement of the awards winners would be made. The exhibitors were requested to be present at the ice palace on the evening of March 7, 1896.

Those who attended were treated to an elegant banquet. The menu consisted of oysters, fish, six kinds of meat, nine kinds of beer and many other side dishes and desserts. Many of the food items were duplicates of those that had been on display in the ice palace.

The banquet was prepared by renowned chef Fred Jacobs who, at that time, was the chef at the Vendome Hotel[35]. Two banquet tables, end to end, had been requested by the Director General. He served as the Master of Ceremonies, and sat at the head of the elongated table. Many toasts were given during the evening meal. Commissioner Hardt lifted a toast to the Director General, complimenting him for his executive abilities in making the ice palace a reality. Messrs. Fred Emerson Brooks, J. Williams Macy and W. W. Coble, were complimentary of the beauty and grandeur of the majestic crystal castle, and the phenomenally short time in which the ice palace was erected.

Beautiful diplomas were awarded to the exhibition winners.

---

[35]By March 7th, John Miller had moved out, and the restaurant at the ice palace closed. The skate-up counter was moved to a room formerly occupied by the band.

Special awards went to:

John E. Miller for design, quality & material of rib-boned badges.

Kuner Pickle Company for quality & purity of pickles in glass.

Hungarian Flour Mills for color, strength and milling of soft wheat flour.

Adolph Coors for bottled export beer.

Capitol Hill Greenhouses (Mrs. R. Manff) for artistic floral design and fine quality of cut flowers.

The *Rocky Mountain News*.

M. Grossman & Company for finest quality and make of Key West Beauty cigars.

Colorado Packing & Provision Company.

Josef Schlitz Brewing Company for Schlitz export beer.

First place awards:

The Colorado Midland Railroad.

Craffrey & Crowell for specially adapted dry climate brooms.

T. J. Underhill for excellent workmanship and material in workshirts and overalls.

John E. Miller for design and workmanship and finish of jewels.

Longmont Creamery, butter display.

Zang Brewing Company for Silver State, Pilsner and Free Coinage beers.

Kuner Pickle Company for flavor of tomato ketchup.

Denver Fire Clay Company for superior quality of all kinds of fire clay material.

Dunwoody Soap Company, excellence of White Water laundry soap.

Adolph Coors for Golden Ale & Stout.

Booth Packing Company received three awards, for natural color of canned vegetables, excellence of export fish and oysters in bulk, and quality of canned fruits and syrups.

The Denver Fish Company received two awards, for New York oysters and for salmon, herring & white fish.

The Denver Tent & Awning, superiority of Proctor's patent for ore sack fasteners.

Solis Cigar Company for quality & workmanship of Dry Climate cigars.

The Denver & Rio Grande Railroad for excellent displays.

Two awards went to the General Electric Company, for superiority of the induction motor, and simplicity of Thomson's arc lamps and incandescent circuit.

W. H. Jackson Photo & Publishing for special panoramic photographs.

The *Denver Times*.

A. E. Meek & Company for fine quality of leather goods.

The *Leadville Herald Democrat*.

Singer Manufacturing Company for excellence of sewing machines.

C. E. Rathe for prime cuts of meat.

Bartlett Bros., taxidermy work.

Neef Brothers Brewing Company also received 2 awards for their Wierner/Maerzen display, and Western export beer.

Booth Furniture Company for display of elegant furniture.

May Shoe & Clothing Company.

M. Grossman & Company for fine quality and manufacture of Perfecto & Victor cigars.

The Colorado Packing & Provision Company (2 awards) for carcasses of beef, mutton & pork, and bacon, hams & lard displays.

The Alamosa Milling Company for Silver Bell flour.

Skinner Bros. & Wright Company for superiority of waterproof horsehide shoes & soles.

George E. Taylor display; E. P. Dilley & Company for purity & medicinal qualities of Silver Brook whiskey.

Horlick's Food Company for nutritional properties of malted milk.

World's Dispensary Medical Association for curative qualities of Dr. Pierce's Golden Medical Discovery.

Chamberlain & Company for healing qualities of eye & skin ointment.

Swift Specific Company for purifying qualities of S. S. Specific.

California Fig Syrup Company for effective constipation remedy of Syrup of Fig.

The Dr. Bosanko Medicine Company for allaying and curing qualities of Dr. Bosanko's remedies.

Johnson & Johnson for greater digestive power by use of Papoid.

Dr. J. C. Ayer & Company for hair restoring qualities of Ayer's Hair Vigor.

L. M. Green for dyspepsia relieving and curing qualities of August Flower.

H. H. Warner & Company for medicinal excellence of Warner's Safe Cure.

Emerson Drug Company for greater properties and headache curing qualities of Bromo-Seltzer.

C. I. Hood & Company for purifying and excellent qualities of Hood's Sarsaparilla. The Dr. Miles Medical Company for efficiency of Dr. Miles new Heart Cure.

Seabury & Johnson for reliability of Belladonna Plasters.

Nance Bros. & White for voice benefiting properties of Frog-in-the-Throat.

Munyon's Homeopohile Home Remedy Company for excellent quality of Munyon's Special XX Rheumatic Cure.

F. S. Cheney & Company for superior curing qualities of Hall's Catarrh Cure.

Carter Medicine Company for quick relieving qualities of Carter's Little Liver Pills.

Wells, Richardson & Company for nerve strengthening qualities of Paine's Celery Compound.

Donald Kennedy for rapid healing qualities of Dr. Kennedy's Healing Ointment.

Potter Drug & Chemical Company for system cleaning properties of Cuticura Remedies.

Scott & Bowne, Manufacturing Chemists for flesh increasing and strength giving elements of Scott's Emulsion.

Second Place Awards:

The Denver Fire Clay Company display.
Bartlett Bros. mineral display.

Honorable Mention:

The Denver & Rio Grande Express display.

The South Park Line display.
Conforth Fish & Oyster Company display.
Windsor Hotel display.
The Albany Hotel display.
George J. Kindel Mattress ad display.
The *(Leadville) News Reporter* display.
The Glenwood Hot Springs display.
Ensminger Bros. display.
Columbine Hotel display.

Displays recognized, but not judged:

C. R. Gallup Floral Company.
The Dunn & Blass Leather Company.
The Denver Produce Company maple syrup.
A. M. Donaldson & Company, Assayers.
Fleischmann & Company.
The Colorado Orchard Company.
Grove & O'Keefe, R. L. James, M & M Company
    paints & colors.
Pabst Brewing Company.
H. Kahn & Company, souvenir display.
H. M. Blakey Company, sundries.
The Singer Manufacturing Company, needlework.
Harvey T. Brown, sundries.
The Silver State Cigar Company.
Bowman & Burleson Candy Company.
The Denver Inc. Liquor Company.
United States Fish Hatchery.

THE CITY'S INDUSTRIAL DAY
March 19, 1896

A Big Time Is Booked for the Palace
in Which All of Leadville
Can Take Part

BEAUTIFUL ARRAY OF FLOATS

On March 8th, the *Herald Democrat* reported plans were being made for an Industrial Day at the ice palace. Merchants were being urged to decorate a float advertising their businesses.

Dennis Taylor, a master parade organizer, was in charge of promoting Industrial Day since his expertise had been utilized for the Colorado Press Day, Elks Day and Miners Day parades.

It was suggested that all businesses get behind Taylor and support the special day. This would give Leadvillites an opportunity to learn the variety and extent of the city's industry and many businesses.

By promoting and backing this event, the merchants would also help the Carnival Association get out of the hole.

It was reported that Leadville had relied on outside support since the opening of the ice palace. Now it was time for the city to do something for themselves, just as they had during Press Club Day. It was noted that the biggest attendance of the carnival was registered that day; but there was some dispute of this. Others argued that

343

Miners Exchange Day brought the biggest number of visitors to the city.

Approximately twenty business houses signed up to participate in the Industrial Day activities.

But it didn't happen . . . Four days later, the *Herald Democrat* reported that the Industrial Day celebration had been postponed, "until a more convenient season." Although Dennis Taylor was vigorous in his attempt to make the day successful the paraders had grown weary of the festivities and had more than they could take to participate in another event.

LEADVILLE BIDS ITS ICE PALACE FAREWELL
The Crystal Castle is Closed

Leadville's Ice Palace was considered the eighth wonder of the world in 1896.

The carnival festivities continued until March 28th. Visitors came from all parts of the United States and Europe. Parades, led by the Leadville Snowshoe Club, escorted the sightseers from the depots to the ice palace with each train arrival and parades were scheduled for every special fete day when cities, clubs, organizations from throughout Colorado and surrounding states were given special recognition. Harrison Avenue was alive with music and gaiety as the revelers marched to the Crystal Castle day and night.

Even though the winter of 1895-96 in Leadville was not the cold and snowy weather usually grumbled at by her citizens, the people came to Leadville by the thousands to behold the majestic playhouse built of ice blocks.

It was rumored that interest in the carnival began to wane in early March, and those that did come to visit brought sack lunches, toured the palace, then went home. This seems somewhat contradictory since there were events held at the ice palace every day of March Some events were special, others not and it may be true that Leadville's citizens grew weary of the festivities, and did not go to the palace as they first had. Attendance was down, and there were those that did make one day excursions, but even to the last day there were outsiders traveling to Leadville to see the beautiful crystal citadel.

January's average temperature was 21°, which lent to the holiday atmosphere, but February turned warmer, averaging 38°. Only ten inches of snow fell during the entire month. Warm days melted the snow and attacked the palace's walls. By month's end, only six inches of snow covered the ground. Two inches of snow fell on the first day of March, followed by an additional 37 inches during the last month of the winter carnival. The average temperature for March, 1896, was an unbelievable 71°! By the end of March the snow was completely gone. The party was winding down and the carnival was coming to an end.

Many suggestions were made on what to do with the ice palace. One suggestion was made to bombard it with cannon and gunfire, blow it sky high, and end it all at once. This raised some concern of the residents near the palace, especially with all the powder magazines close to the castle, those living nearby were worried that the explosion might rock the foundations of the powder magazines and ignite the several thousand tons of dynamite stored there. If so, the detonation would blow more than the palace to smithereens. The fact that the people living near Capitol Hill were unsuccessful in obtaining dynamite insurance caused anxious moments for those homeowners. (There were seventy-seven insurance companies in Leadville at that time.)

The closing was no less sensational and no less beautiful than were the opening day ceremonies. A gigantic fireworks display, and a few closing remarks brought an end to the spectacular ice palace and winter carnival. Those who cared to took advantage of this last night in the ballroom or skating rink. Some of them took one last stroll through the beautiful playhouse, perhaps to store an image of the ice palace that soon would be no more.

The last official ceremony of the Winter Carnival was held on Sunday evening, March 28th. Ironically, as if Mother Nature was sorry for the havoc she wreaked all winter, five inches of snow fell that day and night. Although the temperature midday was 36°, falling to 22° by nightfall, it didn't deter the crowds from attending the closing ceremonies. The snow was beautiful and big flakes fell like soft goose down upon Leadville.

A feeling of sadness permeated the city as darkness enveloped this lofty mountain town. Hordes of people climbed the hills of West Seventh and West Eighth Streets to bid farewell to this magnificent ice edifice that had brought worldwide notoriety to Leadville. Some of the crowd went inside for one last look, but more than half remained outside in the falling snow, awaiting the fireworks display that would bring down the curtain on Leadville's Crystal Carnival.

Murphy's Law prevailed, however. The wet snow put a heavy damper on some of the fireworks. Many of the pyrotechnics were soaked with moisture and would not go off, or fizzled out before they reached the castle walls. A multitude of balloons were sent skyward from the palace's roof, only to be beaten back by the weight of the snow. Yet, in another way, the snowstorm added to the magnificence of the display. The skyrockets and Roman candles were not hindered by the falling snow as they streaked heavenward and rising above the walls and towers of the palace, fiery comet-like trails reflected brilliant colors off the snow crystals before disappearing into the night sky. The corner towers, ablaze with red lights, softened to various colors of pink as snowflakes, dancing like fireflies, drifted to the ground. The palace grounds were breathtakingly beautiful that night. The snow-capped mountains that surrounded Leadville and the ice palace seemed to be aglow with the brilliancy of the fireworks from Capitol

Hill. For every part of the display that was damaged by the storm, it was multiplied a thousand times by the pyrotechnics that could be used.

Attendance that evening was the largest it had been for some time. The ice rink was filled to near capacity with colorfully costumed skaters, lending a festive atmosphere to the castle's closing. A large crowd enjoyed the last ball of the season, and spectators filled the arcades to enjoy one last time in this wonderful ice marvel. Although the crowds tried to maintain a party-like atmosphere, there was an undercurrent of sadness within the palace walls.

As the pyrotechnics turned earthward, and the fireworks died out, the crowds started down the hills toward their homes. Many turned back for one last look at the ice castle that would soon be gone, perhaps trying to mentally photograph it . . . to keep it forever in their memory.

For when green-vestured Spring, too long banished,
Shall unfetter the close-prisoned streams,
We shall mourn our lost palace, then vanished,
To the far, sunset land of our dreams.

— Virginia Donaghe McClurg

THE LAST HURRAHS
Final Events At The Ice Palace

On April 10th, the first and only baseball game was played at the ice palace. For the two days prior to the game, the two teams that had been selected to compete were practicing on the rink with their ice skates, but the idea of using skates was abandoned when it was deemed to be to dangerous. The players were not in favor of having their shins shaved or other body parts being sliced by the sharp edged blades. There was an equipment change; however . . . the baseball used was 1 1/2-feet in diameter and described as the size of a cannonball, and an oversized bat "as large as a barndoor."

In humor, it was reported the only one in any danger was the umpire, Dennis Taylor. It was rumored that he had purchased several bolts of cotton and was having a special uniform made to protect himself. It was conceded that the job was difficult and dangerous, and a fund was subscribed for an insurance policy.

Public skating was allowed before and after the baseball game.

While the people on the east coast complained of terrible heat, Leadville's citizens enjoyed a maypole skating party at the ice palace on May Day. The ice was in excellent condition and a large crowd of ladies and gents spent an evening skating instead of dancing around the maypole.

Plans had been made and invitations were sent. Mr. A. V. Hunter, Mrs. Alfred Thielan and Mrs. Henry Norton served on the reception committee. A maypole was erected in the middle of the rink and wreathed with beautiful flowers and trimmed in colorful ribbons.

Impromptu races were arranged. One of the principal races matched Benjamin F. Follett against Robert H.

Shipley. Shipley was awarded the consolation prize. Another race pitted the Honorable T. A. Dickson and Mrs. Norton against Mrs. Thielan and Ole Burns. Judge Dickson won the honors and was awarded a donut, which he wore around his neck the remainder of the evening. Other races and a variety of entertainment filled the evening program. At 11:00 p.m. the party moved to the dining room for a superb banquet prepared by Caterer Miller. The party broke up in the wee hours of the morning.

Among those in attendance for the last formal affair (the maypole party) were: Messers. and Mrs: Benjamin Follett, Max Boehmer, Alphonse Burnand, Ezra Dickerman, Willis Thompson, Joseph S. Reef, W. H. Woodward, John Stotesbury, H. C. Dimick, Frank A. Keith, Henry Norton, Alfred Thielan, Thomas A. Dickson, Robert H. Blose, Charles Hussey, Mrs. Neils Larsen, Miss Nellie Condon, Mrs. Frank Owers. A number of young ladies were in attendance in addition to gentlemen: Francis X. Hogan, Harry Phillips, J. A. Ewing, John Harvey, Harvey T. Brown, Frank Church, Dr. Bradford Galloway, D. H. Dougan and others.

THE CLOSING CHAPTER
The Last of the Ice Palace Comes Down

After the ice palace closed, the Association had all of the exhibits removed, but the ice rink was used until the first of June when it had become too slushy to skate on.

The average temperature during the spring and summer[36] of 1896 was 48.° It is anyone's guess how long it took the ice palace to melt. Ice melts from the inside out since heat is directed to the center; and the ice "candles," forming combs as in a beehive. This weakens the interior, causing the ice to crumble.

The lumber in the ice palace buildings belonged to the Williams Lumber Company. Because of the economy in Leadville at that time and the unrest caused by the miners' strike, the lumber company managers could not afford to hire security guards to protect the lumber. Some was taken by souvenir seekers or sold. A number of the homes on West Seventh and West Eighth Street contain ice palace lumber in backyard fences, sidewalks, floor joists and door and window frames.

When the miners strike erupted into a riot, a number of men were killed and others were wounded. In September of 1896, the rioting was out of control and the city fathers wired Governor McIntire in Denver to send militiamen to Leadville to stop the fighting. The troops arrived the next day. Some of the lumber that had been used to build the ice palace was removed from the site and used to build floors

---

[36]There were no daily temperatures reported for the month of July. The report being interpolated. Department of Atmospheric Research, Colorado State University.

for the barracks that housed the militiamen at 13th and Poplar Streets.

Although the citizens were not giving much thought to winter sports, or the ice palace, during the summer of '96, there was consensus among a number of Leadvillites that the wooden building should be preserved. One unidentified gentleman's comments were:

> Nearly everyone in Leadville has a financial interest in the Ice Palace. The winter will soon be here and it seems a pity that this great building, enclosing the finest skating rink in the state, should be doomed to destruction. There are people here who would be glad to purchase or lease the building providing they can obtain the necessary financial backing. Hundreds of people have purchased skates and costumes who would gladly purchase a $5 season ticket, and the amount thus raised would purchase the building as it stands. If this could not be done, it might be leased to some responsible party and this winter turned into an ice rink. Of course, the strike has caused everyone to forget, for a time at least, the comparatively, unimportant matter of the ice palace, but now that active steps are being taken to tear it down, I should think some person ought to look into the matter and see what arrangements could be made to preserve the structure. I believe that it is not the wish of the people who contributed to the support of the ice palace to see it entirely destroyed, and it is worthwhile to call attention to the fact that unless something is done, the large buildings which were erected last winter will be destroyed.

On October 17th the Williams Lumber Company let a contract to tear the wooden buildings of the ice palace down. A derrick was erected, and it was reported that, "unless arrangements could be made with the lumber company," demolition of the buildings would begin on Monday, October 19th. There were no takers, and the buildings were demolished.

Many Leadville homeowners, today take pride in the fact that lumber from the ice palace is a part of their beautiful Victorian homes on the former ice palace site.

```
STATE OF COLORADO :
                   : SS.
County of Lake.    :
```

KNOW ALL MEN BY THESE PRESENTS, That the amount of the capital stock of The Leadville Crystal Carnival Association, a corporation organized under the laws of the State of Colorado, is $20,000.00, of which amount $ 18137.⁵⁰ has been paid in. The amount of existing debts is $ 30,391.⁷¹ , consisting of the following items, viz:- *Bills Payable, $12000.⁰⁰*

Sundry open accounts $18391.⁷¹

Witness the corporate name and seal of said Association at the hand of Charles T. Limberg, its Vice-President, this 26th day of February, A. D., 1896.

THE LEADVILLE CRYSTAL CARNIVAL ASSOCIATION.

By _____
                        Vice-President.

```
STATE OF COLORADO :
                   : SS.
County of Lake.    :
```

W. L. Temple, being duly sworn, saith: that he is the Secretary of the above named association; that he has heard read the above and foregoing certificate and knows the contents thereof; that the matters and things therein stated are correct and true.

Subscribed and sworn to before me this 26th day of February, 1896.

My Commission expires Oct. 1, 1898.

_____
                        Notary Public.

Financial Statement, Leadville Crystal Carnival Association February 26, 1896.
Lake County Courthouse

A FINANCIAL FAILURE
Investors/Businessmen Lose Their Money

Whether or not Leadville will ever attempt another ice palace of this magnitude is uncertain but in 1896 there was no doubt. After the ice palace closed on March 28th, it was reported that the carnival season had passed, and as far as the Crystal Carnival Association was concerned, the castle would not be opened again.

The undertaking of the enormous project was staggering and the outlay of labor, energy and capital had been overwhelming. It was doubtful that another man of Director General Tingley S. Wood's caliber could be found, or persuaded to build another ice palace; and his executive abilities plus his willingness to successfully complete a project of such immense proportions, without payment or compensation of any kind, were unmatched. He left his many business enterprises in the hands of others, to head the Leadville Crystal Carnival Association and had spent $22,000 of his own money to finish construction on the ice palace, to keep it open and operating until the end. Other businessmen in Leadville had also bought stock, and had given additional funds to support the effort.

There are no firm figures of how much it cost to build Leadville's Ice Palace. Published figures ranged from $35,000 to $220,000, (which this author believes to be a typographical error.) The construction and affiliated costs plus monies collected were reported as being from $20,000 to $100,000. O'Keefe and Stockdorf, on the backs of their photographs, printed the cost of the ice palace to be $35,000. Noted author and Leadville historian, Don Griswold estimated the figure to be approximately $65,000. Construction cost overruns, the cash prizes, and paid expenses for some of the visitors, all took their toll on the Association and Leadville.

When E. W. Senior first touted the ice palace's construction, he mentioned a possible gain from investments tendered. A corporation was not established and stocks were not offered to the public until Tingley S. Wood assumed the Directorship.

A. V. Hunter, a leading Leadville banker, was asked for his comments on the ice palace and whether he had regretted buying ice palace stock or making additional donations to help keep it going. He laughingly replied, "I've never heard of a man complaining of paying for a good time, and I'll tell you . . . we had one good time!"

Someone approached Director General Wood to get his opinion. A local Leadville paper reported that "If Mr. Wood had his way about it, he would blow the ice palace off the face of Capitol Hill."[37]

Mr. Wood was asked later if he would ever consider building another ice palace, to which he replied, "If I had my way, I would have blown this one to hell!"

On March 26, 1896, the *Grand Junction Sentinel* reported, "While Colorado, as a whole, has failed to support the full measure of appreciation due to Leadville's unrivaled enterprise, the fame of it has spread beyond the seas, and in a way, the eyes of the world have been turned upon the state whose greatness dawned when the Carbonate Camp was born."

A cost study was done in 1985 to determine the financial feasibility of building another ice palace in Leadville. Estimated figures at that time were reported to be $30 million. These costs would be, basically, start-up expenses.

---

[37]*Worksaver Magazine*, Winter, 1984, pp. 12-13.

THE EPILOGUE
A Look Back

On December 28, 1896, the *Leadville Herald Democrat* printed the following article:

The scene is different now. No carnival season to awaken expectancy; no joyous merry makings. The palace is a thing of the past. The crystal walls forever gone, the framework used to build a military barracks. Close to the site of the palace of pleasure now frowns the soldiers' cantonment. Instead of the gay strains of festival music, is heard the roll of drums and the blare of trumpets. The roar of the morning and evening gun echoes over the hills and instead of the merry shouts of the carnival revelers, is heard the stern challenge of the sentry. The contrast is as striking as thoughtful. Strange indeed is the transformation. Stronger is the contemplation of the causes which in this little city, alone in the mountains, brought about the change. Kindly indeed is fate, that the curtain of the future was not raised in those times of peace and pleasure, and the dark and forbidding vistas of the future exposed to view.

TOURISTS FLOODED THE CITY
A Directory of the Visitors

Tourists poured into Leadville after the announcement was out that an ice palace had been built and was ready for visitors.

They came from Colorado, other states, Canada and Europe. Upon hearing of Leadville's Crystal Carnival, a number of passengers on a train passing through Leadville on its way to the coast, stopped to visit the ice palace on January 4th.

Throughout the months of the winter carnival, excursion trains brought the tourists, curiosity seekers and visitors to Leadville. The three railroads, at times, had to add extra cars, some of them five and six coaches long, to bring the excursionists to the Cloud City and special trains brought visitors into the city for special fete days.

Leadville's society pages and hotel registers listed many prominent citizens that came to Leadville that winter of 1896. On Aspen Day James Doyle was afforded much attention. Doyle had discovered Portland mine in Victor and his mine was considered to be the "Little Jonny" of the Victor mining district. After he lost $100,000 in South American mining, he returned, penniless, to Cripple Creek. He reported his mine yielding an average of 200 tons a day, up to $71 per ton and he warned that the Little Jonny was being challenged as the greatest gold mine in the world. He was described as 37 or 38 years old, with a ruddy complexion and a red moustache; shorter than average in height. He came west from New England and many described him to be more Irish than a "New England type."

Colonel Ed F. Browne, president of the Gold Mining Exchange of Cripple Creek, explored Leadville from one end to the other and described it as a hummer. He reflected on the present prosperity of the city, pointing out that it was hurt for a time by "the Sunday school spell[38]," These strict rules of Sunday observance may be a good thing, but I don't believe they apply in a mining camp."

State Senator B. Clark Wheeler of Aspen pronounced the ice palace beautiful beyond his expectations.

Robert F. Hunter, President of the Denver Chamber of Commerce exclaimed, "At our meeting this afternoon we accomplished a great deal that amounted to nothing, but we had a good time, and that is what we came for."

George Rex Buckman, a member of the Colorado Springs Chamber of Commerce, failed in his attempt to make a comparison of Leadville's winter carnival and the August Flower Carnival in the Springs.

Ex-Governor and Mrs. J. B. Grant combined business with pleasure and took the opportunity to see the ice palace sights. Mrs. (Mary) Grant was the daughter of ex-Leadville mining magnate, R. E. Goodell.

W. B. Root, veteran exchange member and president of the Colorado Mining Exchange, was among the stock exchange visitors.

A newlywed couple traveled from London and spent part of their honeymoon in Leadville, visiting the Palace. Alfred Hoff, a gentleman from Frankfurt-on-Main, Germany, made the journey. Leadville's Ice Palace was famous, around the world.

---

[38]In July, 1894, Leadville's saloon keepers tested the Sunday Closure Law.

ELKS DAY — FEBRUARY 15, 1896

Elks Members From Cripple Creek:

Breeson, Jules
Brooks, William
Burkhart, Louis
Burne, Robert
Burns, P.
Donnelson, James
Eick, C. K.
Fitzpatrick, James
Franzer, Oscar
Frederick, John
Gaugh, Charles
Goldstein, M. B.
Goodman, Max
Haas, S. J.
Jenkins, W. M.
Keniter, L.
Kinnear, Mr.

Leader, C. H.
Levy, H. B.
McCloud, John
McKee, Frank
McMurray, W. T.
Mullen, J. J.
Murphy, J.
Nathan, Samuel
Nelson, Tom
Polin, S. J.
Reif, Louis
Richardson, Charles
Sawyer, Charles
Turner, E. M.
Yates, Mel
Yeade, Sam
Zeno, J. K.

Guests From Aspen:

Brown, L. A. W.
Brown, W. O.
Clark, S. B.
Curry, T. A.
Fiske, J. H.
Kech, W. C. F.
Luellen, T. C.
May, J. J.

Pearce, C. H.
Rucker, Judge T. A.
Stilson, C. M.
Swan, P. M.
Tomkins, L. H.
Turley, W. E.
Wachtel, S.
Whitmore, F. B.

Visitors from Denver, registered at the Vendome Hotel:

Baxter, Miss
Bolthoff, W. H.
Dennison, Dr. & Mrs.
Donalson, Mr. & Mrs.
Duncan, J. G.
Eicholtz, L. H. Jr.
Fairbanks, John
Gebhard, Charles
Gorslin, Mrs. E.
Gorslin, Miles
Gregg, Miss
Hurd, Miss
Isbell, O. S.
McNamara, Joseph
McNamara, Miss
McNell, J. L. & Mrs.

Mellon, H. S.
Morey, C. S.
Morey, Mary
O'Connor, M.
Platt, Miss
Rogers, J. W.
Sanderson, Mrs. J. P.
Standart, F. W. & Mrs.
Stebbins, Miss
Struby, Miss
Walker, W. C.
Wayne, Miss
Wilson, Mrs. P. B.
Wolfe, Frank & Mrs.
Young, Miss

From other Colorado cities:

Clayton, J., Central City
Gaymon, Mr. & Mrs. O. K., Dillon (editor of the *Dillon Enterprise*)
Goodman, M., Central City
Gunner, Joseph, Red Cliff
Hames, Sam, Pueblo
Henry, W. J., Red Cliff
King, Nellie, Cripple Creek
Loming, Mr. & Mrs. F. R., Cripple Creek
Mahoney, W. A., Red Cliff
McDonald, Mr. & Mrs. & Son

Himmen, R. H., Central City
Mahoney, W. A., Red Cliff
McDonald, Mr. & Mrs. J. & son, Cripple Creek
Polin, Mr. & Mrs. S. J., Cripple Creek
Retallack, Mr. & Mrs. Joseph, Central City
Smith, John H. Pueblo
Williams, B. S., Breckenridge

From Out-of-State:

Becton, W. W., Boston, Mass.
Converse, V. G., Pittsburgh, PA
Dickinson, F. S., New York
Donnellan, Mr. & Mrs. F. J. & daughter, Salt Lake City
Farma, Mr. & Mrs. F. R., New York
Fangerman, J. B., Cincinnati, OH
Friedburg, J. M., San Francisco, CA
Kerd, Harman, New York
Lunt, George D., Chicago, IL
Meyer, Louis W., Cincinnati, OH
Miller, George, Baltimore, MD
Murray, J. P., St. Louis, MO
Schaefer, Mr., New York
Todd, Mrs. J. A., Chicago, IL
Waxham, E. L., Milwaukee, WI
Wilcox, A. E., Chicago, IL

ASPEN DAY — JANUARY 21, 1896

From Aspen:

Allen, Charles   Arnold. W. W.

Auborne, Bessie J.
Ball, Charles E. & Mrs.
Bell, Charles
Berryman, Charles
Biddle, Mrs. E. S.
Bransford, J. D.
Bruin, Louis
Brunton, Mr. & Mrs.
   D. W. & son
Cramer, Charles
Cramer, Mrs. Charles W.
Chatfield, J. W.
Deveroux, W. H.
Dray, J. P.
Ferguson, H.
Forbes, John
Gutting, Otto
Hall, Mrs. H. S.
Hooper, Miss
Hooper, Mrs. J. D.
Ketherly, Mr. & Mrs. J. W.

King, J. V.
Lumsden, Mrs. J.
Malaby, S. L.
Mason, Mrs. John B.
McElwee, D.
McLarkey, Mrs. A.
Mooney, Miss
Moorhead, William
Perry, Mrs. L.
Petter, Mrs. Sophie
Riland, James L.
Ruggles, Miss Sophie
Sands, Jacob
Schurman, Cabib
Thomas, C. H.
Thomas, William
Williams, James
Wright, Bob
Young, W. M.

From Other Colorado Cities:

Eamon, D. W., Pueblo
Hewitt, James, Pueblo
Henopin, Mrs. T. R. & daughter, Idaho Springs
Hopkins, James, Twin Lakes
Nadford, Fred J., Buena Vista
Smith, L. W., Pueblo
Wiley, Mr. & Mrs. O. W., Pueblo
Wood, Lee S., Rico

From Out-of-State:

Brown, Frank, C., New York
Carlton, J. G., Chicago, IL
Cook, George E., San Francisco, CA
Dunaken, C. A., Kansas City
Goodfriend, B., Mount Vernon, NY
Gregory, W. N., Topeka, KS
Henning, O. W., St. Louis, MO
Hoff, Alfred, Frankfurt-on-Main, Germany
Hoffman, R. W., New York
Smith, Rufus H., Chicago, IL
Sterne, S., New York
Stone, N. A., Chicago, IL

STOCK EXCHANGE DAY — JANUARY 25, 1896

From Denver:

Addlebrook, J. H.
Alkins, W. E.
Allen, Ada
Amens, Miss
Baer, Mr.
Bardwell, J. H. & Mrs.
Beck, W. H.
Beebe, James C.
Boles, O. E.
Bradeheimer, Henry,
    Mrs. & Son
Branigan, Harry & Mrs.
Eastman, H. C.

Freeman, J. E.
Goodell, R. E.
Hughes, J. J.
Hunter, R. Y. & Son
Insley, C. E. & Mrs.
Johnson, F. P. & Mrs.
Jones, A. E. & Mrs.
Jones, J. W.
Lehman, Edwin W.
Macklin, N. B.
McVey, J. C.
Milburn, J. A.
Moore, J. W. & Mrs.

365

Morgan, John G.
Riley, William
Rinehart, A. E.
Romans, Lorenzo
Root, Wm. B., Mrs.
  & Son
Rose, John D.

Senwastur, Ed. E.
Smith, Frank
Smith, Frank C.
Streetor, M. L.
Tessly, Mrs. A. B.
Whitmore, J. D.
Willing, S. D.

From Colorado Springs:

Arkell, Edwin & Mrs.
Buckman, George R.
Goudy, Wm. H. & Mrs.
Gregg, Hal R.
Grover, B. B. & ladies
Hamilton, D. O. & lady
Leipheimer, V.

Lott, George H. & Wife
Pettingill, F. H.
Plumb, J. C. & Mrs.
Pooley, Mrs. E. M.
White, L. W., Jr., and
  Mrs.

From Victor:

Andrews, A. L.
Curley, J. R.
Doyle, James
Golderberg, Walter
Greve, Dr. James

Hall, J. W.
Peterson, W. H.
Reardon, F. M.
Vickers, H.

From Cripple Creek:

Fitting, Miss
Graham, James H.
Hallett, H. W.
Harrington, Stanley

Johnson, Lute H.
McCreere, Helen
Newcomb, E. W.
Queering, Dewitt

Rollins, F. P. & Mrs.
Stovell, Chas. S.
Whinery, J.
Wilson, Allan

From Out-of-State:

Hoffman, R. W., New York
Robertson, C. A. Chicago
Stone, W. A., Chicago

D.D.D. DAY — 2/19/96

Packer, Gilbert, Nottingham, England

A.O.U.W. DAY — 2/29/96

From Denver:

Bail, Mrs. J. J. T.
Ballard, Mrs. C.
Barrett, W. H.
Beal, Harry
Beaman, L. & Mrs., &
  daughter
Blow, A. A. & Mrs.
Brooks, E. J.
Buckwalter, H. H.
Burchinell, W. K.
Donnelly, Clifford
Donnelly, Julia
Elrict, W. R.

Findlay, A.
Frank, Mrs. J. B.
Garberger, Anna E.
Garretson, P.
Goodell, R. E.
Harsh, Miss E.
Hogie, W. H. & Mrs.
Hyman, M. & Mrs.
Jackson, J. C. & Wife
James, George
Leonard, F. G.
Light, E. B.
May, David & Children

McClennan, Miss
McCormack, Miss D.
McGaffey, A. B.
McGaffey, Kenneth M.
Mitchell, J. C.
Orahood, H. M.
Palmer, Miss
Patterson, T. M. & Mrs.
Perkins, W. E.
Poole, John H.
Preis, Joe
Redman, J. H.
Schloss, Miss Eva

Seeley, E. D.
Sheefor, J. D.
Stearns, Miss Mabel
Wagner, A. & Mrs.
Wagner, M. E.
Walter, A. & Mrs.
Wissenhood, C. D.
Wolff, Julius
Wood, Henry E. &
    family
Workendyke, Miss

From Colorado, registered at the Vendome Hotel:

Canfield, C. B., Florence
Crowe, Thomas, Pueblo
Dickens, Charles & Mrs., Manitou Springs
Cole, W. W.
Emmett, W. W., Boulder (brother-in-law of W. W. Coble)
Leddy, Hal
Leddy, Mr. & Mrs. M. A., Manitou Springs
Moore, Granville S., Cripple Creek
Moore, James A., Cripple Creek
Peterson, Hilda, Central City
Sewell, Captain T. C., Cripple Creek
Steele, Mayor Hugh R., Cripple Creek
Company G., Second Regiment

Out-of-State visitors:

Abraham, E., Cincinnati, OH
Cox, Dr. G., Kirksville, MO
Frank, John, Burke, ID
Illoway, J. H., NY
Shackelford, H. D. & Mrs., Cincinnati, OH
Thomas, Mrs. J. P., Titusville, PA

BIBLIOGRAPHY

Newspapers

Aspen Daily Times (September, 1895).

Denver Times (August 19, 1895-October, 1896).

Grand Junction Sentinel (November 26, 1895-February 3, 1896). Mesa County Public Library.

Griswold, Don and Jean. *"Leadville — A City of Contrast." The Leadville Herald Democrat* (December 19, 1969, January 2, 9, 16, 23, 30, 1970-February 6, 13, 20, 27, 1970).

Herald Democrat (July 1895-December 1896). Leadville, Lake County Library and Colorado State Historical Research Library, Denver.

Pueblo Chieftain (November 2, 1895-December 23, 1895).

Periodicals

Branham, Lowell. *"Leadville's Ice Palace," Colorado Magazine* (January-February, 1970), pp. 30-33, 82-85.

Kildare, Maurice. *"Leadville's Ice Palace." True West Magazine* (May-June 1969), pp. 30-33, 49-52.

McMechen, C. Edgar. *"The Brand Book." The Westerners* (June 1951), Vol. 7, No. 6.

Books and Booklets

Blair, Edward. *Palace of Ice, A History of Leadville's Ice Palace, 1895-96*. Gunnison, CO: B & B Printers and Lithographers, 1972.

Davis, Carlyle Channing. *Olden Times in Colorado*. The Phillips Publishing Company, 1916.

First Official Souvenir. *Leadville Crystal Carnival 1896*. Leadville, CO: The Leadville Crystal Carnival Publishing Company.

Griswold, Don and Jean. *Colorado's Century of "Cities."* Smith-Brooks Printing Company, 1958.

Leadville City Directories 1895-1900. Leadville, CO.

Vaughn, Frank E. *The Spirit of Leadville* (Leadville, CO, 1928.

Webster, Noah, LL. D. *Webster's Unabridged Dictionary*, (Springfield, Mass.: G. & C. Merriam & Co., 1889).

Personal Resources

Campbell, Helen. Personal Interview, Denver, 1983.

Dickerman, Ezra D. *Memories of the Leadville Ice Palace, 1895-96*. An interview and unpublished paper, Colorado State Historical Society, Denver, CO.

Fenske, Eva. "City Council Minutes," November 7, 1895-May 25, 1896. City Hall, Leadville.

Griswold, Don. Personal Interviews, Denver, CO, 1992, 1993, 1994.

McNair, Arthur. Personal Interview, Leadville, 1989.

Ossman, June, & Jeanette Mehle. "Lake County Ledgers" and "County Commissioners Meeting Minutes" (October 7, 1895-November 9, 1895, February 27, 1896). Lake County Courthouse, Leadville, CO.

Reichle, Olivia. Personal Interview, Leadville, 1967.

Thelin, Milton. Personal Interview, Leadville, 1968.

INDEX

ORDER FORM

Ice Castle Editions
P.O. Box 280116
Lakewood, Colorado 80228-0116

Please send me the following:

_____ copies of *Leadville's Ice Palace* @ $16.95 plus $3.00 shipping and handling. Colorado Residents, please add sales tax of 7.5%.

NAME _____

ADDRESS _____

_____

CITY, STATE, ZIP _____

I understand that I may return any book for a full refund if not satisfied.

Shipping Charges. Please add $3.00 for the first book and $1.00 for any additional book ordered.

Please complete your shipping label

---------------------------------------Tear here ---

FROM:

ICE CASTLE EDITIONS
P.O. BOX 280116
LAKEWOOD, COLORADO 80228-0116

TO:

_____

_____

_____

_____

_____

ORDER FORM

Ice Castle Editions
P.O. Box 280116
Lakewood, Colorado 80228-0116

Please send me the following:

_____ copies of *Leadville's Ice Palace* @ $16.95 plus $3.00 shipping and handling. Colorado Residents, please add sales tax of 7.5%.

NAME _____

ADDRESS _____

_____

CITY, STATE, ZIP _____

I understand that I may return any book for a full refund if not satisfied.

Shipping Charges. Please add $3.00 for the first book and $1.00 for any additional book ordered.

Please complete your shipping label

---Tear here ---

FROM:

ICE CASTLE EDITIONS
P.O. BOX 280116
LAKEWOOD, COLORADO 80228-0116

TO:

_____

_____

_____

_____

_____